C000260926

Keeping Time

Time, Liturgy and Christian Discipleship

— TIM GORRINGE —

Sacristy Press

Sacristy Press
PO Box 612, Durham, DH1 9HT

www.sacristy.co.uk

First published in 2022 by Sacristy Press, Durham

Sacristy Limited, registered in England & Wales, number 7565667

British Library Cataloguing-in-Publication Data
A catalogue record for the book is available from the British Library

ISBN 978-1-78959-219-1

For Duncan and Angela

Contents

Preface

Sometime around AD 723, the Benedictine monk Bede (672/3–735) began writing a book called *De Temporum Ratione*—the Reckoning of Time. Bede had been in the monastery since he was seven, first in Monkwearmouth, then in Jarrow, and, apart from taking part in worship, spent his time studying, writing and teaching. In a brief note appended to his magnum opus, the *Ecclesiastical History of the English Peoples*, he lists forty-one titles of the books he has written, mainly biblical exegesis. He wrote *De Temporum* to argue for a particular way of fixing the date of Easter. The Celtic Church, he thought, had got it all wrong. In order to do this, he felt he needed to begin with fundamentals—what was meant by time in the first place.

Although he knew Augustine's work, he does not begin with the puzzles about time which the *Confessions* explores but sets out the building blocks of time—days, weeks and months—before getting on to the lunar and solar year, the solstice and the equinox. Erasmus spoke of making the New Testament available for ploughboys, and in the same way, Bede's is an account of time for ploughboys; that is, an account of time as ordinary people experience it in the rhythm of work and play, health and sickness, youth and age. The seasons of the year impose an order on time, and liturgical order finesses this order in relation to the human rhythms just mentioned. Bede believed that fixing the date of Easter needed an understanding of what we mean by time as a whole. The reason he was so concerned was because in his view the date of Easter was itself a sacrament of the fact that all time—in his words, fleeting and wave tossed as it was—was G-d's time and existed as a preparation for "eternal stability and stable eternity".

In this book, I have followed Bede's lead, though my understanding of both history and eternity, and therefore of time, differs from his. He wrote in the Dark Ages, and I write in "the dark ages already upon us" as Alasdair MacIntyre said in 1981. The dangers we, and particularly those now at school, and those being born at this time, face are vastly more serious than anything Bede could have imagined. But he and we share the same Scriptures, and to a large extent share the same creeds, which give us our orientation for how to live and act. He tells us he has transcribed everything Augustine had to say on "the Apostle" and that he has compiled a collection of short excerpts of comments by "the holy Fathers" on the Scriptures. Alongside Augustine, we can assume that many of the figures who appear in this book would have been familiar to him.

Like Bede, I begin with the nuts and bolts of time—the time we experience in getting up in the morning, going to work, noticing the passing of the seasons—before turning to some reflections on it. This constitutes Part 1. Part 2, the bulk of the book, goes through the liturgical year, understood as a crucial part of Christian formation, and therefore shaping our use and understanding of time. In liturgy, as in everything else, the Church is *semper reformanda*, and I have made suggestions here and there for what I consider would be improvements. In Part 3, I turn to the sanctoral cycle—the calendar of saints and martyrs, again making a few expostulations and a few more suggestions.

A note on terminology

Our Christian Bibles, and almost all theological commentary, use the terms "Old Testament" and "New Testament", which derive from Jeremiah's talk about the "new covenant", deemed to be fulfilled in Christ (Jeremiah 31). The problem with the term "Old Testament" is that from the second century onwards it has suggested to some that this part of Scripture is over and done with, that we do not need to bother with it. The Church fought that heresy off, but it remains a strain within the Church, especially in Protestant liberalism. To circumvent that some people use the term "Hebrew bible", but the problem there is that a few parts are in Aramaic and some of the later parts in Greek. I therefore prefer the Jewish term, Tenakh, standing for Torah, Nebi'im and Khetubim, Torah, Prophets and Wisdom writings. I then prefer to refer to the New Testament as the "Messianic Writings", those writings which refer to Messiah Jesus. The full justification for this practice can be found in Gorringe 2020.

I also learned from some of my Jewish students to prefer writing "G-d" for the Creator of all things, and I was pleased to see Elizabeth Schüssler Fiorenza does the same. It highlights the fact that all our language about G-d is inadequate, and it is a way of following the Jewish practice of refusing to pronounce the divine NAME. It also puts a stumbling block in the way of our customary assumption that we know what we are talking about when we say the word.

PART 1

Times and seasons

The dawn of time

When, after ten books in which he had examined and critiqued the Roman and Greek heritage, Augustine turned to his proper theme, the *civitas Dei*, he began from the beginning, asking about creation. His framework is the radical difference between time and eternity, and he followed Plato in saying that because the created world, at every stage, knows mutability, it is obvious that time began with the origin of the world (*City of God* XI:6). Genesis made clear that humans did not arrive until the sixth day, but the authors put the whole of human history (Eve is "the mother of all living"; Genesis 3:20) into the context of the origin of all things. Augustine took the account of the first five days as revealed information ("the Bible never lies"). Today we turn to the astrophysicists but that does not rule out theology. "What are human beings that you are mindful of them?" asks the psalmist. Answering his own question he cites Genesis 1:26—"You have given them dominion over the works of your hands"—and one of the most extraordinary tokens of this difficult phrase is that humans have been able to determine the age of the universe, or at least this phase of it.

Today it is generally agreed that the universe is approximately 13.8 billion years old, or at least, that is the length of time since the Big Bang, which, according to a theory popularized by Roger Penrose, could be a moment in a repeated cycle—as the Stoics and some Indian philosophers once proposed. After the Big Bang, it takes about 370,000 years for the universe to cool sufficiently for neutral atoms to form, and thus for matter to emerge out of radiation. If anything qualified for the *tohu ve bohu* of Genesis 1:2 this would be it, an extraordinary intuitive guess by this and other ancient mythologies of what the conditions of the origin of life might have been.

For about 700 million years, there was no light, so this period is known as "the dark ages". Stars and galaxies began to form between 200 and 500 million years after the Big Bang. With the beginning of light, as far as the Genesis authors are concerned, we have the possibility of marking time. The solar system formed at about 9.2 billion years, and planet earth formed about 4.5 billion years ago. The so-called "Precambrian period" runs from the formation of the earth to 542 million years ago. In this vast period, indeed what Prospero calls "the vast backward and abysm of time", organic matter forms from inorganic, oxygen begins to build up and the development of complex life becomes possible. This possibility includes the life of Jesus of Nazareth. Let us suppose that Christianity is right and that in Jesus G-d, the origin of all things, including time, became human. Of course we can say that this begins with G-d's decision, G-d's election to become human. But then that embroilment, in which the Creator becomes creature, begins in time at this depth and at this infinitely remote period. Jesus of Nazareth, like the rest of us, is stardust; for Augustine, and for the Christian tradition in general, he is the supreme moment of G-d's overarching providence.

In his *A Brief History of Time*, Stephen Hawking spoke of three "arrows of time", the first of which is characterized by the way in which entropy increases, which he calls the thermodynamic arrow of time. The universe is still expanding but at some stage will begin to contract. Earth, as the host of life, will revert to dead matter. The period of expansion, still going on, he calls "the cosmological arrow of time", his third arrow. I will come to the second shortly.

Palaeontologists speak of eleven periods between the end of the Precambrian and the emergence of *Homo sapiens*, a period of more than 500 million years. There were five major extinctions in this period, the last of which, 66 million years ago, and probably caused by an asteroid strike, wiped out the dinosaurs. At the same time, these events sometimes accelerated evolution, the last one favouring mammalian growth. The ancestor of humans, *Homo habilis*, who used stone tools, evolved around 2.8 million years ago. Over the next million years brain size increased, and *Homo erectus*, who used fire as well as stone tools, emerged about 1.9 million years ago during the last ice age, which ended only 11,700 years ago. *Homo sapiens* may have emerged as early as 300,000 years ago (more conservative estimates say 150,000–100,000 years ago), but what is called "behavioural modernity" begins around 40,000 years ago. The oldest cave paintings are earlier than 30,000 BC, and the first bone flutes that have been found are dated to 33,000 BC. By 15,000 BC, humans had settled on all the world's continents. We speak of this whole period, from the emergence of *Homo habilis*, as "hominization", and in this process we move from evolution to history.

Evidence of plant cultivation is found by 30,000 BC, but settled agriculture is generally thought to have begun around 12,000 years ago, with the so-called Neolithic period, with pigs and sheep domesticated about 11,000 years ago, and cattle about 8,500 years ago. Rather than there being a sudden "discovery of agriculture", it is probable that agricultural practices emerged very gradually over huge periods of time, and in different parts of the world. For most of this period, stone tools continued to be the norm, with the Bronze Age starting only about 3300 BC. It is settled agriculture, and the emergence of relatively large and reliable food supplies, which makes the growth of cities possible. Around this period, we find the earliest Sumerian and Egyptian dynasties, relying on industries like weaving, metalwork and pottery, and trading over wide areas. The Sumerians had their own writing. Ur, from which Abraham emigrated, was flourishing around 2600 BC, the period from which we have the first coherent texts. The Akkadian empire, which was the predecessor of both the Assyrian and Babylonian empires which subjugated Israel, replaced the Sumerian about 2270 BC. Codes of law are taken as a crucial advance in hominization, a step away from the blood feud. The code of Hammurabi, who reigned in Babylon from 1792–1750 BC, is seen as a precursor of Israel's Ten Words. The event we know as "the exodus" may have taken place under Ramesses II, who reigned from 1279–1213 BC. According to a currently widely accepted hypothesis the people we know as "Israel" may have been formed of a small group of escaped slaves from Egypt, roving bands of Hyksos coming down from the north, and the peasants who worked to supply the Canaanite city states. This group lived in a loose federation, led in emergencies by charismatic leaders, until the need to combat new arrivals with an iron age technology led to the adoption of "a king like all the nations". David reigned from *c*.1010–970 BC, the period in which the Iron Age began in Palestine. Approximately two centuries later we find Homer, in Greece or modern-day Turkey, and Hosea, Amos and Micah in Israel, at the start of what Karl Jaspers called "the axial age", in documents which still inform modern consciousness. Gautama, the Greek tragedians, Plato, Aristotle, the Stoics and other philosophical schools which followed them, the authors of Second Isaiah and of Job, are all part of this age.

The sense of time

Memory and anticipation, that is to say, the past and the future, are the building blocks of a sense of time (as Augustine suggests in the *Confessions*). They are shared by other mammals, linked to food, which is to say, survival. Philosophers have puzzled over the apparent non-being of past and future, but this would have been meaningless to hunter-gatherers. Memory, the past, was the memory of both feast and fast. As memory, it might be the recall of delicious food which simply by being recalled set the gastric juices flowing. As anticipation, it was looking forward to experiencing the same again.

Gathering food, certainly in nomadic and pre-agricultural societies, requires a sense of time, linked to distance. The major marker of time, at least as far as the authors of Genesis were concerned, was the passage of day and night. Time is linked to distance, as it still is in our ordinary speech. That water hole is one day or half a day's march. The place where we found game is two days' walk away. Today we might say, "The school is just ten minutes away". The ability to measure, crucial in the development of human conceptual ability, thus develops in relation to distance and time. The old measure of a league was an hour's walk, which presupposes, as we shall see, quite a sophisticated understanding of time. Today, geographers speak of "space–time compression" as previously unimaginable distances are traversed in hours or minutes and this affects our moral sense as well, as it feeds the demand for the instant gratification of all our wants.

If the alternation of day and night is the most obvious marker of time, next would be, over a longer period, the phases of the moon. The earliest documents we have, from Egypt and Mesopotamia, all show us that early humans paid keen attention to the night sky, not just the moon, but the position of stars in the zodiac. The authors of Genesis speak of the light of the sun, moon and stars as the means by which created time is measured (Genesis 1:14). On a longer scale again, the passage of the seasons (in most latitudes), the fall of the leaf, and then new growth in spring, gave a sense of a longer time span. The understanding of time is thermometric—based on "the sensible increase and diminution of heat in spring and autumn" (Chambers 1903: 113).

Cutting across these natural cycles is the brevity of the life of humans and animals. The length of a human span, which developed into the notion of a generation, is another kind of cycle, but it marks frets in the rhythm of time:

> As for mortals, their days are like grass;
> they flourish like a flower of the field;
> for the wind passes over it, and it is gone,
> and its place knows it no more (Psalm 103:15–16).

All these time markers are what Bede speaks of as "natural time", as opposed to time established by custom or by authority. In his concern for liturgical time, he looks in detail at all these elements.

The day

The day may be the primary marker of time, but when does it begin? In answering that question, we are already in the territory of *convention* or custom. The Egyptians reckoned from sunrise to sunrise and the Sumerians and Babylonians from sunset to sunset. Looking at the frequent occurrence of the phrase "day and night" (e.g. Deuteronomy 28:66–7; 1 Samuel 30:12; Isaiah 28:19; Jeremiah 33:20), at stories like the Levite of Ephraim (Judges 19) or David's escape from Saul (1 Samuel 19:11), and at some of the Levitical regulations (Leviticus 7:15; 23:5–6) scholars argue that the Israelite day originally ran from morning to morning, like the Egyptian day. Later, under Babylonian influence, the day was reckoned from evening to evening, and this seems to be assumed in the account of creation (Genesis 1:5). This has marked the Jewish day ever since: it begins with the appearance of three stars in the sky. Later, Islam followed Jewish practice (though there are dissenting voices which argue that according to the Qur'an the day begins at dawn), as did the Christian monastic tradition, for which the day began with vespers. Bede argues that though the day began at dawn at the creation, from the resurrection onwards it begins after sunset. First, time moved from light to darkness, but now from darkness to light. The resurrection, he says, "illumines the night". The celebration of Christmas and Easter at midnight, however, shows that the Church by and large reckons the day from midnight to midnight.

Even if the day began technically at midnight (as it did in Rome), practically speaking it began at dawn, when work was possible, and finished when darkness made continued work impossible. When good enough candles were available, the need to meet work commitments might lead to "burning the candle at both ends"—i.e. at both ends of the day, so that weavers, in particular, could work both early and late.

Many cultures, including ancient Egypt, Babylon, Greece and Rome, had lists of auspicious and inauspicious days. Hesiod's *Works and Days*, a peasant poem from the sixth century BC adumbrating good agricultural practice, ends with a long list of such days. How might this idea have arisen? An ingenious suggestion is that the Mesopotamians adopted a 360-day year in the interests of accounting efficiency. The problem was that reality did not map on to this, and "observed coherence with the ideal boded well, noncoherence ill" (Brown 2010: 187). When planets and other heavenly bodies did not behave according to their ideal these events were reported to the king. The notion of what was inauspicious could, then, derive from a failure to conform with the ideal. On the other hand, millennial wisdom also observed when it was good to plant, or cut trees, or lamb or calve, and therefore what times to avoid. Thomas Hardy recorded a superstition, still prevalent in the nineteenth century, that a man born when there was no moon would never thrive. Thus there were other reasons to judge something inauspicious. Neither Israel nor the Church adopted the notion of auspicious or inauspicious days, though superstitions about "Friday 13th" show that the idea still lingers even in the technologically sophisticated West.

Sirach (180–175 BC) can ask:

> Why is one day better than the others,
> While all the daylight of the year is from the sun?
> They were separated by the wisdom of the Lord,
> And he made the times and feasts different.
> Some of them he made exalted and holy,
> And some he counted as ordinary days (Sirach 33:7–9).

All the cultures we know have feast days and holy days, and they are a conspicuous part of the liturgical calendar (they are the subject of Part 3). As we shall see, they mark significant agricultural or historical events, and commemorate people significant to a particular culture. In the liturgical calendar, every such day is a form of thanksgiving to G-d:

> When the Church venerates the saints she is acknowledging
> and proclaiming the victorious grace of the one Redeemer and
> Mediator, Christ. She is thanking the Father for the mercy that
> is bestowed in Christ and that has taken visible, effective form
> in one of her members and thus in the body of the Church as a
> whole (Adam 1979: 200).

Whether measured from dawn to dawn or sunset to sunset the day is never merely a short period of time but something filled with theological and existential significance. The transition from reckoning the day from dawn to dawn to evening to evening was given a theological rationale: creation ends with rest, and each day likewise begins with rest and only then advances to work. Rest, then, has priority over labour, which would have been a polemical point in relation to the Babylonian Atrahasis epic, which taught that human beings were created for unremitting toil, that they were the slaves of the gods. This view of the meaning of human life was deeply pessimistic, but at the same time can be understood as a classic piece of ideology as the obligation to work did not apply to the king and his nobles. Here the ruling ideas of the age were certainly those of the ruling class and alas are still with us, though the mode of expression has changed, with financiers and billionaires in the place of kings, and workers around the globe producing cheap goods for the affluent in the role of those condemned to ceaseless toil.

In the Tenakh, the word "day" (*yom*) is often used to speak of the intervention of G-d, especially in delivering Israel or giving it victory over its enemies (e.g. Exodus 12:17; Judges 19:30). Such and such a day is "the day of YHWH". This day of salvation could then be used of individual deliverance, whether from enemies or from sickness (e.g. Psalms 18:48; 20:2). Gerhard von Rad argued that the phrase "the day of YHWH" originated in the traditions of holy war, and, associated as it was with victory, was thought of as a joyful occasion, but was then taken by the prophets and used as a warning of G-d's judgement on a sinful nation (e.g. Amos 5:18,20). Klaus Koch argues that the prophetic use of the phrase marked a profound change in Israel's understanding of time. Hitherto Israel had looked backward to salvation history and creation in their cultic celebration. By criticizing social, political and cultic conditions as intolerable, however, they relativized the ultimate importance of the divinely given past and instead made hope the foundation of their theology, introducing a sense of incompleteness and a further purpose to be found in world events (Koch vol. 1 1982: 162–3).

The language of "the day of the Lord" is taken up in the Messianic Writings (1 Thessalonians 5:2) where it becomes "the last day" (John 6:39), "the day of judgement" (2 Peter 2:9) or simply "the day" (1 Corinthians 3:13), which is to say the day when Jesus' Second Coming is anticipated, a day for which the whole of creation longs (Romans 8:22) but also a day when evil doers will be punished (Matthew 24:50–1 and often).

The theological use of the word "day" therefore develops in two directions. On the one hand, in its prophetic use and in the Messianic Writings, it is used eschatologically to speak of G-d's coming decisive intervention at the end of time, predicated on G-d's intervention in the past, and especially in the exodus. Simon de Vries contrasts this view of time with an Egyptian view for which time is an endless, meaningless continuum, caught in a seasonal pattern of alteration (but is this not very close to Ecclesiastes?). On the other hand, in the application of the phrase to the deliverance of the individual, which may come on any day whatever, the theology of "the day of the Lord" works to sanctify every day. As we have seen, Sirach distinguishes between holy days and ordinary days, and Paul knew people who had taken this on board:

> Some judge one day to be better than another, while others judge
> all days to be alike. Let all be fully convinced in their own minds.
> Those who observe the day, observe it in honour of the Lord. Also
> those who eat, eat in honour of the Lord, since they give thanks
> to G-d; while those who abstain, abstain in honour of the Lord
> and give thanks to G-d (Romans 14:5–6).

It is clear in Romans that Paul is one of the "strong" who judge all days
alike, but his point is that one must not make a fetish of such issues.
Whichever view you take, what counts is whether you act for the honour
of G-d. Those who judge that all days are alike recognize that any day
could be a day in which G-d was encountered, whether in blessing or
judgement. Of every day we can say, with the Psalmist:

> This is the day that the LORD has made;
> let us rejoice and be glad in it (Psalm 118:24).

In other words that tradition of Christian spirituality which we are
familiar with from, for example, Teresa of Avila and George Herbert,
which finds the presence and reality of G-d in the daily round and
common task, is already implicit in the use of the term "day" in the
Tenakh. The two ways of thinking of "the day" are linked: Christians
must live *now* as "on that day" (Romans 13:13).

That "the day of YHWH" can be any day means that a fundamental
division between secular and sacred time is specious. All time is G-d's
time, and it has a direction, towards the consummation of G-d's purposes
in "the kingdom". This is not contradicted by the cyclical nature of cultic
time, the purpose of which, as we shall see in Parts 2 and 3, is to remind
us of the main framework of faith, of the nature of the G-d with whom
we have to do, and therefore to call us back from the misperceptions of
G-d, the idolatrous projections, to which humans are always prone (as
Calvin put it: "the human heart is a manufactory of idols").

Already in Genesis, the day as a twenty-four-hour period is contrasted
with the day as meaning daylight (Genesis 1:5; cf. Isaiah 10:17; Mark
6:21; Matthew 4:2). Bede says, "Day is air which is lit up by the sun". Karl
Barth reads "night" and "darkness" as that which G-d rejected. According

to him light is the sign and witness of G-d at the heart of all things, and darkness is the opposite. Light and darkness are not peacefully coexistent but mutually exclusive. He can point to the fact that G-d calls light good, and separates it from darkness, which is not similarly blessed (Genesis 1:4); to texts like Isaiah 5:20: "Woe to those who call evil good and good evil; who put darkness for light and light for darkness". Or 2 Corinthians 6:14: "What communion has light with darkness". Or the fact that there will be no night in the heavenly Jerusalem (Revelation 21:25).

But Barth overlooks the numerous texts where "day and night" quite clearly do mean twenty-four hours (e.g. Psalm 1:2); the fact that G-d sometimes commands people to act by night (Judges 9:32; Matthew 2:14); that G-d is wrapped in darkness (1 Kings 8:12; Psalm 18:9); that G-d speaks to the prophets by night (Numbers 22:20; 1 Samuel 15:16); that the Psalmist thinks that G-d creates night in order to feed the wild animals (Psalm 104:20); that the darkness is not dark to G-d (Psalm 139:11); above all that Jeremiah speaks of a covenant with both the day and the night (Jeremiah 33:20).

Barth's account is part of his attempt to give full weight to sin and evil without being forced to concede that G-d created it. On his account, G-d's non willing also has effects, and this is the world of sin, evil and darkness. This suggestion, however, as critics have said from the very beginning, has no warrant in Scripture, and it is surely better to include night in the blessing which comprehends everything that G-d has made, which was "very good" (Genesis 1:31). We are then free to experience darkness, like the author of Psalm 104, and as humans have always done, both as beautiful in itself, and as the occasion both for rest (without which we die) and also for pleasure (Song of Songs 3:1), as positive and creative in its way as daylight.

Lunation and the seasons

After the alternation of night and day, the most obvious marker of time is the lunar cycle (roughly 29.5 days a month). Sirach notes that the word "month" (*mēn*) is the same as the word for "moon" (Ecclesiasticus 43:8), and Bede derived it from the Latin *metiri*, "to measure" (since the moon was used to measure time). The Roman Kalends, the first day of the month, referred to the appearance of the first sliver of the new moon and was the day for accounting (*kalendaria* are account books).

New moons are frequently mentioned together with Sabbaths as sacred days in the Tenakh. In Saul's court, the new moon was a day you were expected to appear (1 Samuel 20:5), and Amos speaks of merchants longing for the new moon and the Sabbath to be over so that they can trade (Amos 8:5), so they were obviously prohibited from trading until the appearance of the moon signified the end of the Sabbath.

The lunar cycle is not endlessly undifferentiated, for what is actually going on in the natural world during a lunation varies according to latitude, height above sea level and relation to the solar year. In other words, when we think about lunations we have to think about the seasons as well. In ancient Israel, only two seasons are mentioned—hot and cold, summer and winter (Genesis 8:22; Psalm 74:17; Isaiah 18:6; Zechariah 14:8; cf. Amos 3:15; Jeremiah 36:22). Bede says the same was originally true for the Saxons, who had only two divisions in the year, summer and winter, summer being the time when days are longer than nights and winter the opposite. Later, three lunations were assigned to each season except in an "embolismic" year, in which there were thirteen lunations, and then summer was granted an extra one.

Hesiod has four seasons and ends the year after the grape harvest in what we call September/October, and the ploughing which follows it. The goddesses of the seasons are the Hōrae (the word from which we derive our "hour"), Order, Peace and Justice. Hesiod presumably wants to say that without these farming cannot prosper. Israel adopted this pattern of the seasons in the Hellenistic period. Egypt, meanwhile, had three seasons, based on the rise and fall of the Nile—flooding between June and September, due to the monsoon in the Ethiopian highlands, planting and growth as the river fell, and then harvest.

People in what we call "the ancient world" knew that the planets moved but thought they moved around the earth. Their astronomy (which was also often astrology) did not tell them that day and night are caused by the earth spinning around its own axis; or that this axis is tilted about 23.5 degrees from the vertical, which combines with the earth moving round the sun to produce seasons. The cycle of the seasons, which means that fruit and grain ripen at more or less the same point of time over an extended period, is what gives us the agricultural year.

The agricultural year

Until the advent of industrial agriculture, the seasons determined the pattern of the agricultural year, and this is what the monthly calendars reflected. The earliest Israelite calendars had Canaanite names: Abib, the month of the ears of corn (Exodus 13:4; 23:15; Deuteronomy 16:1); Ziv, the month of flowers (1 Kings 6:1,37); Etanim, the month in which only permanent water courses flow (1 Kings 8:2); Bul, the month of the great rains (1 Kings 6:38). De Vaux cites a tenth-century calendar, discovered at Gezer, which maps the lunar year against agricultural tasks:

- Ingathering: Two months
- Seedtime: Two months
- Late seedtime: Two months
- Flax gathering: One month
- Barley harvest: One month
- Wheat harvest: One month
- Pruning: Two months
- Summer fruits: One month

Liturgical calendars in the Tenakh use these terms. Thus Exodus 23:16 says that harvest and ingathering must be observed; Exodus 24:22 mentions ingathering and wheat harvest (the Feast of Weeks, Pentecost). Elsewhere we frequently read about the wheat and barley harvests (Genesis 30:14; Judges 15:1; 1 Samuel 12:17; 2 Samuel 21:9–10; Ruth 1:22), and Amos sees locusts swarming at the time of late growth (Amos 7:1). Later, Israel adopted the names of the Babylonian calendar, beginning in the spring (the month of Nisan, March–April, later important in determining the date of Easter). The Gezer calendar is an agricultural (as opposed to pastoral) calendar, related to the growing of crops and vines.

Every agricultural calendar is cyclical, and the pattern, whether for agriculture or for stock keeping, is roughly the same year after year. This cycle is the foundation of the liturgical year, which marks occasions for thanksgiving and for propitiation—and if the Tenakh is our guide, the former are far more frequent than the latter. Although growing food is hard work, a profound sense of thankfulness marks all ancient liturgies.

Dating texts in the Tenakh is problematic, and many scholars today accept a late date for all books, but this is improbable. It is fairly easy to see, for example, a development in the account of the ancient Israelite festivals. In the liturgical calendar in "the Book of the Covenant" in Exodus (Exodus 23:14–17; cf. 34:18–23), three annual feasts are mentioned: Unleavened Bread, Harvest and Ingathering. At these feasts all are commanded to "see the face of G-d", or to "appear before G-d" (Exodus 23:17). This command is interpreted as requiring pilgrimage to a shrine, implausible as a requirement whilst harvest was going on, but possible when completed. In Judges, we read of the young girls dancing in the vineyards at "the feast of YHWH" (Ingathering) (Judges 21:19–21). Later, as we shall see, other festivals were added.

The feast of unleavened bread is not mentioned together with the Passover, and it seems that they were brought together later (they are mentioned as one feast in Ezekiel 45:21). The feast of unleavened bread marked the beginning of the barley harvest and was supposed to run from Sabbath to Sabbath. That bread was eaten "without leaven" meant that it marked a new beginning. As an agricultural feast it was not observed until the occupation of Canaan and may have been taken from the Canaanites (cf. Leviticus 23:10).

Passover, on the other hand, was a nomad festival and the sacrifice of the lamb was probably to secure the prosperity of the flock. The blood sprinkled on the lintels was probably originally sprinkled on tent poles and designed to keep away evil powers, the "exterminator" (Exodus 12:23). All shepherds will tell you that the prime object of any sheep is to die. Steering them clear of this desire is the main object of shepherding and may require more than propitiatory sacrifice. That it was roasted over a fire without kitchen utensils, eaten with unleavened bread and with bitter herbs—herbs picked from the desert—is because the flocks were being driven up to higher pastures. It was celebrated at full moon, because this was the brightest night of the month and the flocks may have been moved up to the hills at night. Perhaps under the reign of

Josiah these two feasts were amalgamated, and Passover was designated a pilgrimage feast by Deuteronomy, which wanted to centralize worship. When the two feasts were brought together, this meant that the start of the feast of unleavened bread on the Sabbath had to be abandoned and it simply followed on from Passover. At this stage, both feasts were given a salvation-historical meaning, as in Exodus 12.

The second feast, seven weeks after this, was the Feast of Weeks, celebrating the wheat harvest (Exodus 34:22). The feast involved offering two loaves baked with new flour and using yeast (Leviticus 23:15–21). As an agricultural feast its date could not at first be fixed, because it depended on the weather (Exodus 23:16; 34:22). It too was connected with the history of salvation by being linked to the giving of the covenant. For the Qumran community, it was the most important feast of the year.

For most Jews, however, the Feast of Tabernacles or Booths (Sukkoth) was the most important of the three feasts (Leviticus 23:39; 1 Kings 8:2,65; Ezekiel 45:25). Josephus calls it "the holiest and greatest of Hebrew feasts". The "booths" were probably shelters made from tree branches whilst the grapes and fruits were gathered. It was the main harvest festival both of grain, olives and wine (Exodus 23:16; Deuteronomy 16:13). It too was given a salvation-historical meaning as a reminder of the temporary shelters people had to use during the exodus (Leviticus 23:43).

A successful harvest could never be taken for granted, but when there was one it was, of course, an occasion for celebration. Harvests, lambings and calvings, essential for life once the hunter-gatherer lifestyle was left behind, were the major markers of time for agricultural populations.

The brevity of life

The second of Hawking's arrows of time he calls "psychological". Hawking claims that our brain measures time in a way where disorder increases in the direction of time—we never observe it working in the opposite direction. In other words, Hawking claims that the psychological arrow of time is intertwined with the thermodynamic arrow of time. I suspect that in reality our awareness of time derives in large part from the fact that our journey from birth to death is inexorable, and that death comes so casually, and to many so brutally early. The Psalms of Israel are full of this sense. In Psalm 39 we read:

> LORD, let me know my end,
> and what is the measure of my days;
> let me know how fleeting my life is.
> You have made my days a few handbreadths,
> and my lifetime is as nothing in your sight.
> Surely everyone stands as a mere breath.
> Surely everyone goes about like a shadow.
> Surely for nothing they are in turmoil;
> they heap up, and do not know who will gather (Psalm 39:4–6).

Eighty years is the maximum we can expect:

> The days of our life are seventy years,
> or perhaps eighty, if we are strong;
> even then their span is only toil and trouble;
> they are soon gone, and we fly away (Psalm 90:10;
>   cf. Psalm 78:39; 103:15–16; 144:4).

The Book of Job is also full of these complaints about the brevity of life:

> Mortals die, and are laid low;
> humans expire, and where are they?
> As waters fail from a lake,
> and a river wastes away and dries up,
> so mortals lie down and do not rise again;
> until the heavens are no more, they will not awake
> or be roused out of their sleep.
> O that you would hide me in Sheol,
> that you would conceal me until your wrath is past,
> that you would appoint me a set time, and
>   remember me (Job 14:10–13; cf. 7:6–7)!

We find a similar sentiment in the Odyssey (Book 11), where Odysseus speaks with the shade of Achilles, reminding him of his glorious mortal existence. Achilles answers:

> Nay, seek not to speak soothingly to me of death, glorious Odysseus—I should choose, so I might live on earth, to serve as the hireling of another, of some portionless man whose livelihood was but small, rather than to be lord over all the dead that have perished.

To characterize this as what Ariès called "tame death", death as a necessary evil, to be met with composure, seems to me implausible. Early humans were only too aware of the liveliness of life and the deadliness of death, and the brevity of an individual life was a key marker of human time. Genesis 2 and 3 mythologize this in their own way. Human beings, the story tells us, were made for immortality but seeking the tree of life they are turned out of paradise. Now,

> by the sweat of your face
> you shall eat bread
> until you return to the ground,
> for out of it you were taken;
> you are dust,
> and to dust you shall return . . .
> therefore the LORD G-d sent him forth from the garden of Eden,
> to till the ground from which he was taken (Genesis 3:19,23).

The consciousness of the brevity of life marks a difference in the awareness of time. The alternation of day and night, the phases of the moon, and the passage of the seasons, are all natural cycles. These cycles form the framework of human life. But human life is not a cycle. Hawking's "second arrow" runs from birth to death, and it is remarked that this applies not just to humans but to all created things. Circularity, then, is crossed by a vertical line, by death. This is another aspect of "nature". Nature is cyclical, but it is not eternal (though Penrose argues that, if conceived as the raw material of the universe, it might be). Human time is a unidirectional arrow measured in terms of the cyclical pattern of the seasons and years. Liturgy comes into being partly as a way of reflecting on, and making sense of, this fact. Early agricultural liturgies may well have been primarily sacrificial, and primarily occasions for thanksgiving and sharing in the gifts of creation. As we have seen, by the time our Scriptures are written, they have acquired stories, they make a claim to cultural memory (self-evidently in the Passover liturgy). Memory gives us not only access to food, as I argued at the beginning of this section, but identity, both individual and cultural. A liturgical calendar is a map of cultural identity, charting a path through the wilderness of time, and relating all created to uncreated time, namely to the origin of all things we call "G-d". Of course there are "gods many and lords many" (1 Corinthians 8:5), and many gods are simply cultural, corporate or even individual projections. We then worship ourselves. Most national ceremonies, even if conducted in Christian churches, involve this kind of self-worship. The G-d witnessed to by Scripture, on the other hand, as we shall see in Parts 2 and 3, calls us to thanksgiving and repentance, to a repeated self-scrutiny, and a repeated obedience.

Ordering time

The decision whether to reckon the day from midnight, dawn or evening is, as we saw, already a matter of convention rather than of "nature". This applies to most of the time markers which we take for granted.

The week

Most cultures have grouped their days, and the prevalence of the number seven in cultures around the world is usually derived from the phases of the moon. De Vaux, however, comments that if a seven-day cycle is uniformly applied it is independent of the lunar months, which are not exactly divisible into weeks, and proposes that, though suggested by the moon's phases, the seven-day cycle acquired an independent significance. In other words, reckoning, as opposed to following the cycle suggested by lunation, comes into play. Since the days in a solar year cannot be divided by seven, one extra day outside the week (a "nonhebdomadal" day) has to be added each year, or two in a leap year. What this shows is that "the year is already determined by the order of creation itself, while the week as a temporal unit is of historical origin and must be subordinate to the year" (Adam 1979: 298).

A sevenfold grouping of days was not the only possibility. Ancient Egyptians divided a thirty-day month into three- and ten-day periods, which appear here and there in Scripture (e.g. Genesis 24:55; Exodus 12:3; Leviticus 16:29; 1 Samuel 25:38). Excavations in Palestine have turned up bone tablets pierced with three parallel lines of ten holes, and it is surmised that these might be calendar markers, though this does not prove that Israel once had a ten-day period of time. Ancient Rome had an eight-day week, where the last day (the *nundinum*) was a market day, characterized by festivity. Elsewhere, thirteen-day, nine-day, five-day and three-day divisions of time are known, but the commonest unit of time is seven. In Mesopotamia and Palestine, the seven-day cycle was of key importance. The Gudea cylinders, dating from the third millennium BC, now in the Louvre, record the rebuilding of a temple to Ningirsu, a god associated with the yearly spring rains, which had seven rooms and was followed by a seven-day festival. Seven-day periods are also found in the epic of Gilgamesh and the poems of Ras Shamra, as well as in the Tenakh (e.g. Genesis 8:10–12; 29:27; 50:10).

As well as the seven-day week Bede discerns seven other "weeks" in Scripture: the first is the week in which G-d created all things. Then there is Pentecost, the "feast of weeks"; the seventh month, in which the Day of Atonement is celebrated; the Sabbath for the land kept every seventh year (Leviticus 25:1–7); the Jubilee, which is seven times seven, plus one, years; the "seventy prophetic weeks" of Daniel which lead up to the birth of Christ; and the week of the world ages, which take us to the end of time. Strictly speaking we have gone beyond convention here, because these are time divisions created by divine fiat, time created by authority. There are human analogies to this, as when emperors establish annual festivities to honour particular events.

Both in Babylonian and Hebrew, the number seven is synonymous with fullness and totality (cf. Proverbs 3:10, where the word translated "plenty" in the NRSV is the number seven). On the other hand, the Babylonian calendar from the seventh century BC picks out the seventh, fourteenth, twenty-first and twenty-eighth days as unlucky days.

The seven-day week was adopted by Greece and Persia, and by Rome after Caesar's calendar reform of 45 BC, where it coexisted with the eight-day period for some time. It later spread to China, India and Japan. What counts as the first day of the week varies around the world. In Europe, and according to the International Standardization Organization, it is Monday; in the Middle East it is Saturday; in North America, Brazil and Japan it is Sunday.

In Greece, the days of the week were named after what they thought of as the major planets: the Sun, Moon, Ares (Mars), Hermes (Mercury), Zeus (Jupiter), Aphrodite (Venus) and Cronos (Saturn). Rome took over this pattern, and the Latin names appear in most Romance languages. In Northern Europe, sometime between the second and the sixth or seventh centuries, the second to the fifth days of the week acquired Germanic or Norse names—Tiw's day (Tiw being the god of single combat), Woden (taken as equivalent to Mercury), Thor and Frige (Venus)—though ironically Germany itself has followed an ecclesiastical ordering, not derived from astrology, in calling Wednesday "Mid-week" (*Mittwoch*).

The Sabbath and Sunday

According to the Fourth Commandment, humans should work six days and rest on the seventh. This is the prime example of what Bede calls time established by authority, namely by G-d's command. The Sabbath command effectively establishes "the working week". In affluent countries there is now usually a five-day week followed by a "weekend", though even here this does not apply to farmers or to workers in the gig economy. The importance of the Hebrew attitude is that, unlike Babylon or Greece, work is affirmed as something proper to human being. Work is required even in paradise (Genesis 2:15) and the writers of the Tenakh, followed by Paul, expect all to work (Exodus 20:9; 2 Thessalonians 3:10). Work is not romanticized—all forms of work involve toil (Genesis 3:18), but there is a promise that finally it will be redeemed (Isaiah 65:23. The Septuagint ("LXX") translated this, following the predominant Greek view, as "work will be outdated"). It seems probable that the story of the great catch of fish in Luke (Luke 5:1ff.) is intended as a messianic anticipation of the end of the alienation of work.

At the same time, although work is proper to our humanness, life is more than labour. "Life is more than food, and the body more than clothing" (Matthew 6:25). That the Song of Songs is the minor scroll at Passover is intended to show that the struggle for liberation is not the be-all and end-all of human endeavour: the joy which is proper to life transcends that. It is in this way that the Sabbath completes the week.

The origins of the Sabbath are unclear. Babylonian, Canaanite and Kenite origins have all been proposed, but without commanding universal or even majority assent. The similarity of the Akkadian *shapattu*, which was a full moon feast held in the middle of the month, to the Hebrew *shabbat* has led some scholars to propose that the Sabbath was originally a monthly full moon feast, which became a weekly feast during the exile. But the *shapattu* was not a day of rest. De Vaux thinks the nearest similarity might be that, just as the Akkadian *shapattu* marked a division in the middle of the month, so the Sabbath marked a boundary between one week and another.

Whenever it is mentioned, the Sabbath is described as a seventh day, on which people rest after six days of work. Two rationales for this are offered. Deuteronomy, a document originating towards the end of the kingdom in Judah, speaks of the Sabbath as what we could call a sacrament of the fact that G-d brought Israel out of slavery in Egypt (Deuteronomy 5:14b–15). The second suggestion, emanating from the Priestly source, is that G-d rested on the seventh day after the labour of creation and thus established a day of rest for all G-d's creatures. For this theology, the Sabbath is a reminder of the covenant G-d made when creation was finished. This meant it was a pledge of salvation (Isaiah 58:13–14), which could be forfeited if either a community or individual failed to keep it (Exodus 31:14; Ezekiel 20:13).

Most communities keep a day of rest and relaxation, though not necessarily for slaves, servants or the working class. The Hebrew Sabbath was marked by the extension to the entire community, including the animals:

> Observe the Sabbath day and keep it holy, as the LORD your G-d commanded you. Six days you shall labour and do all your work. But the seventh day is a Sabbath to the LORD your G-d; you shall not do any work—you, or your son or your daughter, or your male or female slave, or your ox or your donkey, or any of your livestock, or the resident alien in your towns, so that your male and female slave may rest as well as you. Remember that you were a slave in the land of Egypt, and the LORD your G-d brought you out from there with a mighty hand and an outstretched arm; therefore the LORD your G-d commanded you to keep the Sabbath day (Deuteronomy 5:12–15).

In texts which go back to the eighth century BC, the Sabbath is described as a joyful feast day (Isaiah 1:13; Hosea 2:11), when both heavy work and commercial transactions were suspended (Exodus 20:9–10; Amos 8:5). During the exile, when the Temple feasts could no longer be observed, the Sabbath acquired more importance and was gradually hedged about with more and more restrictions. Nehemiah records his shock at finding that normal trading was going on in Jerusalem on the Sabbath and tells us that he had the gates of the city locked to prevent it (Nehemiah 13:15–22). Josephus tells us that the Essenes would not prepare food on the Sabbath, would not light a fire, nor move any household object, "or even relieve nature". Though not as strict as this the Pharisees in the Gospels are depicted as somewhere on this spectrum, which prompted Jesus' comment that the Sabbath was made for human beings, not human beings for the Sabbath, a view echoed by the rabbis in the second century AD.

The first Christians, being Jews, kept the Sabbath, but they also broke bread on the first day of the week, being the day after the Sabbath (Mark 16:2; John 20:19; Acts 20:7; 1 Corinthians 16:2). The Book of Revelation speaks of "the Lord's Day" (Revelation 1:10), generally assumed to be the day after the Sabbath, though sometimes read to mean the Sabbath in view of Jesus' word that "the Son of Man is Lord of the Sabbath" (Matthew 12:8). Justin Martyr wrote: "The first day after the Sabbath, remaining the first of all the days, is called, however, the eighth, according to the number of all the days of the cycle, and [yet] remains the first." Although there are possible mentions of "the Lord's Day" in the Didache, Ignatius and the apocryphal Gospels, it was not until later in the second century that the expression becomes normal as referring to the day after the Sabbath and is explained as commemorating the day of resurrection.

Around 150, Justin gives an account of Christian worship which is held on "the day which is called the day of the sun":

> And on the day called Sunday, all who live in cities or in the country gather together to one place, and the memoirs of the apostles or the writings of the prophets are read, as long as time permits; then, when the reader has ceased, the president verbally instructs, and exhorts to the imitation of these good things. Then we all rise together and pray, and, as we before said, when our prayer is ended, bread and wine and water are brought, and

the president in like manner offers prayers and thanksgivings, according to his ability, and the people assent, saying Amen; and there is a distribution to each, and a participation of that over which thanks have been given, and to those who are absent a portion is sent by the deacons. And they who are well to do, and willing, give what each thinks fit; and what is collected is deposited with the president, who succours the orphans and widows and those who, through sickness or any other cause, are in want, and those who are in bonds and the strangers sojourning among us, and in a word takes care of all who are in need. *But Sunday is the day on which we all hold our common assembly, because it is the first day on which G-d, having wrought a change in the darkness and matter, made the world; and Jesus Christ our Saviour on the same day rose from the dead* (Apology 67).

As we see, the reason for celebrating on Sunday is twofold: it commemorates both the beginning of creation, and the beginning of the new creation in the resurrection.

After the crushing of the Bar Kochba revolt in 135, Jerusalem was destroyed and Jewish practices proscribed. This would certainly have been a cue to put a distance between Christian and Jewish practices, though as a matter of fact Christians in some areas continued to observe the Sabbath for many centuries. Sozomen, in the fifth century, says that Christians in Constantinople "and almost everywhere" observe the Sabbath, but not in Rome or Alexandria. Nevertheless Constantine's decree in March 312 was certainly a decisive moment:

On the venerable day of the Sun, let the magistrates and people residing in cities rest, and let all workshops be closed. In the country, however, persons engaged in agriculture may freely and lawfully continue their pursuits, because it often happens that another day is not suitable for grain sowing or vine planting; lest by neglecting the proper moment for such operations the bounty of heaven should be lost (Schaff 1867: 380).

Constantine had worshipped the unconquered sun, but after the battle of the Milvian bridge became a Christian (though he was not baptized until on his death bed). Many Christians (including Bede) jibbed at the description of the main day of Christian worship as "the day of the Sun", preferring "the Lord's Day", but it became conventional. Following Constantine's edict, the first day of the week (according to Jewish reckoning) was now Sunday and treated like the Sabbath. The tendency to treat Sunday as the Sabbath became embedded. Aquinas wrote:

> In the New Law the keeping of Sunday supplants that of the Sabbath, not in virtue of the precept of the law, but through determination by the Church and the custom of the Christian people. Furthermore this practice does not stand as a figure as did the Sabbath in the Old Law, and so the prohibition of work on Sunday is not as strict as it was on the Sabbath (ST 2a2ae.122,5).

Not only was it not so strict but, in Britain at least, "church ales", festivities which involved a lot of drinking, and were intended to raise money for the repair of the church or the support of the clergy, were common into Tudor times, and were generally held on a Sunday. Whitsun ales continued into the twentieth century. They were usually held either in the church or in a barn nearby.

Luther and Calvin broadly agreed with Aquinas' line, but the Puritans of the following century, who often understood themselves as "the new Israel" and bound by the covenants of the Hebrew Bible, followed a strictness which recalled the practices of Jewish groups in the intertestamental period. Thus the Westminster Confession (1646) taught that the Sabbath (understood to be Sunday) is kept holy:

> when men, after a due preparing of their hearts, and ordering of their common affairs beforehand, do not only observe a holy rest, all the day, from their own works, words, and thoughts about their worldly employments and recreations, but also are taken up, the whole time, in the public and private exercises of his worship, and in the duties of necessity and mercy (Westminster Confession 21:8).

Though there was a reaction to Puritanism, especially in the Enlightenment, this approach to Sunday was embodied in trading laws and cultural practices until the late twentieth century (1979 in Britain), when the god of the market was formally enthroned (by a Methodist Prime Minister!). In 1998, Pope John Paul II felt the need to issue a Pastoral letter, *Dies Domini*, urging the faithful not to confuse "the weekend" with the observation of the Lord's Day. He recognized the value of rest and relaxation but pointed to the centrality of the weekly Eucharist for Christian faith and practice.

Following the Holocaust, Christian theology has given much more attention to Jewish understandings. Teachers like Martin Buber and Abraham Heschel have emerged as important dialogue partners for Christian theology. This has prompted renewed reflection both on the nature of the Sabbath, and on the relation of Sabbath and Lord's Day.

In Heschel's view, Judaism is primarily about the sanctification of time, and "Sabbaths are its cathedrals". He is completely unconvinced by the arguments that the Sabbath has anything to do with the moon (though "Sabbaths and new moons" are frequently mentioned together in the Tenakh). Instead, it is an ordinance of creation. "The Sabbath preceded creation and the Sabbath completed creation; it is all of the Spirit that the world can bear" (Heschel 2005: 21). It has both a positive and a negative significance. In the first instance, it is a day of joy and peace, a day when we are embraced by the divine rest (*menuah*). This is the reason the Eighteen Benedictions are not said on the Sabbath, because the day should not be marred by worry or grief. The command to rest should not be understood as helping one return with renewed vitality to labour. A human being is not a beast of burden (and let us not forget that Exodus and Deuteronomy included beasts of burden in the Sabbath), and the Sabbath is not for the purpose of increasing efficiency. But the Sabbath also has critical significance. Shabbat is a day of harmony and peace between humans, within humans, and with all things. For this very reason, we should not tamper with G-d's world on the Sabbath. We can say that Sabbath has an eschatological significance. In its resistance to the worship of things and of technological civilization the Sabbath is "an example of the world to come".

Learning from Heschel, and also Franz Rosenzweig, Jürgen Moltmann urges a return to primitive Christian practice when both Sabbath and the Lord's Day were observed. Sunday does not, as teachers like Tertullian thought, abolish the Sabbath. On the contrary, it should be understood as a "messianic extension of Israel's Sabbath" (Moltmann 1985: 294). The first celebrates G-d's works in creation and the second the future of a new creation. The Sabbath is pre-eminently a day of remembrance and thanksgiving, whilst the Christian feast of the resurrection is pre-eminently a day of new beginning and of hope. At the same time, he accords an eschatological significance to the Sabbath, arguing that it breaks through the cyclical rebirth of natural time by prefiguring the messianic time and is therefore the sign of the coming freedom from time's cyclical course.

Like Heschel (and with Karl Barth!), Moltmann regards the Sabbath as the crown of creation. The Sabbath teaches us that humans are part of the community of creation. Creation is not simply a stage, and other creatures are not there simply for the sake of human beings. As the Benedicite recognizes, all creatures exist as a realization of G-d's free gift and are part of the celebration of the divine glory. Human history, even including the incarnation, is not the ultimate meaning of creation but rather the new, consummated creation.

Heschel's argument that the Sabbath is a protest against the tyranny of technology becomes in Moltmann a vital part of an ecological doctrine of creation, teaching the sanctity of the created world which has to be honoured if we are to survive. The Sabbath should be observed, therefore, not because, as the Puritans thought, we are subject to the Old Law, but because it is the vital sign and sacrament of the sacredness of creation. At the same time, Sunday should be an assertion of hope for the threatened creation, and for this reason a day when the rule of commerce and of technological civilization is not honoured. Norman Wirzba has developed this, arguing that in their food and work practices, their farming and their economy, Christians need to recover the sense of Sabbath delight in creation as a key part of their response to the global emergency.

Moltmann argues that we have to find a practical way of sanctifying the Sabbath. The Saturday evening devotions which many Christians like to attend always contain something of the rest and happiness of Israel's Sabbath. Worship on Sunday morning can then be set wholly in the liberty of Christ's resurrection for the new creation. It is true that Saturday evening mass has become something which many Roman Catholics like to attend, tacitly adopting the Jewish practice of starting the day in the evening, but in my experience this is so that Sunday can then be a day of leisure, spent with family and friends. The real problem, as John Paul II acknowledged in *Dies Domini*, is that the affluence which has changed cultural patterns so markedly over the past fifty years in Europe and North America has put leisure and enjoyment at the heart of human reality. Ewan MacColl was quite right, in his 1932 song "The Manchester Rambler", to say that for millions of people:

> I may be a wage slave on Monday
> But I am a free man on Sunday.

That is entirely consistent with the Deuteronomists' understanding of the Sabbath, except that they also understood that worshipping the G-d of Life was also a key part of human freedom.

Hours

Peasant cultures do not need to break the day up into smaller units of time. You begin at dawn (or at cockcrow, when that is earlier) and work until dusk. You milk in the morning and the evening and need no clock to tell you when to do so. Sometimes to meet liturgical needs for sacrifices or rituals at particular times of day, sometimes for military reasons to set watches, sometimes for bureaucratic reasons, the advent of cities led to more precise measurements of time, developed independently in Egypt, Mesopotamia, China and perhaps elsewhere.

We have already seen that distance and time go together. In ancient Sumeria, lengths were standardized and applied to time. The basic unit was a barleycorn, six of which were taken as the length of one finger; 30 fingers made a cubit; 12 cubits made a *nindan*, for which the translation "a standard measure" is suggested; 60 cubits made one *UŠ* (a "sixty");

30 UŠ made one *dana*, approximately 10.8 kilometres. Scholars suggest this may represent a rest stop. Each twenty-four-hour period comprised twelve rest stops. So time was measured in units first used for lengths. One *dana* represented one twelfth of a day (Brown 2010). These divisions also corresponded with periods of the watch. The measurement of time, therefore, is also bound up with the need to keep watch. The Latin word for "the watch" is "vigil", and as the tradition of the canonical hours began to develop, vigils were kept on the eve of holy days—an interesting transformation of the connection of time and the watch.

Water clocks were invented as early as 1500 BC, and these could be used to measure the *dana*. Mesopotamians took sixty as their base number and the *dana* were divisible into sixtieths. It may be that our reckoning in terms of sixty minutes and twenty-four hours ultimately derives from the Sumerians. On the other hand, the significance of twelve may also derive from the fact that both Babylonians and Egyptians recognized twelve signs of the zodiac.

A night-day unit is called a *nychthemeron*. Brown suggests that the number of dana in a night-day unit derived from observation of the sun: "In one *nychthemeron* the sun moves through ca. 360°, and in one year the rising or setting point of the luminary does the same. In one month the sun rises 30 times . . . and its rising point has moved through the sky roughly the same distance that the sun moves in one *dana*" (Brown 2010: 189). Thus the *dana* come to measure the months. Units of length based on an average walking pace bring distance and time together, providing the fundamental units for measuring time.

The Sumerians and Babylonians were keen astronomers, as were the Egyptians, and in Egypt time was reckoned in relation to the small constellations which rise consecutively on the horizon. They adopted a ten-day grouping of time because a new star group appears on the horizon at dawn every ten days (Greek *dekanoi*, hence "decans"). The interval between the rising on the eastern horizon of one decanal star and the rising of its immediate follower was an "hour", but the length of this varied with the season. A star clock from the twenty-second century BC shows that twelve hours of darkness were reckoned, and Richard Parker suggests that the division of the day into twelve hours followed by analogy. From 1300 BC, we find instructions for constructing a shadow clock. A sundial from the tenth century BC was discovered in Gezer, and the story of the recovery of Hezekiah mentions one (2 Kings 20:8–11). Ancient sundials had twelve equal segments, and these divided the hours of daylight. A twelfth of daylight, therefore, an "hour" (Greek *hōra* and Latin *hora*), depended for its length on the time of year.

The night, meanwhile, was divided into either three or four watches. If dawn was at 6 a.m. then 9 a.m. was the third hour, and midday the sixth hour when, according to John, Jesus was crucified; 3 p.m. was the ninth hour when, according to all the Gospels, Jesus died; 6 p.m., dusk, was the end of this twelve-hour day. Ancient Israel divided the night into three watches (Exodus 14:24; Judges 7:19; 1 Samuel 11:11). The Romans, like the Babylonians, kept four watches: from sundown to 9 p.m., from 9 p.m. to midnight, from midnight to 3 a.m. and from 3 a.m. to 6 a.m.. The word of Jesus in Mark 13:35 appears to assume a fourfold division.

Bede gives us the smaller divisions of the hour: the *punctus* (one quarter of an hour), the *minutum* (one tenth—six minutes according to our reckoning), the *pars* (one fifteenth, four minutes) and the smallest unit, the *momentum*, which is one fortieth or one and a half minutes. Like the hour itself, these are all conventions.

A poem from the fifth century AD gives us an interesting picture of the day from a non-liturgical perspective but which has resonances with current concerns with "well-being". Then as now we have to assume an affluent household. The people under consideration here did not have to work, and presumably had servants and lived off rent. It names the hours as sunrise (*anatole*), hour of music and study (*mousike*), hour of exercise (*gymnastike*), bath time (*nymphe*), noon (*mesembria*), libations after lunch (*sponde*), prayer (*elete*), eating and pleasure (*akte*), evening (*hesperis*) and sunset (*dysis*). These ten were then topped and tailed with first light (*auge*) and night sky (*arktos*) (Nonnos 1940: 41.263).

The LXX frequently translates the Hebrew word *et*, time, by *hōra*, the word Hesiod uses for the seasons. The "hour" is the right time for things to happen, for the cattle to come back in, the rain to fall and corn to ripen (Genesis 29:7; Deuteronomy 11:14; Job 5:26). G-d determines both the hour of birth and the hour of death (Genesis 18:10; 2 Samuel 24:15). G-d delivers Israel from her enemies at a particular hour (Joshua 11:6; Daniel 5:5).

In the Gospels, the term "hour" is used seventy-six times, and especially in the Passion narratives. John uses the term with special significance. Jesus' "hour" is the crucifixion (John 2:4; 7:30; 8:20; 12:23,27; 13:1). Precisely because this is the case "the hour is coming *and is now here*, when the dead will hear the voice of the Son of G-d" (John 5:25,28). The hour is also coming "when true worshippers will worship the Father in spirit and in truth" (John 4:23). There is also the hour, however, when the disciples will be scattered and Jesus will be left alone (John 16:32). In other words, John can use the term to mean that moment in time when G-d, through the crucifixion and resurrection of Jesus, will inaugurate a new era. The "hour" of the crucifixion we could say is, for John, the very axis of human history.

The term is also frequently used with eschatological reference. No one knows the hour of the last day except the Father (Mark 13:32 and par.). It will break in "like a thief in the night" (Luke 12:39f.). The first letter of John says the "last hour" has come (1 John 2:18) and the angel with the eternal gospel announces the same in Revelation (14:7).

The third, sixth and ninth hours were already special times for prayer in Israel (Psalm 55:17; Daniel 6:10). The early Christians adopted the practice of prayer at regular times of day, and by the second century these were reckoned as seven: "on rising, at the lighting of the evening lamp, at bedtime, at midnight" and "the third, sixth and ninth hours of the day, being hours associated with Christ's Passion". These transitioned into the canonical hours fixed by Pope Sabianus in the seventh century AD. The vigils kept by the Watch were adopted for the evening before a major feast. This routine of prayer has been subject to periodic revision. Vatican II spoke of lauds (morning prayer) and vespers (evening prayer) as "the two hinges on which the daily office turns".

Mumford traced the ordering of time in Europe to the discipline of the monastery, where the regulation of time became second nature. From the monastery it passed to the city. Mechanical clocks were built by 1370, so the difficulties of sundials and water clocks were overcome and the chime of the hours came to define urban life. "Time-keeping passed into time-serving and time-accounting and time-rationing. As this took place, Eternity ceased gradually to serve as the measure and focus of human actions" (Mumford 1946: 18). Mumford thought the clock was the key machine of the industrial age.

The lunisolar year

Early humans, we have seen, understood time in relation to agricultural tasks, and to lunations. Within the month time could be divided by the moon's phases. Thus, in Rome, the Kalends was the new moon, the Nones the first quarter moon, and the Ides the full moon. If you simply follow the phases of the moon there is no reason to count these phases in twelves. A purely lunar calendar, like the Muslim one, quickly loses track with the seasons. However, ancient astronomers already noted that the time from equinox to equinox or solstice to solstice is 365 days, more or less, the length of the Egyptian year, tacitly mentioned twice in Genesis (Enoch lived 365 years, Genesis 5:23; the Flood lasts twelve lunar months and eleven days—365 days, Genesis 7:11; 8:14). From an early period, Egypt followed a solar year, with equal months of thirty days, and five or six days (in the case of a leap year) tacked on at the end. Most other cultures tried to harmonize lunar and solar years. The difficulty is that neither lunations nor solar years can be measured in round numbers. A lunar month averages 29.5306 days but varies owing to gravitational pull. The moment when the moon first appears—taken as the start of a lunar month—varies with the season and the latitude. The solar year, meanwhile, is 365.3422 days. When that figure is divided by the lunar average you have 12.3683, and over three years this means one lunation, so that the third solar year will have thirteen lunations.

The ancient way of dealing with the difference between lunar and solar periods, adopted by Israel amongst many other cultures, was to have a lunisolar year, where the months were based on the moon, but the year on the sun. To deal with the discrepancy various "intercalary" measures were adopted—adding days to make the number up to 365. Israel added an extra month seven times every nineteen years. In Attica, an extra month was inserted every third year. Rome adopted a similar process, but because intercalations were sometimes missed the lunar and solar calendars continued to drift apart, extra months had to be added, and the year began at different times. In 47 BC, Julius Caesar was in Egypt and consulted an astronomer in Alexandria to help him sort out the mess. His suggestion was to add two months to the year we call 46 BC, which made it 445 days long (the *Annus confusionis*!), and from

45 BC on to have 365 days in each year, beginning the new year on the first of January (instead of, as previously, in March), and introduce a leap year adding an extra day in February every fourth year. Caesar kept the existing lengths of the months, which we still have. These are conventions which do not correspond to lunations: they extend the lunar average over twelve periods to make 365 days in all.

This Julian calendar was a great improvement and is still used by some sections of the Orthodox Church, but it still involved a small miscalculation, a gain of 11.25 minutes each year. Over the centuries this built up, and by 1576 the gap between the lunar and solar year was ten days. To deal with this, Pope Gregory XIII, in 1582, skipped ten days, moving directly from 4 October to 15 October, and determined that every year that is exactly divisible by four or 400 is a leap year, but not years exactly divisible by 100. This calendar has been widely adopted as the Common Era calendar. It is still not completely precise, however, and further amendments have been suggested. If every fifth centurial year is a leap year, for example, it will be 30,000 years before the calendar year and the solar year differ!

How our calendar became

The growth of great cities, and the rise of ruling dynasties, introduced new ways of marking time independent of the agricultural year. Irina Ratushinskaya, whom we will encounter later, describes calendars as "a mere convention", which is partly true. As we have seen, it does not apply to agricultural calendars which chart the tasks of the agricultural year against a twelve-month period—from solstice to solstice—and mark the important events of that year either with apotropaic sacrifice (Passover) or with thank offerings. This kind of calendar follows the dictates of the seasons, and it also provides the measure for a person's life (though many people, right up to the present day, do not know how old they are—see Nadine Labaki's film *Capernaum*). All settled societies, however, order their time in other ways as well, marking significant historical events, recalling famous leaders or cultural luminaries, the origin of dynasties, and so forth. These orderings are "mere conventions" to the extent that no one today marks the start of the Sumerian, Akkadian or Babylonian dynasties, as they once did, or for that matter, Trafalgar Day, St Crispin's Day, as the memorial of the Battle of Agincourt, or British Empire Day. In fifteenth-century Florence, 1 November was celebrated as Plato's birthday. As far as I know, that is no longer a feast! What counts as culturally significant is subject to change. Religious conventions—marking time from the birth of Christ, or from the Haj (Mohammed's move to take Mecca)—are amongst the most durable of time markers but even they may be subject to "injurious time".

Do we need calendars? We might reply with Lear's, "O reason not the need!". Without a calendar time could be a wearisome burden from birth to death—as it has been for millions of people, as we shall see later. The Hebrew Sabbath introduced fifty-two breaks in a solar year. To use Anthony Powell's phrase, if there is "a dance to the music of time", these are the bar markings. Feast days, holy days, holidays, days of mourning come in besides because they respond both to a culture's longer story but also to the human need both to laugh and to weep, to dance and to mourn. Sheep (to speak of the non-human creatures I know best) do not have this need: all they want is good fresh pasture and things to browse on. Special days, whether or not connected to the agricultural cycle, impose themselves because humans need not just bar markings but adagio, andante, allegro and so forth. They need both to dance and sit still, to feast and to fast. We have calendars, then, for the same reason that we have "places of the soul". They mark not abstract time but "soul time", time charged with cultural meaning.

In Greece, each city state had its own calendar, basically lunar, and some adopted intercalation and some did not. Athens had two calendars, a twelve-month calendar which included the festivals and a ten-month fiscal calendar. In contemporary Britain, the tax year still runs from 5 April. Our modern division of sacred and secular of course makes little sense in the ancient world but nevertheless there were festivals which were clearly civic or centred on the family. Thus in Greece the Apaturia celebrated the origins of the different states. The Amphidromia marked the birth of a child and was the day on which the child was named.

The earliest Roman calendar had ten months and began in March, named after Mars, the god of war. Presumably this is because, as we read in the second book of Samuel, the better weather conditions meant that this was "the time when kings go out to war" (2 Samuel 11:1). The next month, April, is sometimes thought (by Bede for example) to refer to blossom time (from *aperire*, to open) and sometimes to refer to the Etruscan *Apru*, the name for Aphrodite. Macrobius, followed by Bede, suggests that May and June derived from "elders" (*maiorum*) and juniors, "the first governing by counsel and the second protecting by arms". Bede notes that others derive May from Maia, a fertility goddess, and June from Juno, the goddess of marriage and pregnancy. April, May and June, then, could all be read in terms of fertility, and therefore in an agricultural sense, though they are not defined in terms of agricultural work.

After June, there was a simple numerical count—5, 6, 7, 8, 9, 10. The last four of these, September to December, remain with us (rather confusingly, as "seven to ten" now actually mean "nine to twelve"). After the assassination (and deification) of Julius Caesar, the fifth month was renamed in his honour (July), because that was the month in which he was born, and later the sixth month in honour of Augustus, who defeated Antony and Cleopatra on 1 August.

The original ten-month calendar had early on been supplemented by two extra months—January, possibly from *ianua*, threshold or door, and so the gateway of the year, or from the god Janus, who faced both forwards and backwards, and February, from Februus, the god of purification—associated with Lupercalia, probably a pre-Roman pastoral rite of purification (perhaps a vestige of this remains in "spring cleaning"). Bede contrasts the light of the festival of purification with the propitiatory sacrifices of Rome, and he thinks it also marks the contrast between "the five-year lustration of a worldly empire" and the everlasting time of the heavenly kingdom.

The adding of the two extra months was widely credited to Romulus' successor, Numa, but, as we saw, it was Caesar who wrote this into law. The two extra months were the last months of the year in the old calendar, though Livy tells us that the consular year began on 1 January to mark a rebellion in Hispania in 154 BC. This may be an example of the kind of historicization of earlier agricultural practices which we encounter in the Tenakh. Beginning the year in January effectively made the winter solstice the start of the year, a break from earlier agricultural calendars which began either in spring or autumn.

There were upwards of two hundred festivals in the Roman calendar, some ancient like Saturnalia, Lupercalia, Sementivae (the festival of sowing, 24–26 January), or the original New Year's Day on 1 March when the sacred fire of Rome was renewed. However, there were also festivals like the "Games of the Victorious Caesar", celebrated on 20–30 July from 45 BC onwards, or the Augustan games, from 3–12 October. In the third and fourth centuries of the Christian era, in the debates about when to celebrate Easter, Rome refused to countenance a possible date of 21 April, because this was the traditional date for the foundation of Rome in 753 BC and marked by riotous festivity. Church authorities struggled to get Christians to see that they ought not to celebrate the Kalends of January, and the games that went with them. They thought it was temporizing with the devil, but ordinary churchgoers could see no harm and the political authorities agreed. The ancient festivals were to be observed, as long as there was no sacrifice, no superstition, and no immodesty (Markus 1990: 109).

Throughout the ancient world dates were often counted from the accession of the ruling king. Republican Rome referred to the reigning consuls. In the sixth century the reckoning AD and BC was introduced, becoming general two centuries later.

The Jewish calendar

In Israel, three new festivals were introduced after the exile, not bound to the agricultural year. The first, and most important, is the Day of Atonement, celebrated on 10 Tishri (September–October), the first moon of autumn, whose rites are described in Leviticus 16. This account of sacrifice provided much of the imagery for later Christian understandings of the atonement. It involved both a sacrifice and the driving of a goat outside the city "bearing the sins of the people". Today, celebrated without animal sacrifice of course, it is the most solemn feast in Judaism.

The second festival is Hanukkah (inauguration or renewal), which commemorates the cleansing and renewal of the Temple after its desecration by Antiochus Epiphanes, as described in 1 Maccabees. This was on 25 Kisleu (December). It is mentioned in John's Gospel (John 10:22). It was a joyful feast, celebrated for eight days, and Josephus calls it "the feast of lights". It occurs at a similar time to the Roman feast of Sol Invictus, celebrated on 25 December, but it is not tied to the solstice in the same way.

Thirdly there is Purim, celebrated on 14 and 15 Adar (March), which celebrates the revenge of the Jews of Persia on their enemies. The book of Esther is read, and presents are given. De Vaux calls it "an utterly profane feast ... the Jewish carnival" (De Vaux 1961: 515). Certainly the name of G-d is not mentioned in the Book of Esther, and the book contains no cultic elements. The name comes from *puru*, to cast lots, and it may have derived from a Persian New Year feast. De Vaux believes that it probably commemorates a pogrom from which the Jews escaped in a way which seemed to them miraculous, which may have taken place in the fourth century BC.

In addition to these feasts, today Rosh Hashanah marks the beginning of the Jewish civil new year, celebrated on the first of Tishri (September–October). In the Mishnah Tractate on Rosh Hashanah, four "New Year" days are identified: 1 Nisan, "the New Year for kings and feasts", which is the original beginning of the year in spring; 1 Elul (August–September), the New Year for the tithe of cattle; 1 Tishri for reckoning the years of foreign kings, but also the years of release and of Jubilee—the official New Year for Judaism at present; and 1 Shebat (January–February) for the planting of fruit trees and vegetables. Rosh Hashanah is identified with the feast mentioned in Leviticus 23:23–5 and Numbers 29:1–6, but there it is not identified as a new year feast. The only use of the phrase is in Ezekiel 40:1 where it refers to a spring festival. Though the names of the Jewish months are taken from Babylon, starting the new year in September was not a Babylonian but an Egyptian practice.

The Christian calendar and its predecessors

The Christian calendar, the liturgical year, the subject of the second part of the book, draws on and relates to the calendars of ancient Israel, of ancient Greece and Rome—and therefore in all these relates to the agricultural year of the northern hemisphere—and also marches in parallel to the Jewish calendar. The date of Easter is still calculated in relation to the full moon when Passover is celebrated. Pentecost corresponds to the Feast of Weeks. Christmas is celebrated at the time of the old Roman Saturnalia. In place of the more than 200 feasts of Ancient Rome, there are the more than 200 feasts and commemorations of the liturgical calendar. The liturgical year as a whole is shoehorned into the calendar Julius Caesar determined on coming back from Egypt, which in turn draws on an older ten-month calendar which in turn shows correspondences with many of the calendars of Ancient Greece. The fit was never perfect. The Western world celebrates "New Year" with Caesar's Rome. Its form of dating, however, derives from a sixth-century Scythian monk who much influenced Bede and who calculated the birth of Jesus (probably erroneously) in order to mark the era which derived from him, and who thus gave us *anno domini*. Around the world, many different reference points remain, especially amongst Muslim, Hindu and Chinese cultures, and many Western cultures have opted for "CE" (Current Era) rather than to refer to "the Lord", doffing the cap to cultural difference whilst continuing to exploit and culturally colonize the rest of the world.

Reflecting on time

Meaning in history

We could take the process of hominization to be a clue to the meaning of history. Karl Löwith, on the other hand, in a famous essay, thought there was not the least evidence of such a meaning. "History as such has no outcome" (Löwith 1949: 191). He thought Christianity as a whole, and Augustine as its paradigm author, were by definition incapable of a genuinely historical view. Everything has been accomplished in Christ and all that remains is to see who is saved and who is not. Time is strictly ancillary to eternity and has no independent meaning. He may be right about Augustine, but Irenaeus had a different view, understanding the meaning of time, of human history, as growth from the image to the likeness of G-d (*Apostolic Preaching* xii; *Adversus Haereses* 4.38.1). In understanding time as meaningful, Irenaeus is following the prophets of Israel who discern the hand of G-d in temporal events. The texts which bear witness to Jesus Messiah assume the very same thing, and they pick up ideas from Second and Third Isaiah which suggest that all history, and not just the history of Israel, falls under the divine aegis. In the Messianic Writings, the meaning of history is no longer understood in terms of what happens to the people of Israel but, to use Paul Lehmann's phrase, in terms of making and keeping human beings human. In Jesus, G-d's purposes, that is, G-d's Word, becomes flesh and "Jesus' entire goal was to liberate the humanity in human beings and to help in a breakthrough to the culture of life" (Duchrow and Hinkelammert 2012: 58). Better, G-d's whole purpose in and through Jesus of Nazareth was to do this. According to the Gospel, this is the ultimate meaning of time.

In the last of his theses on the philosophy of history, written in 1940, not long before his suicide, Walter Benjamin cites a biologist who notes that the "paltry fifty millenia" of *Homo sapiens* would constitute something like two seconds at the close of a twenty-four-hour day representing the whole history of creation, and the history of civilized mankind one fifth of the last second of the last hour. He goes on: "The present, which, as a model of Messianic time, comprises the entire history of mankind in an enormous abridgement, coincides exactly with the stature which the history of mankind has in the universe" (Benjamin 1973: 255).

The stature of the history of mankind within the history of the universe seems to be merely an insignificant fragment. Messianic time is redeemed time, but what does this mean in face of "the eternal silence of the infinite spaces", which terrified Pascal as he looked into the night sky? I seem, he said, citing Wisdom 5:14, "as the remembrance of a guest that tarries but a day". Pascal met this terror with a revelation of the G-d of Abraham, Isaac and Jacob, G-d revealed in and through a narrative, and not the god of the philosophers; he met it, in other words, through the Scriptures of Israel and Church.

In the famous ninth thesis of his ruminations, Benjamin recalls Paul Klee's *Angelus Novus*, looking back over the past and seeing "one single catastrophe which keeps piling wreckage upon wreckage", a pile which grows skyward. Benjamin is talking about human history, but equally we can think of the whole of time, from the dawn of time to the present, with all the extinctions and what seem to have been false starts—one vast pile of wreckage, the *tohu ve bohu* of Genesis 1. The angel wants to awaken the dead, says Benjamin, and make whole what has been smashed but in fact only the Messiah can do this. To articulate the past historically, Benjamin says in Thesis 6, means "to seize hold of a memory as it flashes up at a moment of danger". "The Messiah comes not only as the redeemer, he comes as the subduer of Antichrist. Only that historian will have the gift of fanning the spark of hope in the past who is firmly convinced that *even the dead* will not be safe from the enemy if he wins. And this enemy has not ceased to be victorious" (Benjamin 1973: 247).

What I want to suggest is that the *lectio divina*—the reading of Scripture which is the heart of the liturgical year—is the action of fanning the spark of hope. It does this as it calls into being a community which lives by the dangerous memory of the crucified Messiah. It recalls the Messiah both as the redeemer and as the subduer of Antichrist. John's Gospel brings together both the need to struggle for the truth and the promise that the dead are not consigned to oblivion. The two cannot be separated. Lazarus is only raised if the truth is maintained. John's reflections on truth commit the Church to an ongoing hermeneutic ascesis and on the basis of that to an ongoing witness. That witness is concerned with meaning in history or, to use the phrase of Ephesians and Colossians, "redeeming time" (Ephesians 5:16; Colossians 4:5).

Time and history

We have seen how the sense of time may have arisen, memory and anticipation articulated through the natural rhythms of creation—the passage of day and night, lunations, and the seasons. We have seen the emergence of conventional or cultural time, marking time through weeks, months and hours, and then the efforts to correlate solar and lunar periodicities. Over and above these regularities are the stories spread over decades, generations, centuries through which cultures—and mostly the ruling class—articulate their self-understanding. Alongside calendars, mapping regularities, these narratives provide another mapping of time which we call "history". History, as it emerges in the great Greek historians, but also in the work of the Deuteronomic editors of the so-called "historical books", and, self-consciously, in Luke's two-volume work, is not simply a chronicle of events but seeks to interpret these events, to think in terms of pattern or meaning. History is time interpreted.

In the history of Israel, the foundation narrative is the exodus, and the long process of the occupation of Canaan which followed. On the far side of that is the Patriarchal history, to which the Primeval history is then appended, the claim that this history is no longer tribal but universal. On this side is the rise and fall of the monarchy, the split of Israel into two kingdoms, the destruction first of the Northern and then of the Southern Kingdom, the end of the Judean monarchy, the exile, the return of Nehemiah and Ezra, and the attempt to rebuild a Jewish state, the fallout of Alexander's conquests, the revolt against Hellenization under the Maccabees and the civil war which followed. Löwith felt it was possible to speak of a philosophy of history in relation to the Hebrew

prophets, who saw G-d punishing and rewarding Israel for obedience
or disobedience:

> The possibility of a belief in the providential ordering of world-
> historical destinies depends on ... belief in a holy people of
> universal significance, because only peoples, not individuals,
> are a proper subject of history (Löwith 1949: 195).

He failed to understand that for Paul, and the authors of Hebrews and
1 Peter, *ekklesia* was now this "holy people" which also had a history.
Luke sketched the early chapters of this history in his account of Paul's
journey to Rome. Löwith thought that Christians were not a historical
people, because for them the promise of salvation was individualized,
and it is quite true, as we shall see in a moment, that Augustine, who for
Löwith was the normative Christian theologian, thought like this. But to
excise the historical dimension from Christianity is to posit an absolute
breach between Tenakh and Messianic Writings which would have been
impossible for both Jesus and Paul. The mid twentieth century gave up
the "Whig view of history", the idea that we can discern a triumphant
march of progress, but it gave up meaning in history at the same time.
From a Christian point of view, we have to ask, why would G-d enter
history if history had no meaning?

Lecturing in Cambridge the very same year as Löwith published
his book, Herbert Butterfield could tell his audience that Christianity
was a historical religion in the technical sense that it presents us with
religious doctrines which are at the same time historical events or
interpretations, and its most daring assertions are all rooted in ordinary
history (Butterfield 1949: 3). Certainly the Messianic Writings record
events which happened under Augustus and Tiberius, and the Procuracy
of Pontius Pilate. Both the Jewish and Christian scriptures discern the
hand of G-d in these events. They represent an interpretation of events in
which G-d should be understood as an actor. They invite us to understand
our own history in this way. This interpretation is the foundation of the
liturgical calendar of both Israel and the Church.

The scaffolding of the Spirit

In ordinary conversation, we are always qualifying time. We speak of "a good time", "a bad time", "a wonderful time", "a terrible time". Of the French Revolution, Dickens said: "It was the best of times. It was the worst of times." We say of many things that they are "a waste of time". When we are bored, we speak of "killing time". Middle-class parents aim to give their children "quality time" around the edges of their work. Time is a great healer, we say, but it also destroys. As we get older, we say we are living on borrowed time, and many now apply that to the whole of humanity, given the dangers of the global emergency.

Shakespeare, who mentions time constantly in his plays and poems, speaks of Devouring Time, never-resting time, this bloody tyrant, Time, sluttish time, of humans being subject to Time's love or Time's hate. Flirting with Orlando, Rosalind illustrates how time ambles, trots, gallops and stands still. Urging Achilles to action Ulysses remarks:

> Time hath, my lord, a wallet at his back,
> Wherein he puts alms for oblivion,
> A great-sized monster of ingratitudes
> (Troilus and Cressida, Act 3, Scene 3).

Only continued action, he argues, keeps "honour bright".

Macbeth, after his wife's death, laments the futility of time:

> Tomorrow, and tomorrow, and tomorrow,
> Creeps in this petty pace from day to day,
> To the last syllable of recorded time;
> And all our yesterdays have lighted fools
> The way to dusty death (*Macbeth* Act 5 Scene 5).

The distinction of times is the burden of the famous passage in Ecclesiastes which discerns a season for everything, whether love or hate, mourning or dancing, war or peace (Ecclesiastes 3:1–8). The problem with this is that everything is put on a level, as if G-d endorsed both, so that if we are involved in war, we can simply shrug our shoulders and say: "Well, there's a time for everything"—and people often do precisely that. This ignores the clear trajectory of Scripture which says that there are some things for which there is no time—all forms of idolatry, for example—and that G-d wills some things and not others.

A poem in Isaiah, citing agricultural examples, notes the proper time for ploughing, sowing and so forth (Isaiah 28:23–9; cf. Job 4:8). G-d teaches us this knowledge, says the poet. This might be what von Rad calls the doctrine of "the proper time", but it should not be run together with Ecclesiastes, which is really the so-called wisdom of realpolitik.

Another sense of "the proper time" is the notion of a decisive moment for which Aeschylus and Plato, amongst others, use the word *kairos*. The Messianic Writings sometimes use it in this sense: Jesus comes into Galilee preaching the gospel of G-d and saying "the time is fulfilled (*peplērōtai ho kairos*), the kingdom of G-d is at hand" (Mark 1:15); he tells the Pharisees and Sadducees that they cannot discern "the signs of the times" (Matthew 16:3); the devil leaves Jesus "until an opportune time" (*achri kairou*, Luke 4:13); Paul says that "at the right time" (*kata kairon*) Christ died for the ungodly (Romans 5:6); the author of Ephesians bids people to "make the most of the time, because the days are evil" (Ephesians 5:16).

In the decades after World War II, some scholars claimed that the idea of the decisive moment characterized a distinctively Christian view of history as opposed to the "Greek" view centred on *chronos*, chronological time. It was this teaching which lay behind South Africa's Kairos Document, and later the Kairos Europa movement, the one challenging apartheid, the other the neoliberal economy. James Barr showed that the distinction between Greek and Hebrew senses of time was nonsense, but he did not sufficiently emphasize that the Messianic Writings as a whole clearly do believe a decisive moment has arrived in Jesus, and that his coming marks a turn in the ages. The scholars Barr criticized were right to claim this but wrong to base it on the use of the word *kairos*.

The distinction of times is the very stuff of human experience (which is why the passage from Ecclesiastes is so famous and even turned into a folk song). As a way of making sense of that reality theologically (an attempt which I think Ecclesiastes abdicates), I want to propose that time, in all its distinctions, might be thought of as the scaffolding of the Spirit, to use a phrase from R. S. Thomas (in his poem *Emerging*).

Time, both as *chronos* and as *kairos*, in the passage of the seven ages of man, and in the passage of the rise and fall of kingdoms and cultures, is the scaffolding which the Spirit of G-d uses to fashion human lives and human history, understood in Irenaeus' terms as hominization. Such an understanding, however, is diametrically opposed to the normative Christian understanding of time.

Time and eternity

Although Plato could, in the Laws, speak of time (*kairos*) in terms of a decisive moment, his central intuition is that time and chance cannot be the heart of reality. We must, says Timaeus, distinguish between that which always is and never becomes, on the one hand, and that which is always becoming and never is, on the other. The first can be understood rationally, the second is only the object of opinion, and never fully real. The maker of all things is eternal and fashions this world as "a moving image of eternity". Time accompanies creation, and we use the three tenses, past, present and future, improperly for what changes is never truly real. That which is eternally the same and unmoved, which we call "G-d", does not become, but simply is. This understanding of the relation of time and eternity profoundly marked Christian reflection.

Drawing especially on Plotinus' commentary on Plato, Augustine devoted the eleventh book of his *Confessions* to the question of time and eternity, effectively importing a Platonic metaphysic of time into Christianity. G-d, says Augustine, exists in the sublimity of an eternity which is always present. Citing Psalm 102:27 ("You are the same and your years do not fail"), he writes:

> Your years neither go nor come. Ours come and go so that all may come in succession. All your "years" subsist in simultaneity, because they do not change . . . your "day" is not any and every day but Today, because your Today does not yield to a tomorrow, nor did it follow on a yesterday. Your Today is eternity (*Confessions* XI:13).

Taking up Plato's problematic, he asks how we can speak of the present when it is always immediately receding into the past:

> The cause of its being is that it will cease to be. So indeed we
> cannot truly say that time exists except in the sense that it tends
> towards non existence (XI:17).

The problem with this teaching is that it seems to call the importance of time into question. If time is unreal, why do we bother about it? Drawing on Plotinus, Augustine understands time psychologically. Aristotle said time was a form of measurement—but of what? Augustine answered— of memory and expectation. The impression made upon the mind by passing events is what you measure. "That present consciousness is what I am actually measuring." In this way, Augustine saves the appearances, he retreats from absolute scepticism. The three tenses all exist "in the soul". "The present considering the past is the memory, the present considering the present is immediate awareness, the present considering the future is expectation" (XI:26). Measure is in the mind. Augustine gives the example of reciting a psalm off by heart:

> Before I begin, my expectation is directed towards the whole. But
> when I have begun, the verses from it which I take into the past
> become the object of my memory. The life of this act of mine is
> stretched two ways, into my memory because of the words I have
> already said and into my expectation because of those I am about
> to say. But my attention is on what is present: by that the future
> is transferred to become past (XI:38).

That process, he argues, can be applied both to the whole life of a person and indeed to the whole of history. So it seems there is some resolution of the problem of the fleetingness of time. But then Augustine recalls that to be human is to be scattered in times whose order we do not understand. "The storms of incoherent events tear to pieces my thoughts, the inmost entrails of my soul, until that day when, purified and molten by the fire of your love, I flow together to merge into you" (XI:39). The psalm analogy only takes us so far. With G-d everything is different:

> You are unchangeably eternal, that is the truly eternal Creator
> of minds. Just as you knew heaven and earth in the beginning
> without that bringing any variation into your knowing, so you
> made heaven and earth in the beginning without that meaning a
> tension between past and future in your activity (XI:41).

The most celebrated version of this account of time in modernity is probably to be found in T. S. Eliot's *Four Quartets*, and especially in the first of them, *Burnt Norton*, where the *Confessions* are in the background. The evanescence of the past and the non-being of the future can only be healed at the still point of the turning world which is the uncreated light of G-d the Creator. The four poems all return again and again to the unreality of worldly time, the destiny of which is eternity:

> Before the beginning and after the end.
> And all is always now.

The time-eternity contrast continues to frame Augustine's argument in the *City of God*. On the one hand, Augustine seems to affirm the importance of the arrow of time in repudiating the Stoic cyclical doctrine of time. He argues that it is hopeless, for hope and faith are essentially related to the future and a real future cannot exist if past and future times are equal phases within a cyclical recurrence without beginning and end. Belief in the cyclical doctrine paralyzes hope and love itself (XII 14;18). Thus the supreme importance of a person's time is affirmed, but in the overall scheme of the book the contrast remains Platonic. Augustine is the star witness for Löwith's claim that Christianity is not a historical religion. The earthly city is the stage on which persons act out their way either to salvation or damnation, and the heavenly city is participation in G-d's eternity. The history of the earthly city does not contribute to or alter in any way the story or the reality of the heavenly city. Though Augustine values the peace which the earthly city can offer it in no way relates to the kingdom of G-d. The heavenly and earthly cities overlap, and Christians have a duty to work for the common good, but the common good does not provide even a parable of the kingdom. What happens in human time is that wheat and tares together grow, both inside and outside the Church, and who will finally be saved remains a mystery. We must think of ourselves as *peregrini*, pilgrims or resident aliens. Furthermore, Augustine runs the providence of G-d together with predestination in such a way that, although free will is affirmed, it is impossible to see what content can be ascribed to it. This, too, empties history of meaning.

Augustine's teaching on time and eternity is in stark contrast to the teaching on hope and time in the Messianic Writings. The fervent hope for the Second Coming which we find there—Maranatha, Come Lord Jesus!—is transformed into a concern about what happens to the individual after death. Eschatology is individualized and loses its connection with history.

G-d's time

The antithesis of time and eternity remained a theological given for more than one and a half millennia until Karl Barth challenged it in the first volume of his doctrine of G-d published in 1937. The abstract opposition of time and eternity, going back to Plato, he regarded as a "Babylonian captivity". He liked Boethius' definition of eternity as "total, simultaneous and complete possession of unlimited life", but felt that this had hitherto not been properly exploited. The key to understanding it he saw to be the incarnation, when G-d takes time to G-dself. G-d subjects G-dself to time in such a way that to know G-d as the eternal one "we must cling utterly to G-d's temporality". The fact of the incarnation means we cannot understand G-d's eternity as pure timelessness. True eternity, we learn from the incarnation, includes the potentiality of time. At the same time, created time, our time, acquires in Christ "the character and stamp of eternity".

G-d's eternity, according to Barth, is not itself time but it is the absolute basis of time. We can speak of a "temporality of eternity", a pre-temporality, a supra or co-temporality (*Überzeitlichkeit*, i.e. accompanying our time) and a post-temporality.

Pre-temporality means that G-d's existence precedes the time of all things—the origin of the universe as Stephen Hawking or Roger Penrose understand it. There was a time when the universe did not exist, and this was the pre-time or eternity of G-d. Traditionally theology discussed this under the question whether G-d created time along with the universe, or whether time preceded it. Barth is clear—G-d created time with the universe.

The supra-temporality of G-d means that G-d embraces time on all sides. This embrace is not timelessness. Eternity does not will to be without time but causes itself to be accompanied by time. Every epoch, every lifetime, every passing hour is in eternity "like a child in the arms of its mother". We have to speak of a supra-temporality of G-d if we are not to speak secretly of a timeless G-d and therefore of a godless time, hypostasizing the "now" of our time. G-d's eternity accompanies time so that time acquires its hidden centre. This is what speaks to Macbeth's sense of the futility of time, for this means there is no merely empty time. The past is that *from* which we are set free, and the future that *for* which we are set free by G-d.

Finally, G-d is post-temporal. This is what addresses Hawking's first arrow of time, entropy, the fact that this planet, and all its life, will one day fail as the light of the sun fails. G-d is, when time is no more. The post-temporality of G-d corresponds to what theology conventionally spoke of as eschatology.

Returning to Boethius, we can understand eternity as the simultaneity and coinherence of past, present and future. The simultaneous possession of unlimited life means that there is no tension between G-d's pre-, supra- and post-temporality. In G-d, these times exist, but are held together without the threat of death, which marks our time.

The upshot of this doctrine is that we no longer have to think of human life in terms of an individual's passage from time to eternity. The whole of human time is embraced by G-d's time and this fact, Barth argues, makes political speech possible. Political action is grounded in the hope which follows from the fact that G-d is our future, and it is this which makes the privatization of faith impossible. At the same time, Barth, as strenuously as Augustine, insists that human history cannot be confused in any way with the kingdom of G-d. The question we have to ask is, what is the significance of the obedience to the divine command which is the heart of Christian ethics? The point of discipleship is not individual salvation. The obedience of a Christian happens within a social body, a community, and it bears witness to a salvation which applies to all people and all reality. It has effects. We cannot speak of a "Christian" state or culture but at the same time G-d's Word does not return void (Isaiah 55:11). It makes history (Jeremiah 1:9–10). That history, it seems to me, Irenaeus understands in terms of humanization.

Time as gift

Looking at the qualities of time, we noted that although we often speak of marvellous or precious time, time is also often characterized as "devouring"—the image of Saturn devouring his children, or, in the image of Father Time, wielding the scythe of death. If G-d embraces time in eternity, however, the way is open to understand time positively. Barth speaks of time, beautifully, as "the hidden rustling of the Holy Spirit". We will have to ask, however, to what extent we can speak like this, given the atrocities committed in time.

Creation itself is gift (as we shall see in Part 2, Creation Season), and since time is part of creation this applies to time as well. That G-d becomes human in Christ and takes time to G-dself means that it is not a "dark backward and abyss" but "the garment and form of grace", the scaffolding of our existence in and through which G-d encounters us. The hours, days and years which we have are "the declaration of the acts of G-d's righteousness and mercy, of G-d's wisdom and patience, whose witness and object we are privileged to be in virtue of our existence in time" (Barth 1960: 526). Time, therefore, is gift, and gift evokes gratitude. The Rule of the Iona Community centres on members accounting to each other for the use of their gifts, their money—but also their time. In many ways, this is the most difficult of the three, even though money is the true sacred of our society. There are times when we use our time well; but the "sin" which we confess each day is our crass misuse of time (which is different from the leisure without which life stops altogether).

We can spell out the reality of time as gift in relation to the antinomies which bemused Plato and Augustine. They were struck by the fact that we have no *nunc stans*: as we say "now", the moment becomes past. But "that G-d is present to us is what fills our present". That our present is embraced in G-d's present reality is our *nunc stans*, and this is what stands against what appears to be the futility of so much of human life. Because we are embraced in G-d's present "now is no time for dreaming about past or future. Now is the time to awake, to receive or act, to speak or be silent, to say Yes or No . . . Now we must step out and act as the people we really are" (Barth 1960: 532).

We are people who are shaped by our past, often full of mistakes and wrong paths, failures and regrets. But in G-d's eternity yesterday is also today and tomorrow. Because G-d loved us then, and meets us not only with judgement but forgiveness, we can live with our past and not be overwhelmed by it.

Similarly the future may be bright and enticing, but also ominous and forbidding. The threat of climate change brings intense anxiety to many young people today. But again, "come what may, we shall be what we shall be with and under G-d". This knowledge does not say, "sit down, O men of G-d, you cannot do a thing", but summons us to gratitude and responsibility:

> Teach me to do your will,
> for you are my G-d.
> Let your good spirit lead me
> on a level path (Psalm 143:10).

Fallen time

In his reflections on vocation, Barth discusses the time each individual has as "the unique opportunity". Every act of a person must be measured and tested by the question whether it is a seizing or neglecting of the unique opportunity presented to them. This is marked by an acceptance of the time into which we are born, and an openness to others in that time; by the fact that we know we have no time to lose but know how to make and take time; and by the fact that we do not fear death.

The trouble with this teaching is that it assumes a large degree of autonomy, and this is something most humans have never had. When Simone Weil worked in a factory in France, she found time an "intolerable burden", and this has been true for uncountable millions of people. In some sense, all human time is "fallen", that is to say, marked by frustration, loss, very often by oppression and despair. To illustrate this, I offer three examples. The first is a well-known account from the British Parliamentary Commission to look into labour in the mines in 1842. The whole report could be cited, but this story has caught people's imagination. In the mines, when the coal was hewed out, children known as "hurriers and thrusters" had to drag it in tubs to the cage, where it was taken to the surface. Hurriers had to wear belts attached to a heavy chain which passed between their legs and was attached to the coal tub. Thrusters (often girls) had to push the tub with their hands and foreheads and often lost their hair doing it. The Commission interviewed a seventeen-year-old girl called Patience Kershaw and these were their notes of the interview:

> My father has been dead about a year; my mother is living and has ten children, five lads and five lasses; the oldest is about thirty, the youngest is four; three lasses go to mill; all the lads are colliers, two getters and three hurriers; one lives at home and does nothing; mother does nought but look after home.
>
> All my sisters have been hurriers, but three went to the mill. Alice went because her legs swelled from hurrying in cold water when she was hot. I never went to day-school; I go to Sunday-school, but I cannot read or write; I go to pit at five o'clock in the morning and come out at five in the evening; I get my breakfast of porridge and milk first; I take my dinner with me, a cake, and eat it as I go; I do not stop or rest any time for the purpose; I get nothing else until I get home, and then have potatoes and meat, not every day meat. I hurry in the clothes I have now got on, trousers and ragged jacket; the bald place upon my head is made by thrusting the corves; my legs have never swelled, but sisters' did when they went to mill; I hurry the corves a mile and more under ground and back; they weigh 300 cwt.; I hurry 11 a day; I wear a belt and chain at the workings, to get the corves out; the getters that I work for are naked except their caps; they pull off all their clothes; I see them at work when I go up; sometimes they

beat me, if I am not quick enough, with their hands; they strike
me upon my back; the boys take liberties with me sometimes
they pull me about; I am the only girl in the pit; there are about
20 boys and 15 men; all the men are naked; I would rather work
in mill than in coal-pit.

The Commission commented: "This girl is an ignorant, filthy, ragged, and deplorable-looking object, and such an one as the uncivilized natives of the prairies would be shocked to look upon" (Scott & Baltzly 1934: 89).

I cite this story because Patience Kershaw can stand for the labour of most human beings who have ever lived, and probably many millions alive at the moment. Whether you think of the slave labour of antiquity, the serf labour of medieval Europe, the labour of the factories or the mines, and indeed of the fields (Ronald Blythe's interviewees in *Akenfield* told him that before World War I in Britain farm hands were quite literally worked to death), most humans since the rise of agriculture and the growth of cities and of empire have lived in poverty, oppression and exploitation. The very idea of making the most of "the unique opportunity" for these people is a callous joke.

The second story comes from the final days of Donald Trump's presidency which saw on the one hand a rush to pardon his cronies, but on the other hand a rush to execute prisoners on death row. One of these, Lisa Montgomery, committed a dreadful murder, but spent her first fifteen years being abused by her alcoholic mother and raped, beaten and urinated on by her stepfather. While still in school, her mother forced her into an abusive marriage to her own boyfriend's son. She had four children in five years and was then sterilized. After divorce, her ex-husband filed for custody of the children, and she committed the murder in an attempt to get a child. After conviction she was diagnosed with psychosis, bipolar disorder, PTSD, dissociation from reality, and brain damage from old head injuries (*Private Eye* 1537: 18). She was sent to death row and executed one week before Trump left office.

The point of this story is to raise, in an extreme way, the question of the conditions of responsibility. What we know of social history indicates that through most of human history, up to and including the present, routine cruelty has made sane and healthy relations for millions of people difficult if not impossible. And there is a sliding scale, for part of what the doctrine of original sin has to say is that all of us are damaged.

The final story is from the seventeenth century. John Evelyn, devout, well-educated, a Fellow of the Royal Society, in touch with the best medical advice of the day, lost his five-year-old son to what he called a "quartan ague", though whether it could really have been malaria we have to doubt. The boy was obviously precocious, and pious like his father. Evelyn was distraught, but the story can stand for the commonplace death of children throughout history, and today commonplace in the world's slums and shanties, in refugee camps and all areas affected by war. Most humans who have ever been born, we can surmise, never lived to be able to think of taking advantage of "the unique opportunity". This fact so distressed the French theologian and priest Jacques Pohier that it left his picture of God "in fragments".

What these stories illustrate is that we cannot talk abstractly and universally about "human time" and the ethics of the use of time. What comes first is an understanding of what it means to be human, and therefore of what conditions and relations make that possible. I said at the beginning of this section that the overall meaning of history should be understood, in the light of Scripture, in terms of making and keeping human life human, and I noted this process was not finished. If it is true that with human beings evolution becomes history, and if it is true that G-d engages with human history in Jesus of Nazareth, then this process of humanization involves the concrete consequences of Jesus' life and teaching. This is only partly set out in the witness and work of the Church. We cannot claim that every move towards the recognition of fuller humanity derives from that witness and work, but some of it does, and it behoves those of us who are Christian to recognize such moves when we see them. Such a move, preliminary but necessary, was the UN Declaration of Human Rights of 1948, which tried to set out what belonged to the very foundation of being human concretely in terms of rights to food, housing, education, medical care, respect for beliefs and convictions and freedom from assault. These things flesh out time, or make the possession and use of time possible. This concern for the concrete is in complete accord with Torah, and especially with the desire of Deuteronomy for a different and more just society and economy.

Lacking such concrete provisions, it is nonsense to talk of meaningful time.

The stories also invite us to return to Benjamin's talk of a memory flashing up at a moment of danger. Turning this round, Johann-Baptist Metz wanted to speak of a "dangerous memory", namely a memory in solidarity with the dead and the conquered which "breaks the grip of history as a history of triumph and conquest" (Metz 1980: 184). It is a memory of suffering which provides an orientation for action, and the fundamental form of this memory, for Christians, is the crucifixion. The memory of Christ in each Eucharist is not meant to lull us to sleep, to send us away in a pious rapture, but to provide a dangerous insight for the present, for in the crucified Jesus we meet all the other human crosses, right up to the present.

This raises the question of the sense and structure of liturgical time. John Baldovin rightly points out that liturgy cannot do everything and that it is unrealistic to expect that an hour or less in church each week can attune people to the value system the gospel invites us to. It is superficial, he argues, to preach about world hunger without providing a means in parish life actually to do something about it: "A parish with no active, extra-liturgical, adult-education-and-action committee is not likely to do much of substance in terms of addressing the many issues of justice" (Baldovin 2000a: 438). Liturgical time, that is to say, "going to church", only makes sense within a broader commitment of time understood as a demand of discipleship. In the first place this challenges a highly individualized Christianity where fifty minutes a week, plus help at fêtes and festivals, is the most that people are prepared to consider. Even for the committed, the pressures on people's time—in a peasant or farming community the pressure of unremitting work 365 days a year, in an urban or suburban setting the demands of work, the need to give time to the family, activities in music-making, sport, social and political activism and so on and so forth—mean that this is a big ask. Lots of non-church-based social and political activism may be more important than anything which happens from the church, and some means of integrating this into the communal life of the church needs to be found. These remarks provide the context for thinking about the liturgical year in the next part of the book.

PART 2

The Christian Year

The liturgical year and the lectionary

The liturgical year has its roots in the agricultural year, according to the Tenakh. On that cycle of agricultural festivals is superimposed the commemoration, or celebration, of historical events. Why do we celebrate them year on year when they are not cyclical events? When we celebrate the Eucharist on a Sunday, we remember Christ's death and resurrection, and the giving of the Holy Spirit. Why, then, have special feasts for those events? When we pray, we pray to the Father, through the Son, in the Spirit. The Trinity, in other words, is fundamental to the life of faith. Why then have a special feast for it? That question goes back at least to the eleventh century. Part of the answer might be that, as we have seen, agricultural festivals, which are by nature cyclical, attract historical interpretations: a lambing festival becomes Passover, a wheat harvest becomes Pentecost. More profoundly, the round of festivals marks the time of a particular culture. Humans imbibe their particular culture through language, of course, but also through the routine of festival, and they have festivals because it is a need of the soul to mark time, especially given the succession of generations and the brevity of life. "Time is the true hero of every feast, uncrowning the old and crowning the new" (Bakhtin 1984: 219). It is no surprise that festivals of different religions and cultures in the same hemisphere happen at around or indeed at precisely the same time. They are all meeting a similar need.

John Baldovin asks us to think about what Christians mean by the celebration of time. If we speak of every Eucharist as a "celebration", it diminishes the term. A celebration, he argues, is really a festivity, and he cites as a definition "an exuberant manifestation of life itself standing out in contrast to the background rhythm of daily life . . . the feast is the communitarian, ritual and joyful expression of common experiences and longings, centred around a historical fact, past or contemporary" (Baldovin 2000b: 375/6). On this definition only Easter, Christmas and possibly Harvest—at least as we currently celebrate them—qualify as "feasts" but cross-cultural studies make very plain the need for human communities to mark time through festival.

In addition to marking time, we can say that liturgical calendars have a pedagogical function. As we saw in Part 1, Irenaeus thinks of the education of the human race as the purpose of history:

> G-d directs all things to achieve the end of humankind's perfection and human edification; and to display G-d's own character, so that G-d's goodness may be demonstrated and G-d's righteousness fulfilled, and that the Church may be conformed to the image of G-d's Son, and humankind may at length reach maturity, becoming ripe, through these experiences, for the vision and enjoyment of G-d (*AH* 4.37.7).

The calendar gives us a structure for exploring the significance of the great stories of our faith in some depth year after year. In a community where worship is more than pious recreation, the calendar, which at its heart is the reading of Scripture, is the fundamental mode of formation. Its purpose is to help disciples towards living fulfilled time or, in the words of Ephesians and Colossians, "to redeem the time".

In terms of the shape of the year, Passover morphed into Easter, the axis of the Christian liturgical year, and the Feast of Weeks, finally, into Pentecost. Earlier in the year, a period of preparation for baptism developed, not necessarily connected with Easter, which became Lent. This provides the first main block of the Christian year. Debates about the date of Christ's birth went on for some centuries, as we shall see, with 6 January an early and important candidate. In the fourth century, most of the Church (but not all) fixed on 25 December, to which a period of baptismal preparation was affixed (for baptism on 6 January), and this gave the second block of time, from Advent to Epiphany. All the other Sundays were designated "Ordinary Time" until 2015 when "Creation Season" was introduced, running through the whole of September to the feast of St Francis on 4 October.

How important is the celebration of the liturgical year? On the one hand, the Church is a body, which meets together to worship and to read and reflect on Scripture. The Jewish calendar was part of its inheritance, and in the Tenakh the major festivals were regarded as what Bede called "commanded time". Quite apart from the command, however, worship is something which is as natural as breathing, if we have faith, and we do it together. On the other hand, we are reminded during Advent and Lent of the prophetic critique of the cult and the warning that if it is divorced from the doing of justice and righteousness G-d "hates and despises" it. Practically speaking what this means is that the way in which Christians are formed by the liturgical cycle has to have constructive (rather than reactionary!) political and economic consequences if those same Christians are to offer credible and authentic witness in the contemporary world (Baldovin 2000a: 431).

We need to hold these two perspectives together. Karl Rahner spoke of the Eucharist as "a small sign, necessary, reasonable and indispensable, within the infinitude of the world as permeated by G-d", a sign which reminds us of the limitlessness of G-d's grace, and which should on no account be considered to be the only place where G-d was present. It does not dispense us from striving in the night of the world as Jacob strove with the angel. Rather it brings home to us the fact that this struggle of life is a striving like Jacob's (Rahner 1976: 169,175). This seems to me to get the balance exactly right: in liturgy we are engaged in that which is a small sign, but at the same time necessary, reasonable and indispensable. Every word here needs to be given its full weight.

In Jewish tradition regular readings from the Tenakh, especially at festivals, probably began in the synagogue, which developed during the exile in Babylon (though the Talmud says such readings went back to Moses!). In medieval Judaism, the Torah was read through once a year, and Nebi'im and Khetubim (Prophets and Wisdom) were read selectively. Christianity took the practice of Scripture reading over. For the earliest Christians, "Scripture" meant the Tenakh. During the second century, we find evidence that the four Gospels, the letters of Paul, and other letters, some of which were finally included in the canon and some not, were being read as Scripture by the Church. Justin Martyr, in a passage cited in Part 1, talks of the reading of the apostles and prophets "for as long as time allowed". By the fourth century, the canon we now use had been agreed on. A second-century proposal to ditch the Tenakh was fought off, though it has presented a recurring temptation, especially in Protestant liberalism. The Tenakh as a whole was and is read as sacred Scripture with the proviso that the ceremonial regulations no longer applied. As a matter of fact, though the "Ten Commandments" were even taken into the Protestant liturgy most of the social and civil proscriptions of the Torah were also dropped, except, of course, for the few passages supposedly condemning homosexuality.

The Church, then, adopted a lectionary based on both Tenakh and Messianic Writings. Readers of the lectionary are referred to in the third century, and the Bishop of Marseilles had a lectionary produced in the fifth century. At the same time, Benedict, in his rule, established that the Psalms should be read through weekly. The development of the daily office in the monastic orders, and especially the Benedictine, probably helped develop the lectionary which, however, differed from area to area, and has always been subject to reform. Cranmer proposed that the Psalter should be read monthly, the Messianic Writings twice a year, and the Tenakh once, but this was, of course, only possible for clergy. Even very devout, and reasonably wealthy, Anglicans, like John Evelyn, would not have managed to do this. Most lectionaries had a one-year cycle, but at Vatican II a three-year cycle was adopted, focussed on the Scripture readings for Sunday Mass, and intended to increase biblical literacy for the laity. This was adopted by many Protestant churches and became the Revised Common Lectionary in 1992. Further proposals, for a four-year cycle, or a narrative cycle, have since been advanced.

In my account, I will follow the Common Lectionary. This has a three-year cycle based on the three Synoptic Gospels, where the bulk of Matthew, Mark and Luke are read in succession over three years, in connection with related readings from the Tenakh, and with the Acts of the Apostles read between Easter and Pentecost, and the Epistles and Revelation read consecutively, and not usually related to the other two readings, throughout the year. John's Gospel is read during Lent, Easter and Pentecost and otherwise interpolated through the year. Selected psalms, or portions of psalms, are provided for the gradual. It is thereby hoped that lay Christians will become familiar with most parts of their Scriptures (though they will still be hazy about large parts of the Torah, Joshua, Judges, Chronicles and much else). The readings are not determined by "theme", a common Protestant practice which leads to concentration on a handful of purple passages, often grouped around substitutionary atonement.

In determining the passages read, the assumption seems to be that congregations have limited attention spans, and that services should not last more than fifty minutes. All the best narrative parts of Scripture, especially in the Tenakh, are thereby lost. The liberation theologians, in the 1970s and 80s, proposed the reorganization of church around the idea of "base communities", an idea which had many resonances in Europe and North America as well. These communities were organized around the Word, around the sacraments (when possible), and around new ministries exercised by lay people (both women and men). They were not priest-centred, but participative, and oriented towards what was understood as "integral liberation", liberation of the whole person in all dimensions. It seems likely that such communities offer the real future of the Church, and it is to be hoped that, in such communities, a deeper and more ruminative study of the Word, in the context of worship, will be possible.

In what follows, I will comment on the major sections of the liturgical year, looking in various ways at the set readings for all sections except for ordinary time (which I propose calling "ministry time"). I am not attempting a full exegesis for the texts for each Sunday of the year: this is the purpose of commentaries, and one of the points of having full-time clergy, I suppose, is that there should be at least one person in the community whose job it should be to consult these and pass on the discussion to those too busy otherwise to do so. Rather, I am trying to suggest pointers to illuminate the significance of each moment of the liturgical cycle in terms of formation. Before turning to that task, I want to say a word about the use of collects.

Not all traditions use collects, but in those that do the Gloria in the Eucharist is followed by a "collect" just before the first reading from the lectionary. At the end of the fourth century, as we learn from Augustine (Sermon 325), the Eucharist began with a greeting from the celebrant, followed at once by the readings. However, according to Jungmann (1959: 288–98), it was the building of great basilicas which led to the growth of the early part of the Eucharistic rite. Bishops and their retinue might have a long way to come in, so they were accompanied by song. The celebrant then invited the people to pray: "first the people pray; then the priest sums up their prayer in the oration". The prayer of the people could be a litany with the refrain, Kyrie Eleison. This was later abbreviated simply to a "kyrie", but the celebrant's summarizing oration (the collect) remained. This drew on ancient rhetoric, distinguished by conciseness and beautiful rhythm. Other accounts speak of the way the collect sums up the theme of the scriptural readings.

There are a number of problems with the current use of collects. First, many Christian gatherings are very small, and in no need of rhetorical devices adapted to great basilicas. Second, though the rubric before the collect suggests private prayer may be called for, the prayers of the congregation generally come later, and whoever leads them does indeed, in some form of words, gather those prayers up, or "collect" them, at the end. Third, the collects often fail to bear on the Eucharistic readings, and so do not illuminate what is going on. Fourth, the attempt to preserve the style and wording of the ancient collects leads to prayers often written in a form of churchspeak incomprehensible to either humans or angels, which leave everyone present perplexed. If we are to have a prayer after the Gloria and before the readings, first, let it be in words, as Cranmer wanted, "understood by the people", and second, let it sum up or point towards or reflect on the biblical readings.

Advent

The advent of Advent

There is some obscurity about the advent of Advent, related to the late appearance of the celebration of Christ's birth on 25 December. Martin Connell speaks of three basic and sometimes interrelated traditions of keeping Advent. One is scriptural, preparing for the infancy narratives at Christmas; one is ascetic; and the third is eschatological. The ascetic tradition may be related to a forty-day preparation for baptism at Epiphany, on 6 January. It is a survival of that tradition which determines that Advent is kept as a penitential season, without flowers or the Gloria, with purple vestments (when used), and traditionally as a season of fasts.

As we shall see when we turn to Christmas, we find a six-week preparation for Christmas in the fifth century, the first five weeks of which are known as *de adventu*—"on the theme of the coming". Advent was widely kept from St Martin's Day, 11 November, to Christmas, a period of seven weeks. Gregory the Great (d. 604) reduced this period to four weeks, the first of many liturgical reorderings.

In Milan, in the Ambrosian rite, and in Spain in the Mozarabic rite, Advent is still kept for six weeks, whereas the rest of the Western Church follows Gregory's organization. However, there are four Sundays between the last Sunday after Trinity and Advent Sunday. The first three of these all have readings with eschatological themes, drawing on the so-called "little apocalypse" in the Gospels, and six of the nine Epistle readings are taken from 1 and 2 Thessalonians, which assume a "Second Coming". Thus the "eschatological" reading of Advent is firmly adopted.

The Sunday next before Advent breaks the cycle, and is the celebration of Christ the King, instituted by Pius XI in 1925 partly in response to the question of who had political power in the papal state, and partly in reaction to growing secularism and nationalism. In its current place, it is intended to mark the end of the liturgical year but is susceptible to an eschatological reading, shown by the fact that two of the three Gospel texts are from the eschatological discourse, and a text from the first chapter of Revelation is one of the Epistle readings. It fits the Advent theme, not as Pius XI intended it, but insofar as it serves as a critique of all earthly rule.

If we turn to the four Sundays of Advent, the first continues the eschatological theme, with the accent on the Second Coming. The second and third Sundays turn to John the Baptist, the Forerunner, whilst the final Sunday has the annunciation to Mary and Matthew's account of the angel's word to Joseph. All of the texts from the Tenakh, without exception, are strongly eschatological, as are most of the epistolary passages.

What this shows, I think, is that from the last Sunday of "ordinary time" (an expression which should be abandoned, as I shall argue later) until the second Sunday of Advent the lectionary focusses on eschatological themes, and especially the so-called *Parousia*, or "Second Coming", and then turns its attention to the "first coming", in the flesh, which it will celebrate at Christmas. In effect, the new liturgical year begins on the fourth Sunday *before* Advent, and a change to recognize that would be welcome. In the early Church, a seven-week Advent is known, and in practice, in terms of the themes offered for reflection, we now have an eight-week Advent. This makes excellent theological sense, as I shall now go on to argue.

Advent as the beginning of the year

Some scholars argue that the eschatological character of the Advent texts, and the location of Advent within the Roman liturgical books, suggest that at one stage it *ended* the year rather than began it. The Christian year began, then, with the mass on Christmas Eve. If this suggestion is correct this would mirror the position of eschatology in Christian doctrine throughout the medieval period, and into the mid twentieth century. In Aquinas' *Summa Theologiae*, for example, eschatology comes right at the end, added by another Dominican after Aquinas' death. Eschatology is an appendix. It concerned itself with "the four last things"—death, judgement, heaven and hell. This understanding was represented in the dooms over chancel arches which were found in churches throughout medieval Europe: Christ is at the apex, with the book of judgement open on his lap. On his right hand the blessed, including many of the poor, are taken up into heaven. On his left hand, the damned, including many bishops and kings, are cast down into hell. The famous carol Dives and Lazarus embodies the same understanding which represents a form of social critique, in line with that of the prophets, which otherwise was virtually impossible in that society, with its hierarchical ideology. It tells us that the ideology was nowhere taken for granted. The emphasis on coming judgement, which we know weighed heavily on many Christians into the twentieth century, provided a new rationale for Advent as a penitential season.

This account of eschatology was fundamentally changed in 1964 by Jürgen Moltmann's *Theology of Hope*, and I suggest that this puts Advent as the beginning of the Church's year into a completely different light. To begin the Church's year with Advent is not (excuse the pun) adventitious: on the contrary, it means that the Church adopts an entirely different approach to time to that of secular society. How come?

Moltmann began his reappraisal of eschatology by taking aim at what he called the "epiphany of the eternal present", the god who is always the same and always equidistant from our present, no matter when that is—effectively the view of Augustine's *Confessions*. The problem is that the contemplation of this god does not make a meaningful experience of history possible, but negates it. This in turn makes nonsense of the idea that we know G-d in and through the G-d who becomes flesh. We find in Scripture not the eternally present god but, to use Paul's phrase, the "G-d of hope" (Romans 15:13). The G-d known in the exodus and resurrection, Moltmann argued, "is" not eternal presence, but promises G-d's presence and nearness to the one who follows the path on which they are sent into the future. Augustine speaks of the *cor inquietum*, the restless heart which always seeks for G-d, but biblically we should speak of the *promissio inquieta*, which keeps looking for signs of the kingdom. It is the story of the crucified and risen Messiah which constitutes a "disturbing promise" contrasting the present godless situation with the promised future in which, as the Advent texts promise, all things attain to right, life, peace, freedom and truth, and in which, furthermore, death is conquered.

Following classical precedent, Augustine divided time into six epochs, but the first five finished at the birth of Christ, and there then remained only one epoch until the end of time. In the twelfth century, the Calabrian abbot, Joachim of Fiore (1135–1202), made the momentous suggestion that time should be understood in a Trinitarian way, in three overlapping ages: from Adam to Christ (but bearing fruit through Abraham), which was the age of the Father; from Christ to the end of the twelfth century or the beginning of the next (inaugurated by Uzziah, bearing fruit through Zechariah, father of John the Baptist), which was the age of the Son; and the age of the Spirit, inaugurated by St Benedict but only now about to begin. This opened up an expectation of G-d's new and decisive action in history, through a figure, who might be Francis or might be the Emperor Frederick Barbarossa, and which triggered a string of millennial movements right into the twentieth century. The "Third Reich" of Adolf Hitler looked back to this idea. In the Church, it changed the understanding of sacraments from signs of individual conversion and piety to witnesses to the reality of G-d's incoming kingdom.

Now it could be seen that the Tenakh, rather than an "old" dispensation which we have had done with, was full of expectation, and it was this which accounted for the eager hope, "living wholly and utterly in Advent", as Karl Barth put it, of the first community. To live by such a hope meant working here and now to make something of the promised redemption of all things become visible. In the Messianic Writings, it is above all Paul who speaks of hope. According to him faith without hope is empty (1 Corinthians 15:14). G-d gives the believer hope (Romans 15:13). The Spirit of the One who raised Christ from the dead dwells in believers, and their hope is an earnest one for the whole of creation "groaning in bondage". "In hope we are saved" (Romans 8:9–24). The love which comes from Christ "hopes all things" (1 Corinthians 13:7). And according to 1 Peter, Christians are reborn to "a living hope" (1 Peter 1:3). The one who hopes finds him or herself on the side of the homeless, the restless and the rightless "for the sake of the diviner right that is coming" (Moltmann 1965: 224). As opposed to the idea that hope might be deceptive, we have to say that hope alone is to be called realistic, because it is hope which takes seriously the possibilities with which all reality is fraught. Hope is not utopian in the sense of daydreaming of a place which does not exist, but seeks to give a place to realities which at present lack one but may acquire one. This is the substance of the prayer: "Your kingdom come on earth".

All this means that far from being the *last* chapter of any theology eschatology should be understood as *the key signature of all theology*. This is exactly what we affirm when we begin the Christian year with Advent. *Hope, Yearning, Longing for a world made otherwise, is the key signature of the entire Christian year.* This is exactly what Christians affirm when we announce the key signature of our faith in Advent and perhaps it is an inner recognition of this which accounts for the fact that we have so many wonderful Advent hymns, which proclaim the Maranatha, Come Lord Jesus, when established churches everywhere have quietly forgotten it.

This is not what was intended when Advent became the start of the liturgical year, but it turns out to be a happy choice. It means, too, that while Advent certainly strikes the note of prophetic judgement, it is not about fear in relation to what is going to happen to me after death, nor about eagerly anticipating the end of this aeon, but about a joyful embrace of the divine promise, precisely the theme of the last Sunday of Advent in the annunciation to Mary.

To take Advent as the start of the liturgical year involves a different mapping of the year, as proposed in the diagrams below.

Advent brackets the cyclical pattern of the liturgical year and subsumes it under the arrow of time: all time, it says, is heading in one direction, towards "a new heaven and a new earth", "the kingdom of G-d". Cultures and belief systems which adopted the idea of reincarnation, or reiterated cycles of time (e.g. Stoicism, Hinduism) could understand the death of the individual within a cyclical framework. According to the gospel understanding, however, all people are judged by whether they lived in solidarity with the least and met their basic needs (Matthew 25:31–46, the Gospel for the Sunday next before Advent). They are judged, in other words, in terms of their actions in a unique experience of time.

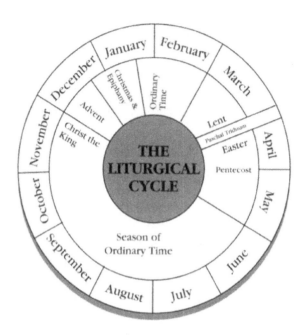

Liturgical cycle as it currently is (above) and as proposed (below)

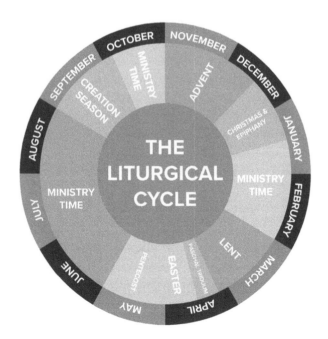

The Advent lectionary

Scholars tell us that YHWH was in origin a West Semitic mountain god. The first great prophet we meet, Elijah, is a man of thunder, lightning and earthquake. When we come to the writing prophets, they often take over this imagery. So, for example, on the Second Sunday before Advent in Year A we read:

> The great day of the LORD is near,
> near and hastening fast . . .
> That day will be a day of wrath,
> a day of distress and anguish,
> a day of ruin and devastation,
> a day of darkness and gloom,
> a day of clouds and thick darkness,
> a day of trumpet blast and battle cry
> against the fortified cities
> and against the lofty battlements (Zephaniah 1:14–16).

And on the First Sunday of Advent in Year B we read:

> O that you would tear open the heavens and come down,
> so that the mountains would quake at your presence—
> as when fire kindles brushwood
> and the fire causes water to boil—
> to make your name known to your adversaries,
> so that the nations might tremble at your presence!
> When you did awesome deeds that we did not expect,
> you came down, the mountains quaked at
> your presence (Isaiah 64:1–3).

What is happening here is that storm and earthquake imagery is being used poetically to speak of G-d's judgement in a historical, political context. Towards the end of Israelite prophecy, under the pressure of persecution, prophecy morphs into apocalyptic which uses this imagery to strengthen resistance to the idolatrous claims of world empires and to urge the faithful not to resign themselves to fate. We find this, for example, in the passages from Daniel set for the Second Sunday before Advent and the Sunday next before Advent in Year B. This imagery is picked up in the so-called "eschatological discourse" of Jesus set for the Gospel on the Fourth Sunday before Advent, Year A (Matthew), the Second Sunday before Advent, Year B (Mark), and the first Sunday in Advent in Year C (Luke). Mark is the earliest of these, and Matthew and Luke are dependent on him. It has been cogently argued that Mark 13 is an apocalyptic message arising from the desperate fight for Jerusalem in AD 69/70, urging Christians not to join that particular struggle because it is misdirected. But, like the prophets, it uses apocalyptic imagery, taken from Daniel, about the coming of the Son of Man and the end of all things—stressing, nevertheless, that no one knows the day or the hour (Mark 13:32 and par.). These texts advocate neither fatalism nor escapism, but "a revolutionary commitment to the transformation of history, which always demands political vigilance and discernment" (Myers 1988: 341).

Now the Epistles for many of these Sundays draw on earlier texts which quite clearly *do* expect Christ's Second Coming, the *Parousia* (Third before Advent in Years A and C; Second before Advent in Year A; Advent 1 in Year A; Advent 2 in Years B and C; Advent 3 in Years A and B). So, in Third before Advent, Year A we read:

> the Lord himself, with a cry of command, with the archangel's call and with the sound of G-d's trumpet, will descend from heaven, and the dead in Christ will rise first. Then we who are alive, who are left, will be caught up in the clouds together with them to meet the Lord in the air; and so we will be with the Lord forever (1 Thessalonians 4:16–17).

The week after that we hear Paul reminding the same group that "the day of the Lord will come like a thief in the night" (1 Thessalonians 5:2). In the first week of Advent Paul reminds his readers in Rome that "salvation is nearer to us now than when we became believers; the night is far spent, the day is near" (Romans 13:11–12). The following week the second letter of Peter tells us that the day of the Lord will come like a thief, and then the heavens will pass away with a loud noise, and the elements will be dissolved with fire, and the earth and everything that is done on it will be disclosed (2 Peter 3:10).

The Messianic Writings are full of such texts, and there is no doubt that, in the wake of the resurrection, the early Church did feel that the end of all things was at hand. We know that the community to which 2 Peter is addressed complained about the delay of Jesus' coming in glory, and we know that Paul's congregations speculated about it. At the same time, they also felt an urgency to spread the word of the death and resurrection of Messiah Jesus, to live a life appropriate to that, and to live in the light of what they acknowledged as the gift of the Spirit. As we see in Romans 8, the early community lived with a vivid sense that a brave new world was breaking in right now, under our feet. For them, the hope of Christians is the visible breath of that morning air. I believe that is how we should primarily read these texts. Ched Myers has also suggested that we should read these texts as speaking of the moral, spiritual, social and political unsustainability of the world to which the gospel is addressed, an unsustainability which is even more pronounced for us than it was in the first century (Myers 2015).

Alongside these eschatological or apocalyptic texts there are also texts of prophetic judgement (Fourth before Advent in Years A and C; Third before Advent in Year A; Advent 1 in Year A; Advent 3 in Year B). The text for the Third Sunday before Advent in Year A is Amos 5:18–24—the tremendous denunciation of the cult:

I hate, I despise your festivals,
and I take no delight in your solemn assemblies.
Even though you offer me your burnt offerings and grain offerings,
I will not accept them;
and the offerings of well-being of your fatted animals
I will not look upon.
Take away from me the noise of your songs;
I will not listen to the melody of your harps.
But let justice roll down like waters,

and righteousness like an ever-flowing stream (Amos 5:21–4).

This text is not simply a historical comment on the cult of ancient Israel, but a comment on our own liturgy if it is divorced from the practice of justice.

Alongside these texts are parables from the Gospel which likewise emphasize the need for just behaviour (Fourth before Advent in Years B and C; Third before Advent in Year A; Sunday next before Advent in Year A).

Two of the weeks of Advent are devoted to John the Baptist. The Year C readings are from Luke, and in the second service for Advent 2, we have the account of the annunciation to Zechariah: like a Nazirite, Zechariah's son will touch no wine or strong drink, he will come with "the spirit and power of Elijah", he will be filled with the Holy Spirit, and he will "turn the hearts of parents to their children, and the disobedient to the wisdom of the just (*dikaios*), to make ready a people prepared for the Lord" (Luke 1:17). Ched Myers and Elaine Enns point out the parallelisms and the gender politics in the annunciation to Zechariah and to Mary. The first annunciation is patterned on the story of Abraham and Sarah, but here, instead of the woman being reproved ("and Sarah laughed . . . ") it is Zechariah who is reproved and silenced for his incredulity. The men are silenced, and the women find their voices.

The story moves straight on to the annunciation to Mary. Mary at once takes off to Elizabeth's house. Two village women meet. They are nobodies, not the stuff of history, but G-d works through them to move history on its axis. "When Elizabeth heard Mary's greeting, the child leaped in her womb" (Luke 1:41). "G-d sneaks into the world in a somatic and social landscape" (Myers and Enns 2015). Elizabeth cries out ecstatically: "Blessed are you among women, and blessed is the fruit of your womb". The word "blessed" is used three times ("blessed is she who believed . . . " Luke 1:45). This village woman recognizes "the blessing, the mystery and the conspiracy of life". Mary responds with the song of praise we know as the Magnificat (Advent 4 in Year C), a reworking of Hannah's song in 1 Samuel 2. Both songs speak of G-d's upside-down world, where the powerful are dethroned, the hungry are given bread, and the rich sent away empty. Mary says: "G-d has looked with favour on the lowliness of G-d's servant" (Luke 1:48). G-d works through the least, at the margins, not at the centre. As the psalmists repeatedly said: "G-d has shown strength with G-d's arm; G-d has scattered the proud in the imagination (*dianoia*—understanding, mind) of their hearts" (Luke 1:51). It is Jeremiah above all who talks of the "evil imagination" (*sheriruth*, stubbornness) of the heart (Jeremiah 3:17; 7:24; 9:14; 11:8; 13:10; 16:12; 18:12; 23:17). This stubborn imagination is something like hubris, the belief that (some) humans have ultimate power, can do what they want. Nebuchadnezzar had it, and became like an animal, eating grass. We see it in the world rulers and the CEOs of our own day. The power of G-d is nothing like this. Here we see it in a woman giving birth.

When the adult John the Baptist appears (Advent 3 in Year C), the same formula is used as is used of the eighth- to sixth-century prophets: "the Word of G-d came to . . . ". There was a belief that prophecy had ceased, but now it is heard again. Luke situates his account of the Baptist in real political space: in the reign of Tiberius, when Pilate was governor, Herod Antipas was ruling Galilee, his brother Philip neighbouring Ituraea, and Lysanias ruling Abilene, when Annas and Caiaphas were high priests (Luke 3:1–2, cf. Myers and Colwell 2012: 174). This forms a stark contrast to the infantilized image of the nativity of the contemporary Western Christmas (just look at the Christmas cards!). John is active in the Jordan valley, but all the Gospels apply the words of Isaiah/Malachi to him: "in the wilderness prepare the way of the Lord". Once again we are at the margins, not at the centre. John addresses the whole people, not simply in a message of individual repentance, but in response to the question, "what should we do?", he replies: share with one another and don't exploit others.

The Advent antiphons

The Magnificat is an Advent song, a song hailing the dawn of a world made otherwise, and in the monastic office is sung each day at vespers (which Bede, we remember, thought was the beginning of the day). The psalms and canticles would be accompanied by an antiphon, and from 17 to 23 December, beginning in at least the eighth century, the Magnificat was accompanied by seven antiphons, one for each day, drawn from Isaiah, expressing hope for the renewal of the world. An eighth antiphon, celebrating the annunciation to Mary, was sometimes added, pushing the first day back to 16 December. They are known as the "O" antiphons because they all begin with hailing Jesus by one of his Names, and they all embody the Advent prayer, Maranatha, Come Lord Jesus. They are known to most ordinary Christians in the West as paraphrased in the hymn, "O Come, O Come Emmanuel", but when Percy Dearmer and Ralph Vaughan Williams published *The English Hymnal* in 1906 (banned by the Archbishop of Canterbury—a rare accolade!), they included antiphons for use in parish churches throughout the year, and the Advent antiphons were amongst them. They are a beautiful way of preparing for the celebration of Christmas. The first, taken from Isaiah 11:2–3, is *O Sapientia*, O Wisdom:

> O Wisdom, coming forth from the mouth of the Most High,
> reaching from one end to the other,
> mightily and sweetly ordering all things:
> Come and teach us the way of prudence.

Many scholars argue that the most primitive Christology was a Wisdom Christology, and even if that is not the case wisdom themes were certainly prominent. In Proverbs, Wisdom is said to dwell with prudence (*ormah*, translated by *boulē*, counsel, in the LXX) (Proverbs 8:12), but Paul rethinks what is meant by wisdom, understanding it in terms of the cross (1 Corinthians 1:18–25). This in turn redefines the "prudence" of discipleship.

On 18 December, we sing *O Adonai* ("Lord", a reference to the divine NAME), drawing on Isaiah 11:4–5:

> O Adonai, and leader of the House of Israel,
> who appeared to Moses in the fire of the burning bush
> and gave him the law on Sinai:
> Come and redeem us with an outstretched arm.

According to Paul, perhaps citing an already existing hymn, Jesus is the bearer of the divine NAME (Philippians 2:5ff.) which was already known by the ancient Israelites in the exodus (1 Corinthians 10:1–5). The redemption known in Christ, which seeks completion, is a continuation of that revelation to Moses, and the new law in Christ continues that of the first law (Matthew 5:18).

On 19 December, *O Radix Jesse*—O Root of Jesse (Isaiah 11:1; 52:13–15):

> O Root of Jesse, standing as a sign among the peoples;
> before you kings will shut their mouths,
> to you the nations will make their prayer:
> Come and deliver us, and delay no longer.

At some time in the tenth century BC, the tribes of YHWH, who had a bronze-age technology, found themselves facing an opponent with iron-age weapons (and David defeated their champion using a stone-age weapon!). Their response to repeated defeat was to set up a monarchy, a move bitterly contested at the time (1 Samuel 8:10–18; cf. Hosea 8:4), and which produced repeated disappointment. Finally the kings of Judah are carted off into exile and disappear. Some Jews still longed for a new king "like all the nations", but the group we know as "Second Isaiah" instead looked for a servant who would astonish the nations, who would redeem in an absolutely unlooked-for way. The first Christian community believed this promise was fulfilled in Jesus and looked for the fulfilment of his absolutely alternative rule.

On the 20th, *O Clavis David*, O Key of David (Isaiah 22:22; 42:7; Psalm 107:10,14):

> O Key of David and sceptre of the House of Israel;
> you open and no one can shut;
> you shut and no one can open:
> Come and lead the prisoners from the prison house,
> those who dwell in darkness and the shadow of death.

The first Isaiah uttered a prophecy directed at a steward he believed was corrupt, and prophesied that one, Eliakim son of Hilkiah, would take his place and be a father to the inhabitants of Jerusalem. This antiphon combines that prophecy with one of Second Isaiah's prophecies about the Servant, which refers to the situation of the exile (where some may have been in prison) but also echoes Psalm 107, which speaks of prisoners "in misery and irons, in darkness and 'the shadow of death'" (*tsalmaveth*—profound shadow; NRSV translates "gloom"). It is impossible not to think of Isaiah 25:8 as well, which promises that G-d will

> destroy on this mountain
> the shroud that is cast over all peoples,
> the sheet that is spread over all nations;
> he will swallow up death forever (Isaiah 25:6–7).

The Christian community believes that Jesus has accomplished this in his resurrection.

On the 21st, *O Oriens*—O Dayspring or Morning Star (Isaiah 9:2; Zechariah 3:8):

> O Morning Star,
> splendour of light eternal and sun of righteousness:
> Come and enlighten those who dwell in
>   darkness and the shadow of death.

Above all, in John's Gospel Jesus is identified with the light that scatters the darkness, the darkness of lies and propaganda, of group (and especially national) hysteria and delusion, but also of self-deception.

On the 22nd, *O Rex Gentium*—King of the Nations (Isaiah 2:4; 9:6; 64:8):

> O King of the nations, and their desire,
> the cornerstone making both one:
> Come and save the human race,
> which you fashioned from clay.

As we know from our Christmas readings the first Isaiah speaks of a coming ruler whose name will be

"Wonderful Counsellor, Mighty G-d,
Everlasting Father, Prince of Peace".
Of the increase of his government and of peace
there will be no end,
upon the throne of David, and over his kingdom,
to establish it, and to uphold it
with justice and with righteousness
from this time forth and for evermore (Isaiah 9:6–7).

Earlier he has told us that

He shall judge between the nations,
and shall decide for many peoples;
and they shall beat their swords into ploughshares,
and their spears into pruning hooks;
nation shall not lift up sword against nation,
neither shall they learn war any more (Isaiah 2:4).

And in a later passage he refers to the familiar image of G-d fashioning human beings out of clay. Those who put the antiphon together, at some stage during "the dark ages", knew that human beings needed saving (the Latin has *et salva hominem*) from their own self-destructive impulses.

Finally, on the 23rd, *O Emmanuel* (Isaiah 7:14; 42:1,6; Romans 15:12):

O Emmanuel, our king and our lawgiver,
the hope of the nations and their Saviour:
Come and save us, O Lord our G-d.

The writer of this antiphon begins with Isaiah, but then his mind turns to the catena of quotations in Romans 15, some of which come out of Paul's own head, but which express the sense of Scripture nonetheless. "Isaiah" says, according to Paul:

The root of Jesse shall come,
he who rises to rule the Gentiles;
in him shall the Gentiles hope.

Paul conflates the promises of Second Isaiah that the servant (possibly Israel) will be a light to the Gentiles, and replaces "light" with "hope"—an Advent theme. In the cries given voice in these antiphons—the repeated Come!, Come, our Deliverer!—both the Messianic hope of Israel and the longing of Christian people, the substance of Advent, was and is expressed.

Christmas

Why 25 December?

The celebration of the birth of Christ does not appear as a feast until the fourth century and there has never been a universally agreed date for it. Clement of Alexandria, at the turn of the third century, cites views that Jesus might have been born on 20 April or 20 May. In Egypt and the East, it was celebrated on 6 January, which is when the Russian Orthodox and Armenians still celebrate it.

The 25 December date appears in the fourth century and was adopted fairly widely by the end of the century. The two suggestions for choosing this date are, first, the "history of religions" approach, which suggests that it was chosen because, under the Julian calendar, it was celebrated as the solstice (the Council of Nicaea corrected this to the 21st) and had also been named as the festival of the unconquered sun by the emperor Aurelian. The idea is that the date was chosen to try and wean people away from pagan celebrations. The other suggestion, already implicit in Clement, is that people tried to calculate the day by correlating the Gospel stories with Roman and astrological records, relating the dates of conception and death (assuming, because Jesus was perfect, that these would occur on the same day). In his *History of the World*, the third-century historian Julius Africanus dates both the creation of the world and the conception of Jesus on 25 March and this, too, would give us (after nine months) 25 December.

The fact that Christmas as an independent feast appears around or after Nicaea also suggests that the (widely contested) decision that Christ was *homoousios* (of one substance) with the Father may have had something to do with it. Certainly the fourth century sees the consolidation of much liturgical practice, which is hardly surprising, since it marked what was hoped to be a final end to persecution and, for good or ill, a new relation to the State. The suggestion that the nativity stories in Matthew and Luke might pull against the Nicene decision signally misses the point of that decision, as I shall argue below.

Whatever the reason for the choice of 25 December, the fact that Christianity first spread north and west meant that much of the emotional force of the Christmas celebration was borrowed from midwinter. In the northern hemisphere, it is at this time that the year turns towards longer and warmer days, when hens start laying again after a month or so off, when evergreens are a reminder that life still goes on, and this is a cue for the celebrations of a Saturnalian kind. As Thomas Hardy put it (in *The Return of the Native*):

> To light a fire is the instinctive and resistant act of man when, at the winter ingress, the curfew is sounded throughout Nature. It indicates a spontaneous, Promethean rebelliousness against the fiat that this recurrent season shall bring foul times, cold darkness, misery and death. Black chaos comes, and the fettered gods of the earth say, Let there be light.

Many Christmas carols express this spirit. If Christianity had spread first in the southern hemisphere (where 21 December is the longest day), then the theme of light might still be there, but the tone of the celebration would be very different. At the same time, it has to be granted that, especially under the influence of consumer capitalism, Christmas has reverted for many, if not for the majority, to a parody of Saturnalia, centred on consumption, with a light and largely sentimentalized dressing of nativity themes.

In the Gospels, we have three different responses to the birth of Christ but all, as Ched Myers notes, represent a quite different picture to the domesticated versions of contemporary Christmas celebrations. These stories "invite us to reimagine Christmas as a time to resist not only the delusions of our consumer society, but also the rule of Domination in the world" (Myers 2004).

Matthew's story

Matthew begins his Gospel with a genealogy on the lines of the early genealogies of Genesis. He traces Jesus' descent from Abraham (so, a proper Jew), in three lots of fourteen generations—from Abraham to David, from David to the exile, and from the exile to the birth of the Messiah. Doubtless these perfect numbers would have proved convincing to Matthew's readers.

We get a pretty good idea of Matthew from his Gospel. He is the one who sticks in the "unchastity" clause in the story about divorce (Matthew 19:9); he is the one who salivates about outer darkness with wailing and gnashing of teeth. The angel announcing Jesus' birth comes to Joseph, not to Mary (who would talk to a woman after all?!). So we would expect a patriarchal cast to the genealogy, but he surprises us. Four women break the sequence: Tamar, who had to disguise herself as a prostitute in order to get her marital rights from Judah (Genesis 38); Rahab, a "Madam" who helps the Israelite spies (Joshua 2); Ruth, a Moabite widow, who "uncovers the feet" of Boaz (a euphemism) to make a marriage which enables both her and her mother-in-law to survive (Ruth 3); and Bathsheba, who commits adultery with David. Since Jewish tradition counted Tamar as an alien, Rahab was a Canaanite, Ruth a Moabite and Bathsheba married to a Hittite, the point might be that they are Gentiles, and so prefigure the Gentile mission. On the other hand, it might be that Matthew is saying that G-d works through women who are, to say the least of it, not perfectly respectable. The genealogy reminds us of "a central truth of incarnational theology": "God's redemptive purpose works in and through real human situations, in all their ambiguity—especially through courageous women willing to defy oppressive social conventions in order to embrace the alternative vision of G-d" (Myers 2012: 163/4).

In this connection, we can recall the second-century legend that Jesus was the son of Mary by Pantaenus, a Roman soldier. We have to ask, what does it mean for G-d to take flesh? Does it require a virgin birth? (not to mention perpetual virginity!) And if G-d works through normal human processes, and from the margins, what could be more marginal than a child conceived through a relation with a loathed and despised oppressor? This is not, however, what either Matthew or Luke wants to say. Matthew cites Isaiah 7:14 where the first Isaiah prophesied that in the time it took for a young woman (*almah*) to conceive and wean her child the forces threatening Judah would all be dissipated. In the LXX, "*almah*" was translated *parthenos*, and Matthew insists that after betrothal Joseph "had no marital relations" with Mary before the birth of Jesus (Matthew 1:25). Rather, Mary was "found to be with child from the Holy Spirit" (1:18). Later, these details became the centre of a Marian theology and a miraculous birth, but we need to remember that all conception was regarded as a gift of G-d (Genesis 18:10–12; 25:21; 29:31; 30:2; 1 Samuel 2). In John, we read that all who believe are born "not of blood nor of the will of the flesh, nor of the will of man but of G-d" (John 1:13). Also the pagan culture of the time knew conceptions without a human father (this was supposed to be true of Alexander, for example). "The fact of such a birth therefore did not single Jesus out as unique, it simply placed him in the company of the great men of the age" (Schweizer 1976: 33).

The angel tells Joseph that the boy is to be called "Joshua", "G-d-saves" (in Greek *Iēsous*). Matthew supplies the meaning of the Hebrew name in parenthesis and also cites Isaiah 7, to say that in Jesus G-d will be with us. The point of the whole birth narrative, then, is that through this child G-d is acting as G-d did in the exodus, as a deliverer, setting human history on a new axis.

Matthew then tells the story of the Magi, which I shall deal with under Epiphany, but it follows directly from that story that Mary and Joseph have to flee to Egypt. To be sure, this is probably a theological fiction to emphasize that the word of Hosea 11:1, "Out of Egypt I have called my son", is fulfilled. At the same time, it ranks Jesus and his parents amongst the countless millions of refugees in human history, and amongst the Palestinians, Syrians, Rohinga and others who so desperately seek security and a new life in our own day, and meet with so determined a refusal.

Luke's story

Just as Luke situates John the Baptist's preaching in socio-political space, so is the birth of Jesus situated. Caesar Augustus orders a universal tax, which requires a census, and people need to be registered. Joseph, according to the story, has to go from Nazareth, in Galilee, to Bethlehem in the south, taking Mary, who was near her term. Josephus tells us that the tax brought about a revolt, and Luke mentions that its leader, Judas the Galilean, died, "and all who followed him were scattered" (Acts 5:37). Myers and Enns point out that a poll tax was often impossible for the poor to afford, and such a journey (a journey impossible today because of Israel's anti-Palestinian walls) would be a profound hardship. The world into which Jesus was born, they comment, resembles modern-day Afghanistan or El Salvador, and Luke's story defies the trivialization of most Church accounts and especially of their depiction on Christmas cards (Myers and Enns 2015).

On reaching Bethlehem, no lodging place (*kataluma*) has room for them, but someone offers them shelter with the animals (probably in a longhouse, where part of the house was used to keep animals, which gave warmth to the rest), and the newborn infant is laid in a feed trough. The "ox and the ass" of Christmas carols are read into the story from Isaiah 1:3. "The scandal is not a miraculous virgin birth but the social space of this political geography. The push and pull of empire still forces people to leave their homes in order to survive", but "in such circumstances the G-d of the Bible for ever kick starts the process of redemption" (Myers and Enns 2015).

Whilst the newborn is cared for an angel announces the birth to shepherds, who are looking after their flocks. As with Matthew, the importance of the story is theological, not historical, but were it historical the time for shepherds to be with their flocks would be spring rather than winter, when flocks were on their way to higher pastures, and also when lambing took place. Clement's suggestions about the date of Christ's birth would then come into play. Later Judaism spoke of shepherds as people of no account, but David was a shepherd when anointed by Samuel, and the shepherd metaphor was constantly used of the kings of Israel. In any event, shepherds were people well acquainted with byres and feed troughs. The angel announces a new messianic order, "peace to those with whom G-d is well pleased", "a close mimicking of Roman imperial propaganda, a subversive appropriation of political language" (Myers and Enns 2015). The shepherds set off to check out the "word" (*rēma*, word or saying) of the angel and to make known what they had been told. They interpreted the events for those around. All were amazed but Mary "treasured all these words and pondered them in her heart" (Luke 2:19). After the angel, the shepherds are the first evangelists. In Luke's whole story (including Acts) this moment is a pivot: he begins in Rome, with the emperor Augustus, he goes to Nazareth and Bethlehem, to the birth of a child who is an entirely different sort of king, laid in a feed trough, and then a movement, beginning with shepherds, takes place which ends back in Rome (Acts 28:14–31) and eventually displaces Caesar. Read in the light of proper biblical literacy the story contradicts our sentimentalization and domestication of the Christmas tradition and helps us "resist the toxic culture of Christmas" (Myers and Enns 2015).

John's poem

What we call the Prologue of John's Gospel is the text which has to be read at some point on Christmas Day, whether at midnight or in the morning. On the face of it, it is a million miles away from the nativity stories of Matthew and Luke and takes us into a world of theological speculation. Is this the case? The answer to this depends on the framework of interpretation we adopt. Philo, Stoicism, Neoplatonism, the Mandaean writings, Gnosticism, and much else besides have all been invoked to understand the Prologue. In my view, it rests solidly on the Tenakh. I agree with those exegetes who argue that John is part of a Jewish community which accepts Jesus as Messiah and therefore finds itself at loggerheads with fellow Jews who most emphatically do not. When the expression "the Jews" is used in John, it is this latter group which is meant. The opening verses, in my view, represent a Christian Midrash, if you like, on the first four verses of Genesis, and the thought of the "Prologue", if that is how we should think of it, then ranges widely over the whole of the Tenakh.

The author (with tradition we call him "John") begins his Gospel exactly as Genesis begins in the LXX—*En archē*. But where Genesis says that all was formless and void, and darkness was upon the face of the deep, John says there was "the Word". What Word is this? Genesis 1 has a sevenfold "And G-d said", by which G-d creates, and G-d communes with G-dself at the creation of humans (Genesis 1:26). John also knew what Gerhard von Rad called the "theology of the Word" in the writings of the great prophets—the Word which "came" to Hosea, Amos, Micah, Isaiah and all the rest, and through which G-d makes history (Jeremiah 1:9–10). John understands that it is this Word which is at the beginning, through which all is created (John 1:3).

Like many of the first Christians, John was especially familiar with the Wisdom writings. He read in Proverbs that G-d created Wisdom at the beginning of G-d's work, "the first of G-d's acts long ago!":

> When he established the heavens, I was there,
> when he drew a circle on the face of the deep,
> when he made firm the skies above,
> when he established the fountains of the deep,
> when he assigned to the sea its limit,
> so that the waters might not transgress his command,
> when he marked out the foundations of the earth,
> then I was beside him, like a master worker;
> and I was daily his delight,
> rejoicing before him always,
> rejoicing in his inhabited world
> and delighting in the human race (Proverbs 8:27–31).

In Sirach, he read that Wisdom was eternal, created before all things, and G-d chose Israel as the place for her tent (*skēnēn*), and she made her dwelling (*kataskēnōson*) there (Sirach 24:3–12). In Wisdom of Solomon, he read that Wisdom is "a pure emanation of the glory of the Almighty", that she renews all things, passes into holy souls and makes them friends of G-d.

Compared with the light, she is found to be superior:

For it is succeeded by the night,
But against wisdom evil does not prevail (Wisdom 7:29–30).

John applied such images to the Word. Word and Wisdom were ways of speaking of the same thing.

What is it that G-d brought into being? All reality. All living things. According to the second creation story, G-d created human beings by breathing into the dust of the earth "and Adam became a living being" (Genesis 2:7). John knew from the prophets that G-d was the source of life (Jeremiah 2:13; 17:13). He found in his Scriptures that life was a source of joy and delight (Job 22:26; Jeremiah 15:16; Psalms 16:11; 43:4) and, drawing on that tradition, Jesus, in John, says that he has come to bring precisely this—fullness of life (John 10:10). He knew from Deuteronomy that humans do not live by bread alone "but by every word that proceeds from the mouth of G-d", something that profoundly shaped his own view of Jesus (Deuteronomy 8:3; cf. 32:47 "This word is your life"). He knew from the Psalms that life comes from fellowship with G-d (Psalm 67:3), that G-d gives life and saves from death (Psalms 16:11; 27:1; 31:4). Is it any surprise that, having begun with the Word he goes on: "in him was life" (John 1:4)? But with the scroll *Bereshit* (In the beginning) open before him, he of course sees that the very first work of G-d is the creation of light, and its separation from darkness. The NAME is my light and salvation, says Psalm 27:1; the justice of G-d is a light to all peoples, says Isaiah (Isaiah 51:4). John echoes that verse. The light the Word brought into being (through him all things came into being) is the light of all people (John 1:4). But the Word separated light from darkness. In his Scriptures, he found many metaphorical uses of darkness to stand for human obduracy, wickedness and sin (e.g. Proverbs 2:13; 4:19; Ecclesiastes 2:14). He also found the promise that the people who walk in darkness will see a great light (Isaiah 9:2). That promise, John believes, is now fulfilled: "The light shines in the darkness, and the darkness has not overcome it" (John 1:5).

So far, a Midrash. But John now goes decisively further: "the Word became flesh" (John 1:14). This is a real stone of stumbling. The community in which he grew up knew, of course, that no one can see G-d and live. G-d is not and cannot be a creature. To deify the creature is idolatry—the heart of wickedness according to his Scriptures. What on earth could it mean? Perhaps John hardly knew—perhaps the whole early Christian community hardly knew. For throughout the Messianic Writings we find the claim that it is Jesus "through whom are all things and through whom we exist"(1 Corinthians 8:6); that the light of the knowledge of the glory of G-d shines in the face of Jesus Christ (2 Corinthians 4:4); that Jesus has been given the NAME above every name (Philippians 2:5f.); that "Christ is the image of the invisible G-d, the firstborn of all creation . . . in him were created all things in heaven and on earth, visible and invisible, whether thrones or dominions or principalities or authorities; all things were created through him and to him" (Colossians 1:15–16). And so on. John's "the Word was made flesh" is his version of the claim that G-d is encountered in human history which rings through the Messianic Writings, and which follows from the resurrection. The author of Hebrews began his letter:

> Long ago G-d spoke to our ancestors in many and various ways by the prophets, but in these last days he has spoken to us by a Son, whom he appointed heir of all things, through whom he also created the worlds. He is the reflection of G-d's glory and the exact imprint of G-d's very being, and he sustains all things by his powerful word (Hebrews 1:1–3).

John writes: "We have seen his glory, the glory as of a father's only son, full of grace and truth" (John 1:14). We can see why Martin Hengel could say that with regard to the development of Christology more happened in the first twenty years than in the entire later development of dogma.

Do these claims mean, as has been repeatedly claimed, that the faith of Israel was now left behind, that Hellenism, or Platonism or Gnosticism took over from the simple (and today we can also say "political") gospel? My own view is that this entire development is rooted in the Tenakh, that the first Christians believed that what Abraham Heschel calls "the pathos of G-d" took flesh in Jesus. "Do not think I have come to abolish the law or the prophets", says Jesus in Matthew's Gospel. "I have come not to abolish but fulfil" (Matthew 5:17). For John, that fulfilment entailed flesh-taking, the ultimate expression of G-d's *hesed* (solidarity). That means that all the passion for justice, righteousness, truth and peace of the Tenakh is embodied in Jesus—and so the Church has always believed when it has been true to itself. So the nativity stories of Matthew and Luke—Messiah born to a peasant girl, the baby laid in a feed trough, refugees on the run from state terror—are not done away with in John's Prologue but are *presupposed*. John will have quite enough to say about state terror in due course (which we shall encounter in the readings for Good Friday). Meanwhile, the Messianic Writings had set a problem for those who came after. Jesus, Reb Joshua, someone with a family, brothers and sisters, followers who knew him well, one of whom betrayed him, was *worshipped*! Surely, this was the most brazen idolatry? What we call "Christology" is the record of the stumbling attempt by the community to say that G-d's faithfulness, witnessed to by Torah and prophets, entailed flesh-taking, and that this did not amount to the deification of a creature nor to the death of G-d—the end of G-d being G-d.

Incarnation

I have attempted an account of the development of Christology, and a defence of the classical formulae for it, elsewhere, and I shall not repeat it here but simply make a few observations. At the heart of the whole question is what we mean by G-d and how we think G-d engages with that which is not G-d. The two words which have been used to think about this both derive from the Tenakh, and they are "Spirit" and "grace". If there is anything in the claim that G-d reveals G-dself to Israel, then G-d is personal (which is implied in the idea of G-d as "Word") and G-d is known in justice, mercy, truth, patience and love.

After the end of the first century, as Christianity spread around the whole of the Mediterranean, and to Gaul and to Britain, Christians argued about how to make sense of "the Word made flesh". When Constantine became sole emperor and became a Christian (though he reserved baptism for his death bed), he wanted to make sure that his subjects all agreed about their central ideological commitment and summoned a council in Nicaea (modern-day Iznik in Turkey) in AD 325 to sort out differences. At issue was whether Christ should be understood as a

demi-god—divine, but less than the Father—or whether he was equal
with G-d (*homoousios*—of the same substance). The Council agreed the
latter but struggles with the opposing party went on for another sixty
or seventy years. Further attempts at restatement and disagreements
followed and another council was called at Chalcedon (modern Kadiköy,
also in Turkey) in 451. The agreed statement resolved by this council
ran as follows:

> In agreement . . . with the holy Fathers, we all unanimously teach
> that our Lord Jesus Christ is to us one and the same Son, the
> same perfect in G-dhead, and the same perfect in manhood;
> truly G-d and truly human; the same of a rational soul and body;
> consubstantial (*homoousion*) with the Father in G-dhead, and
> the same consubstantial (*homoousion*) with us in humanity
> (*anthropoteta*); like us in all things except sin; begotten from
> the Father before the ages as regards his G-dhead, and in the
> last days, the same, for us and for our salvation (born) of Mary
> the Virgin, the *Theotokos*, as regards his humanity; one and the
> same Christ, Son, Lord, only-begotten; made known in two
> natures (*phuseis*) without confusion, without change, without
> division, without separation; the difference of the natures being
> by no means removed because of the union, but the property
> of each nature (*phusis*) being preserved, and coalescing in one
> person (*prosopon*) and one concrete being (*hypostasis*) not parted
> or divided into two *prosopa*, but one and the same Son, only-
> begotten, divine Word, the Lord Jesus Christ; as the prophets of
> old and Jesus Christ himself have taught us about him, and the
> creed (*symbolon*) of our fathers has handed down.

Far from this being an account of how we are to understand the
incarnation it is really a series of buoys which marks out the reefs and
shoals of the harbour of Christian faith. The points it wants to make are:

- G-d cannot cease to be G-d.
- It is clear from Scripture that Jesus was truly human.
- To be faithful to Scripture we have to say that "G-d was in Christ".

- To propose an admixture of the divine and the human would be pagan mythology.

The declaration tells us what we have to avoid, and only implicitly what we should believe. No account of how it might be that G-d could take flesh in a fully human being is implied. Far from representing a Babylonian captivity to Greek philosophy it bends Greek philosophical terms out of all recognition in trying to speak of G-d's act in Christ.

Although accepted by the Western Church, the definition settled nothing. Another 150 years later an attempt to address the issue was made in terms of thinking of G-d shaping our personal reality. G-d, it was argued, not only brings all reality into being, but shapes it as well. G-d does this through the "Spirit", a way of talking of G-d's engagement with created reality. The difference between the human being Jesus and ourselves, it is argued, is in his openness to being shaped by G-d, to the extent that we can say "the Word became flesh". At the same time, the human being Jesus is not "adopted" by G-d but "elected", chosen from all eternity for this particular task, so that the shaping of this person can be understood as a becoming of G-d.

Karl Barth argued that we cannot define G-d as by definition incapable of radical solidarity with the creature. He wrote:

> We may believe that G-d can and must only be absolute in contrast to all that is relative, exalted in contrast to all that is lowly, active in contrast to all suffering, inviolable in contrast to all temptation, transcendent in contrast to all immanence, and therefore divine in contrast to everything human, in short that he can and must be only the "Wholly Other". But such beliefs are shown to be quite untenable and corrupt and pagan, by the fact that God does in fact be and do this in Jesus Christ (Barth 1956: 186).

Following the ancient discussion of the Church, Barth is prepared to talk of a union, not of natures but of "essence" (*Wesen*), but the "essence" of G-d is "the free love, the omnipotent mercy, the holy patience of the Father, Son and Holy Spirit" and the "essence" of a human being is that which makes a human being a human being as opposed to G-d, an angel or an animal. This "essence" in Jesus is determined "wholly and utterly, from the very outset and in every part, by the electing grace of G-d". This is not apotheosis, the deification of human essence, because "It is genuinely human in the deepest sense to live by the electing grace of G-d addressed to all people" (Barth 1958: 89). Because the human essence of the Son of G-d always remains human essence we have to talk of the *humanity* of G-d. This is to understand the depth of the divine solidarity with the creature, as expressed in Christ.

Theology is not chemistry. The incarnation cannot be understood as something produced in a divine laboratory. Chalcedon offered no formula, because there is no such thing. What the first generation of Christians left us is a challenge to understand what we mean by the word "G-d" in the light not just of the Tenakh (which gave Jesus his own understanding) but also in the light of crucifixion and resurrection, of the crucified G-d. In the Hebrew lexicon, "solidarity" is offered as one of the possible meanings of *hesed*. What we clumsily call "the doctrine of the incarnation" is the record of the stumbling, inadequate, but nevertheless necessary and always renewed attempts to do that.

The Christmas octave

Christmas was celebrated for twelve days. Twelfth Night, the eve of Epiphany, was a day for more festivity and for the inversion of traditional social mores, as the last day of Saturnalia had been in Rome. In his study of the early Christian liturgy, Josef Jungmann observes that "immediately after December 25th we celebrate feasts which have very little to do with Christmas"—the feasts of St Stephen and St John the Evangelist. T. S. Eliot, in *Murder in the Cathedral*, written in 1935, much more perceptively sees the profound connection between these festivals.

In those Christian traditions which use hangings and vestments all the hangings and colours are changed from white to red on 26 December—the colour of martyrdom. It may well be the case, as Jungmann argues, that St Stephen was commemorated on 26 December before Christmas was celebrated on the 25th, but if so, the timing was fortuitous. For we turn at once from festivity to the cost of discipleship—something already recognized in Luke's nativity stories: "A sword shall pierce your own heart also" (Luke 2:35). If we remember St Stephen, there can be no offensive triviality to Christmas for we are asked at once to remember the martyrs—something we shall think more about in Part 3.

On 27 December, we celebrate the feast of St John the Evangelist— obviously, because we have just listened to his extraordinary Prologue which, as we have seen, has set the Church thinking for the whole of its existence.

On 28 December, we remember Herod's massacre of the innocents. Again it is prompted by a story in the Tenakh, Pharaoh's slaughter of Hebrew boy children in order to find a "final solution" for the refugee problem (Exodus 1:22), and by Jeremiah's later reflection on that, in the light of his own situation: "Rachel weeping for her children" (Jeremiah 31:15). Perhaps this story, too, is a theological fiction, but again it reflects theologically on only too true a reality of human history: children holding the hands of their parents as they are herded into the gas chambers; Genghis Khan annihilating entire cities; the slaughter of every man, woman and child in Magdeburg in 1631 by "Christian" soldiers of the Imperial army; the deaths of countless children in modern-day El Salvador, Syria, Gaza, Iraq and Yemen. The slaughter goes on and on. The biblical stories tell of stratagems of survival—children floated down the Nile, families fleeing for safety to the country of an ancient oppressor. "Against the presence of Power is pitted the power of Presence: G-d with us" (Myers 2004).

29 December is the date of the murder of Thomas à Becket, Archbishop of Canterbury, by thugs loyal to the King, Henry II, just as Oscar Romero and the Jesuit martyrs of El Salvador were murdered by thugs serving the ARENA government. The calendar rubs our noses in the leitmotif of the Gospels: "Whoever will be my disciple must take up their cross and follow me" (Mark 8:34). It reminds us that this is not a moralistic imperative, but a warning of the likely consequences of belief, consequences which still follow, not least in countries which bear the name of "The Saviour".

Carols

Myers and Enns draw our attention to the revolutionary canticles of Luke's narrative—the Magnificat, the Benedictus, the Nunc Dimittis—and speak of them as the ancestors of our carols, contrasting them unfavourably with the sentimental piety of our own carols. I want to say a word about this.

The authors of the *English Hymnal*, Ralph Vaughan Williams and Percy Dearmer, joined forces with Martin Shaw and in 1928 produced the *Oxford Book of Carols*, for which Percy Dearmer wrote the preface. Dearmer was a lifelong socialist, brought up in the tradition of William Morris' Arts and Crafts movement, and influenced by the first Folk Music revival. In the First World War, he and his wife both volunteered for ambulance service at the front, where his wife died of typhus. After the war, Dearmer was given a post at Westminster Abbey, where he promptly set up a soup kitchen for unemployed people. The preface to the *Oxford Book* is a characteristically pugnacious and brilliant account of what a carol is. Dearmer understood carols as folk poetry, full of hilarity, often lamentably "re-written by well-meaning clergymen into frigid expositions of edifying theology". The origin of the carol is in the folk dance, dancing in a ring. "The typical carol gives voice to the common emotions of healthy people in language that can be understood and music that can be shared by all" (Dearmer 1928: v). The carol dances because it is so merry and "to take life with real seriousness is to take it joyfully, for seriousness is only sad when it is superficial. It is the antidote to a morose pharisaism." Dearmer cites the Puritan Hezekiah Woodward, who in a tract of 1656 spoke of Christmas Day as

> The old Heathen's Feasting Day, in honour to Saturn, their Idol-God, the Papist's Massing Day, the Profane Man's Ranting Day, the Superstitious Man's Idol Day, the Multitudes' Idle Day, Satan's—that Adversary's—working Day, the True Christian Man's Fasting Day ... We are persuaded, no one thing more hindereth the Gospel work all the year long, than doth the observation of that Idol Day once in a year, having so many days of cursed observation with it (Dearmer 1928: xii).

Now Myers quite rightly attacks the trivialization and domestication of Christmas, and it is true there are Christmas hymns, which we call carols, which drip with sentimentality: "the little Lord Jesus, no crying he makes". Good old second-century Docetism never goes away. Many of the Christmas hymns we sing make the northern hemisphere winter the centre of the story: "In the bleak midwinter, frosty wind made moan". And so on. But the true carol, especially the medieval carol, is the expression of ordinary people—shepherds!—rejoicing, singing and dancing, over the divine solidarity with their own kind:

> He neither shall be born
> In housen nor in hall
> Nor in the place of Paradise
> But in an ox's stall
> He neither shall be christened
> In white wine nor in red,
> But with fair spring water
> As we were christenéd.

I suspect that this carol, like so many traditional songs and poems, and like the Gospel periscopes, originated in oral tradition and was only later written down. It does not come from people for whom "an ox's stall" was a sentimental picture on a Christmas card, but from people who had to put fresh straw or other bedding in day by day, and filled the manger (from "*manger*", to eat, so feeding trough) because the animals had to work, who had muck on their shoes. There is plenty of sorrow in these carols—the Coventry Carol, for instance—for their authors knew sorrow, oppression and death first hand. But they also knew fullness of life, despite everything, and they learned from the nativity stories that G-d was with them, and so they sang and danced for a moment, one day, when they were freed from labour, tramped around the wealthier farms at night to sing carols and collect alms and celebrated the G-d who speaks first to the poor. Carols belong on the street rather than the cathedral choir stall. Sung on the street, in cities, towns, villages, and around the farms, they are a paradigm of what "evangelism" might mean—a free communication of glad tidings which imposes on none but which witnesses to light in the darkness.

In his preface to the *Oxford Book*, Dearmer charts the near demise of the carol in the nineteenth century, but it was in 1880, in Truro, that the now almost universal "nine lessons and carols" started, ironically with the intent both of getting away from singing around people's houses, and with getting people out of the pubs. The nine lessons borrow the pattern of lessons from the Easter vigil, but focussing on the nativity stories and without the Eucharist. The format is popular but at present it can form part of the bourgeois captivity of the Church, a church which has lost its moorings in poverty and the call to discipleship and exists in amiable complicity with the principalities and powers. On these lines the carol becomes something polished, a matter of high art and not of the street. As such it loses touch with what it celebrates and its origins. Its lifeblood dries up and survives—as always—on the periphery, in pubs in West Yorkshire, and in so-called "folk" groups which tune in to earlier peasant idioms in both music and theology. This is not a matter of taste, but a question of where the gospel is indigenous, and where it can flourish, and as the carol cited above notes, this is not "in housen nor in hall".

Epiphany

The sixth of January

Liturgiologists tell us that the sixth of January is a more ancient feast than 25 December, and originally it celebrated the baptism of Christ. A textual variant of Luke 3:22 cited the whole verse of Psalm 2:7: "You are my son, this day I have begotten you" in the voice which spoke at the baptism. This would obviously suggest an adoptionist Christology, rejected as heretical after Nicaea, but again we have to ask, what does it mean for G-d to engage with G-d's creation? To understand the "birth" of Christ as dating from the baptism is, in another way to Matthew and Luke, to understand G-d's engagement through the Spirit. It is not self-evidently absurd and has to be understood as part of the Church's ongoing search for understanding.

As with 25 December, it may have replaced a pagan festival, the birth of the god Aion, in Egypt, also born of a virgin, celebrated on this day. As well as the account of Jesus' baptism the story of the wedding at Cana was also read at this time, and this might correlate with an Egyptian celebration of the waters of the Nile, or a feast of Dionysus, on 5 January, which also thought of water turning into wine. Pliny talks of a spring which produced wine on the Nones of January, more or less at this time. Earlier enthusiasm for understanding Christian festivals as replacements for pagan feasts, for example in Jungmann, has, however, now been replaced by scepticism, as the evidence for correlations is considered to be weak.

In the West, by the fourth century, the taking of the gospel to the Gentiles had come to be the main theme at Epiphany, though readings about the baptism of Jesus and the wedding at Cana were also included. Commemoration of the baptism of Christ was only moved to the Sunday after Epiphany in 1969.

The Gentiles

The Tenakh reading for Epiphany Sunday is Isaiah 60—the coming of the peoples to the light which Israel offers, bringing gifts—including gold and frankincense (v. 6).

The Gospel is the story of the coming of the Magi (astrologers), a story which is fabulously complex and replete with allusions to the Tenakh. One of Matthew's themes throughout his Gospel is the parallelism between Moses and Jesus, and the worry of Pharaoh about the infant Moses is in the background. Josephus has a story about an Egyptian astrologer, or astrologers, predicting the birth of a coming saviour of Israel, and Pharaoh summoning them to find out more. In the background is also the story of Balaam, who came from the east and saw the star (the messiah) rise out of Jacob (Numbers 23:7; 24:3-4,15-17).

Astonishingly, Persian astrologers actually came to Nero in AD 66 on account of prophecies in the stars, to worship him as king of the universe, and returned by another route. As we saw in Part 1 of this book, astrology played an extremely important role both in Egypt and Babylon. In virtue of their skill, astrologers may well have been important Crown counsellors in Persia. Israel was forbidden to use astrology, but astrological lore was widely accepted. The astrologers in Matthew's story want to "worship" the newborn king—prostrate themselves before him. Herod summons his theologians to see what they make of it, and they respond with a garbled, or edited, version of Micah 5:2 which promises a leader (*hegemon*) who will shepherd Israel, the traditional task of Israelite kings (Matthew 2:6—the last line is a quote from 2 Samuel 5:2). Herod, of course, is alarmed because he is King of the Jews himself (Matthew 2:1-2) and knows that his claim is contestable because he is of Edomite origin.

The Magi find Jesus and offer him royal gifts (that there are three is what leads to the idea of "three kings", alongside texts like Psalm 72:10,15 and Isaiah 49:7 and 60:3,6,10). Warned by a dream, they evade the security forces and escape back over the border to their own country.

For Matthew, the fulfilment of prophecy in the Tenakh is always important, but two themes are in the background. One is the authority of Jesus. He is Messiah, the rightful king of Israel, but a king unlike any other, as Matthew's Gospel, along with all the others, demonstrates. The nervousness of Herod ("he was troubled", 2:3) represents the nervousness of all representatives of the status quo at a fundamental challenge to the reigning order, and their determination to stamp it out by all means necessary (a determination co-opted and enthusiastically endorsed by the Church from at least the fourth century on).

With the whole early Church, Matthew is also concerned with the accession of the Gentiles, and this is what the later Church mainly took from the story. The Magi represent the recognition by pagan wisdom that in Jesus G-d is revealed or made manifest. Epiphany (*epiphaneia*) is the manifestation of Christ's glory. This is the theme of the Epistle for the day, from Ephesians 3. It is not certain that this letter is by Paul—it could be by a close follower. The author speaks of "the mystery of Christos" (v. 4). We know that Christos became used as a proper name quite early on, but it is a literal translation of Hebrew *mashiach*—anointed one, which is to say, the one through whom G-d accomplishes G-d's purposes. This mystery—the mystery of the fulfilment of G-d's purposes—had not previously been made known to all humankind but now "the Gentiles have become fellow heirs, members of the same body, and sharers in the promise in Messiah Jesus through the gospel" (v. 6). It was Krister Stendahl who argued that this was far more the centre of Paul's concern than the idea of justification, as Luther believed. We need to recover the astonishment of this promise.

Since the rise of settled societies, humans seem always to have needed boundaries, and to have thought in terms of in groups and out groups. Greeks thought of themselves over against "barbarians"—everybody else. In the same way, Jews defined themselves over against Gentiles. Paul, in Galatians and 1 Corinthians, and the author of this passage if not Paul, disallowed these distinctions. Jesus, the new Adam, had introduced a new era which recognizes one common humanity: all are included. He is not saying that all humans are de facto Christians, members of a new religion. He is not saying they are all included in *ekklesia*, the Church. He is announcing the First International—the end of boundary-marking between humans. When we come to Pentecost, we shall have to speak about how this applies to culture. But for now we have to notice the breathtaking radicalness of this proposal.

We could perhaps say that some such idea was "in the air". Rome had its own law, the *ius civile*, which applied only to Roman citizens. Conquered peoples lived under their own customary law—one of the issues at stake in the trial before Pilate according to John. This arrangement led to no end of problems, especially in trade relations, and what emerged as a compromise in the second century was the *ius gentium*, the law of nations, which was quickly identified with Stoic *ius naturale*, natural law. Later, in Justinian's Institutes (AD 533), followed by Aquinas, this was identified with the law of G-d. The difference from Paul's proposal is that Paul believes that all humanity now live in the light of, and by the norms of, Messiah Jesus. We can see what this means if we look at his radically revised account of the virtues (Galatians 5), and of the need to live by faith, hope and agape (1 Corinthians 13). Virgil, in his Fourth Eclogue, less than a century before Paul, believed that Augustus ushered in an era of world peace. Paul knew exactly what that peace entailed. He announced a quite different peace, ushered in by a Roman crucifixion. The announcement of that peace was the good news, *euangelion*, gospel, to those who had previously been known as the Gentiles.

The way in which early Christians understood this can be seen in the document we know as "the letter to Diognetus", dating, most probably, from the end of the first century. For Christians, says the author, "every native land is a foreign land *and every foreign land a native land*". There are no boundaries in the new order—just one common humanity. The idea of the "church universal" was a way of honouring this, albeit marking itself from other religions, but the rise of "national" churches in the fifteenth and sixteenth centuries made a complete mockery of it, even to the replacement of Christianity by polytheism, as Karl Barth pointed out in relation to the behaviour of different churches in World War I. By and large, what passes for Christianity is a form of polytheism in which various small communities, usually identified by race or nation, worship their own image and confuse their own image with the good news of Jesus of Nazareth, the second Adam, the progenitor of all humans irrespective of race or culture.

The Baptism of Jesus

Honouring the ancient theme of 6 January, the baptism of Jesus is the Gospel for the Sunday after Epiphany (John's account is on the Second Sunday).

The Church fixed on baptism when thinking of the birth of Christ because of the voice from heaven. Mark's account of Jesus' baptism is the briefest, and it is described from Jesus' point of view. He was baptized by John in the Jordan, and just as he was coming out of the water, he saw the heavens torn apart and the Spirit descending like a dove. The first phrase derives from Isaiah 64:1: "O that you would tear the heavens and come down", but the significance of the dove is unclear. The dove was regarded as a symbol of the Spirit brooding over the waters, and the voice of the Holy Spirit was also compared to the cooing of a dove. Then a voice came from heaven—the voice of Psalm 2:7, a royal psalm—"you are my son", but also an allusion to Isaiah 42:1, "I will put my spirit upon him". It is possible that, as with the citation of Psalm 22 on the cross, the remainder of the verse is implied:

> He will bring forth justice to the nations,
> He will not cry or lift up his voice in the street,
> A bruised reed he will not break (Isaiah 42:1–3).

Into this account, Matthew inserts the demurral of John the Baptist—"I have need to be baptized by you"—and Jesus' reply: "it is proper for us to fulfil all righteousness". Jesus fulfils G-d's will. As opposed to Mark, the experience here is not that of Jesus but the voice proclaims (so that all can hear): "This is my Son". Luke adds that Jesus was praying after his baptism and then the Spirit descended "in a bodily form" as a dove and proclaimed him G-d's son (Luke 3:22).

In John's account, it is John the Baptist who is the witness: "I saw the Spirit descending from heaven like a dove, and it remained on him" (John 1:32). John is told by G-d: "He on whom you see the Spirit descend and remain is the one who baptizes with the Holy Spirit" (John 1:33). In all four Gospels, the story is a divine epiphany in the light of which the rest of the story must be read. In this sense we can see why the story was the centre of Epiphany reflection. For upwards of three centuries, however, this story was more than that and appears to have been the principal account of Jesus' divine "begetting", which once again raises the question of how we understand the divine engagement.

Of course, there are many other dimensions of the baptism story. In Matthew and Luke, but especially in John, it makes the point that Jesus is the one to whom we have to look, not John the Baptist.

The imagery of the heavens opening and the dove descending can be understood as "his induction into the eschatological office of the Son of G-d" (Schweizer 1971: 39).

Myers reads Jesus' acceptance of the baptism of repentance as his renunciation of the old order, a break with the values and structures of society. His baptism is a declaration of resistance, a resistance to which Christ's disciples are also called (Myers 1988: 129).

The Wedding at Cana

At some point between Epiphany 2 and 4, the story of the wedding at Cana is always read, again following the practice of the early Church. The reason is once again clear: the story concludes "and he manifested his glory" (*kai ephanerose tēn doxan autou*). This glory, already mentioned in the Prologue (1:14), reappears later in the Gospel as the cross (12:23).

For its first 1500 years, the Church by and large read Scripture allegorically, so it had no problem with this story, though its meanings are multiple. The story begins, "On the third day"—foreshadowing the resurrection. It concerns a wedding, an image used frequently in the Synoptic Gospels. Jesus replies to the question about why his disciples do not fast with a counterquestion: "Can the wedding guests fast while the bridegroom is with them?" (Mark 2:19). This is another way of saying that the kingdom is "already now at hand" (Mark 1:15). Jesus, in Mark, goes on to talk about new wine and old wine skins, and this image is picked up in John's story. The old wine runs out, the new wine is better than the old, and there is a vast supply of it: 120 to 180 gallons, "filled to the brim" (cf. Luke 6:38: "Give and it will be given to you. A good measure, pressed down, shaken together, running over"). There is little doubt that the Church saw in this story (probably originally a parable) the superiority of its gospel to what was offered in the Tenakh, and that this was bound up with the offer of salvation to all people, or the inclusion of all people in the promises to Israel.

The Presentation of Christ in the Temple

The Epiphany cycle ends with "Candlemas", so called because candles, symbols of Christ as the light of the world, were blessed on this day for use the rest of the year. Formally the feast is known as "The Presentation of Christ in the Temple", earlier as "The Purification of the Blessed Virgin Mary". As such, it made sense to women who had to be "churched" after a birth and understood themselves as doing what Mary also did. According to Leviticus, a woman had to be purified thirty-three days after the birth of a boy (it was longer for a girl, cf. Leviticus 12). Luke tells us that Mary and Joseph undertook this, and, a mark that they were not well off, offered the minimum sacrifice of two pigeons. The current name of the feast, however, reflects more accurately the sense of the story, which is not about Mary but about Jesus.

Jesus is circumcised after eight days and given the name Jesus (unlike Matthew, Luke does not explain it). Then, at the time of his mother's purification, he is "presented to the Lord"—an echo of Hannah dedicating Samuel to G-d (1 Samuel 1:11,22–8). The Holy Spirit takes the initiative for the fifth time in Luke's narrative. Like John the Baptist's parents Simeon is righteous and devout, "looking for the consolation of Israel" (Isaiah 40:1ff.). The Spirit had told him he would not die before seeing the Messiah and guides him to the Temple. The child is presented to Simeon, who praises G-d in the song which has been used in Christian worship since the fifth century:

> Master, now you are dismissing your servant in peace,
> according to your word;
> for my eyes have seen your salvation,
> which you have prepared in the presence of all peoples,
> a light for revelation to the Gentiles
> and for glory to your people Israel (Luke 2:29–32).

The Epiphany theme occurs once more: the liberating work of G-d is "for all peoples". This is Israel's vocation, her glory (Isaiah 49:6).

As with the shepherds, Mary and Joseph are "amazed" at the words. Simeon then turns to Mary: "a sword will pierce your own soul too". The child is a sign that will be opposed—the common experience of the early Church. A woman's voice is also added, the widow Anna, "praising G-d and speaking about the child to all who were looking for the redemption of Israel" (Luke 2:38). She is, then, the second evangelist, after the shepherds: another nobody.

The themes of Epiphany—the calling or manifestation of Jesus, salvation to the Gentiles, the glory of Jesus known in the cross—are rightly celebrated but are compromised if they are conflated with the claims of the Church. The Church witnesses to Christ, to G-d's purposes not only for humankind but for all creation, but it does so through a mass of compromises, and even downright denials, which occlude the original story. Hence the need to foreground Scripture, the original telling, in this case the witness to an understanding of G-d who is known in crucifixion, scorned and put to death, then as now, by the ruling authorities.

Ordinary time

The weeks from the Presentation to the beginning of Lent, and then from Trinity Sunday (!) to the first Sunday of September, and then from 4 October to the First Sunday of Advent, are known as "ordinary time". The word derives from late Latin *ordinalis*, order in a series—so, first, second, third, etc., an ordinal number. Unfortunately the use of "ordinary" in English derives from *ordinarius*, orderly, usual, and has the meaning, "of the usual kind, not singular or exceptional" and even "commonplace, somewhat inferior" (OED). When we encounter the phrase "ordinary time", this is what springs to mind, but of course this is theologically impossible, for no time is ordinary in this sense—all time is graced, all time is gift, though it can be wickedly abused.

As it stands, "ordinary time" is all those Sundays not part of the Easter or Christmas cycles, and now also the Creation Season, and the lectionary on those Sundays goes through the bulk of the Gospels. What is happening here is exactly what happens in the creeds: the story of Jesus is reduced to "born of the Virgin Mary, suffered, died and was buried, on the third day he rose again, he will come again in glory". The ministry of Jesus, the teaching, healing and conflict stories, are all left out. It has long been realized that this is grossly inadequate.

We can listen to a Roman Catholic critic, Jon Sobrino. He objects that the creedal abbreviation is much too abstract. We do not find in the creeds, he says, the historical categories that are typically highlighted in the Messianic Writings: the conflict-ridden reality of Jesus, his temptations, his ignorance, and the internal acts and external process of development that he experienced. We lose sight of the fundamental data in the Synoptic Gospels, i.e. that the truth about Jesus is not to be found primarily by relating him to the eternal Logos, but rather by relating him to the Father (Sobrino 1978: 202, 331).

Moltmann agrees. This abbreviation means that we lose sight of the fact that socially Jesus is the brother of the poor, the comrade of the people, the friend of the forsaken, the sympathizer with the sick. He heals through solidarity and communicates his liberty and his healing power through his fellowship.

He accordingly wants to augment the creed, after "and was made human", somewhat as follows:

> Baptized by John the Baptist,
> Filled with the Holy Spirit:
> To preach the kingdom of G-d to the poor,
> To heal the sick,
> To receive those who have been cast out,
> To revive Israel for the salvation of the nations, and
> To have mercy on all people (Moltmann 1990: 150).

I have suggested that immediately prior to that a creed ought to read:

> For us and for our salvation
> he was born a Jew,
> shaped by the traditions and afflictions of his people
> (Gorringe 2020: 278).

If the creed was amended like this, the liturgical year should follow it. The Gospels are not adequately described as "passion stories with extended introductions", and the traditional structure of the year, with only two great cycles, around Easter and Christmas, missed out much of what was essential in the Gospels, and especially Christ's prophetic ministry. The use of the term "ordinary" in an obsolete sense only compounds the difficulty. I would propose that those weeks outside what are now three great blocks (including creation) might be known as "Ministry season". Whatever term is used needs to refer equally to Jesus' teaching, healing and conflicts. This material is indispensable to understand both passion and incarnation. The lectionary tacitly recognizes this but obscures it by the existing terminology. Here as elsewhere it urgently needs reform.

Lent

Just as Advent begins the first block of liturgical time which runs to the end of Epiphany, so Lent begins the second block, running to Pentecost or, as I shall argue, Trinity Sunday.

The origins of Lent

Until recently, it was assumed that Lent originated as a time of baptismal preparation for Easter, but liturgical scholars now doubt this. Summing up the debate of the past forty years, Bradshaw and Johnson suggest that Lent arose out of, first, a post-Epiphany fast, suggested by Jesus' own post baptismal fast in the desert; second, a three-week preparation for Easter baptism in Rome and North Africa; third, a three-week preparation for baptism in general, unrelated to Easter. The origins of Lent, then, have relatively little to do with Easter. However, after Nicaea, Easter became the preferred time for baptism in almost all churches, and thus the various fasts came together under one umbrella and Lent as we know it took shape. Only when infant baptism took the place of adult baptism, and public penance was replaced by individual confession, sometime after the fifth century, did Lent become solely the preparation for Holy Week and Easter.

The English word "Lent" (shared with Dutch) means "spring season", as in the well-known middle English poem "Lenten is come with love to toune":

> Lenten ys come with love to toune,
> With blosmen & with briddes roune,
> That al this blisse bryngeth;
> Dayes eyes in this dales,

Notes suete of nyhtegales;
Uch foul song singeth.

The poem is entirely secular and suggests that the origin of the name "Lent" from a word meaning "length"—so, the lengthening of days during spring—seems likely. By contrast, ecclesiastical Lent has always been associated with fasting and discipline.

Advent, we saw, is a time of hope and expectation; Christmas amazes us with the humility and solidarity of G-d; Epiphany celebrates the First International, the proclamation of the messianic order to all people, and therefore the announcement that all peoples are sisters and brothers. With Lent, however, we are with the first disciples after Caesarea Philippi. Jesus is ahead of us. We have acknowledged him as Messiah, without really knowing what that means. He talks to us about the way of discipleship, about the need to take up our cross. We are alarmed, doubtful, confused. Writing long before the reordering of Vatican II, Jungmann remarked that in the Lent lectionary we miss "the clear logical sequence, the strictly planned progress of thought" that might be expected and "the ideas are knit together only very loosely" (Jungmann 1959: 260). There is truth in that, but in fact what is happening is the preparation for the renewal of our baptismal vows on Easter Sunday. All the Lent readings are preparing us for that, asking us whether we really understand what we are doing, whether we are prepared for the cost of discipleship. If we live in the northern hemisphere, the natural world around us is crackling with new life as we journey, as the poem just cited records, whilst in the south it is closing down: in the one case a parable of Easter and in the other of Good Friday.

Ash Wednesday

In Scripture, sprinkling with ashes is a sign of shame, humiliation or mourning (2 Samuel 13:19; Job 2:8; 42:6). Jesus uses the phrase "sackcloth and ashes" to speak of archetypical repentance (Matthew 11:21=Luke 10:13).

Once Lent was adopted as a penitential preparation for Easter, it seems that, to begin with, public penance was required for mortal sin, which required wearing sackcloth and being sprinkled with ashes. The practice of public penance faded out by the eleventh century and ashes were then sprinkled on all believers at the beginning of Lent. Usually, at the imposition of ashes, we use the words (drawn from Genesis 3:19): "Remember, O mortal, you are dust and to dust you shall return", a *memento mori.* An alternative is Mark 1:15: "Repent and believe in the gospel". Given the seriousness of the global emergency, and given our common responsibility for it, this seems more appropriate. What might be meant by repentance is spelled out in Isaiah 58:

> Is not this the fast that I choose:
> to loose the bonds of injustice,
> to undo the thongs of the yoke,
> to let the oppressed go free,
> and to break every yoke?
> Is it not to share your bread with the hungry,
> and bring the homeless poor into your house;
> when you see the naked, to cover them,
> and not to hide yourself from your own kin (Isaiah 58:6–7)?

To do these things, we understand today, is to address the global emergency, to change our economic and therefore our political system. Lent study groups could helpfully reflect on this, taking as a guide someone like Naomi Klein. Isaiah 58 is a giant warning sign not to imagine that liturgy is what human beings are made for, and that by performing our liturgical obligations we do what G-d asks of us. The monastic tradition speaks of worship as the *opus Dei,* but it can only be described thus with severe qualifications. According to the prophetic tradition of Israel, first comes letting the oppressed free; when that is in train, then you can talk about worship with integrity. Today we have to recognize that social justice includes climate justice. "Sharing bread with the hungry" is not charity but seeing that our economic practices do not destroy the livelihoods of billions of people around the world, and also write off the future. In this context, prayer and worship assumes a new seriousness, as the struggle to deal with the climate emergency involves a struggle with the principalities and powers, a struggle which is beyond us, and where hope is in very short supply.

The first option for the Gospel on Ash Wednesday is Matthew 6:1–6,16–21, a warning against ostentatious religious practice, but then:

> Do not store up for yourselves treasures on earth, where moth and rust consume and where thieves break in and steal; but store up for yourselves treasures in heaven, where neither moth nor rust consumes and where thieves do not break in and steal. For where your treasure is, there your heart will be also (Matthew 6:19–21).

This is a pointed text for those of us who live in affluent parts of the world. Where exactly is our treasure? In what do we really trust? And what would a "fast" mean in relation to our banking, the assumptions we take for granted about "national defence", our assumptions about the things we cannot possibly live without. Since we are following Jesus "on the way" what changes does this require us to make?

Lent 1: The Temptation narrative

After his baptism, according to Mark, Jesus is "thrown out" or driven out (*ekballei*) by the Spirit into the wilderness:

> And he was in the desert forty days tempted (*peirazomenos*) by Satan, and he was with the wild beasts, and the angels ministered to him (Mark 1:12–13).

The forty days, of course, look back to the wilderness wanderings. The testing, or tempting, occurs three times later in the Gospels, each time by opponents (Mark 8:11; 10:2; 12:15). Whilst in Gethsemane Jesus, finding Peter asleep, warns him to watch and pray "that he may not be brought to the test (*peirasmon*, 14:38; the same word is used in the Lord's Prayer in Matthew 6:13). Jesus is with the "wild beasts", reminiscent of the terrible beasts of Daniel 7, which stand for merciless war against G-d and G-d's people. Myers quotes C. Cargounis:

> The concept of the wild beast does not stand for any one king, but rather for the sum total of power as exercised by several earthly rulers who are inspired and directed by the invisible *archōn*. The wild beast … consists of the complex made up of the invisible guardian, the human delegate and the entire state mechanism that makes possible the execution of the *archōn*'s projects, in short, the genius of a nation (Myers 1988: 130).

Matthew and Luke spell the temptations out at length. Luke changes the order of the second and third temptations so that he can end in Jerusalem. He comments that Satan left Jesus "for a while" (4:13), and Satan reappears, leading Judas to betray Jesus (22:3). As so often, the story is constructed around a dense set of references to the Tenakh.

The first test, after a forty-day fast, is to turn stones into bread, the bread and circuses through which the Roman plebs were pacified, turning the stone of the harsh facts of social and political life into the fast food of leisure and entertainment. Jesus cites Deuteronomy 8:3, "Humans shall not live by bread alone but by every word which proceeds from G-d's mouth"—the word of truth which tolerates no lie.

The second test looks back to the "testing" of G-d in the wilderness, in the escape from Egypt. The story is one of the major leitmotifs of the exodus narrative. The people of Israel are happy to escape slavery, but they don't want to pay a price for it. They don't want the long road to freedom. This is the same test: ask G-d to see that you come to no harm, no matter what you do. This is a question about the nature of G-d and G-d's ways. Can the kingdom be attained just like that, without suffering, without the cross, without the arduous traverse of history? Surely G-d would want that? Jesus is equally sure G-d does not want that and cites Deuteronomy 6:16, "You shall not put G-d to the test".

The last test in Matthew's telling is to worship Satan, who can gift him "all the kingdoms of the world, in all their greatness" (4:8). It is a devastating comment on the so-called greatness of empire, built on the back of violence and military force: it is the province of Satan. Jesus cites the Shema, in abbreviated form: "The Lord is our G-d, the Lord alone. You shall worship the Lord your G-d with all your heart and soul and strength . . . G-d shall you serve."

Dostoevsky later took this story (in *The Brothers Karamazov*) and turned it into a parable against the Church, a Church which infantilized people, which turned its back on the long road to freedom, and wanted to rule by mystery, magic and authority. From the fourth century on, the Church has repeatedly fallen for the third temptation, and indeed Mark represents James and John already falling for it (Mark 10:35–6).

Paul Lehmann speaks of "the darkness of the gospel", its obvious unfitness to deal with the reality of power or, as Bismarck complained, the impossibility of running a state according to the ethics of the Sermon on the Mount. "To the weakness of power, Jesus juxtaposes the power of weakness. To the exercise of power, he juxtaposes the refusal of power. To the pervasiveness of power, he juxtaposes the transfiguration of power" (Lehmann 1974: 25). This confrontation is the theme of Holy Week.

Lent 2: Abraham

All three years give us the call of Abraham for the second week of Lent— called to leave Ur and seek a promised land. We have to read this in terms not only of the partial fulfilment of the promise, but also of Jeremiah's advice to the exiles to build houses and dwell in them (Jeremiah 29:5), and also with an eye to the warning of Hebrews that we have not yet arrived (Hebrews 11:39). All the same, the need to be prepared to surrender our securities, to set off on a journey in faith trusting only in the promise (the theme of the Epistle, Romans 4) is fundamental to discipleship. In Year B, the Gospel puts us firmly on the road to Jerusalem already mentioned:

> He called the crowd with his disciples, and said to them, "If any want to become my followers, let them deny themselves and take up their cross and follow me. For those who want to save their life will lose it, and those who lose their life for my sake, and for the sake of the gospel, will save it. For what will it profit them to

gain the whole world and forfeit their life? Indeed, what can they
give in return for their life (Mark 8:34–7)?

"Denying ourselves" does not mean giving up sweets or alcohol or any
of the treats we take for granted. It refers to the temptation to deny Jesus
in situations of danger—precisely what Peter later does. To confess that
one is a follower of Jesus may require you to deny yourself, that is, to
risk your life:

> The threat to punish by death is the bottom line of the power of
> the state; fear of this threat keeps the dominant order intact. By
> resisting this fear and pursuing kingdom practice even at the cost
> of death, the disciple contributes to shattering the powers' reign
> of death in history. To concede the state's authority in death is to
> refuse its authority in life (Myers 1988: 247).

We will see examples of this in Part 3.

Lent 3: The Wilderness

Jungmann's complaint about the Lent lectionary might be justified here,
for the three readings from the Tenakh and from the Gospel all lead in
different directions, but these are nevertheless rich texts. Two of them
(Exodus 17:1–7; 1 Corinthians 10:1–13) speak of Israel putting G-d to
the test in the wilderness—a major theme in Torah—preferring being
well-fed, albeit in slavery, to the toil of liberation. If we are reasonably
comfortable, we all know this problem.

The Tenakh reading for Year C is the astonishing text from Isaiah 55:

> Ho, everyone who thirsts,
> Come to the waters;
> And you that have no money,
> Come, buy and eat!
> Come, buy wine and milk
> Without money and without price.

Why do you spend your money
For that which is not bread,
And your labour for that which does not satisfy?
Listen carefully to me, and eat
What is good,
And delight yourselves in rich food (Isaiah 55:1–2).

All the commentaries recognize that this text looks to the Wisdom tradition—Wisdom sitting at a street corner and inviting people to come and eat (Proverbs 9:5; Ecclesiasticus 24:19). But this does not explain the reference to cash. Scholars have recently pointed out that the advent of a cash economy is deeply bound up with the "axial age". It was one of the factors which stimulated the writing of Greek tragedy, and it lies behind this text, too. The advent of such an economy marked the end of an older economy of reciprocity, where it was basically "from each according to their ability to each according to their needs". Instead, as the prophets complain, those with money were now endlessly on the look out to exploit (Amos 8:4–6). Money isolated people and deepened class divisions. The prophet therefore takes a conventional Wisdom text, but adds the promise that in the world structured around Divine Wisdom no money is necessary. He is pointing backwards—or forwards—to a different kind of economy, an economy of grace, realized, according to Luke, after Pentecost (Acts 4:32). He is offering wisdom, but wisdom is not something that one simply acquires in a study, but something which shapes daily life according to the standards of justice.

The Gospel given for this Sunday is the story of the barren fig tree, in Luke (13:1–9). Originally, doubtless, this referred to the rejection of the Messiah by Israel, but when we fail to work for a world made otherwise we, too, become barren fig trees. Jesus ends the parable with a warning: "If it bears fruit next year, well and good; but if not, you can cut it down" (Luke 13:9).

Lent 4: Once upon a time

In England, at least, Lent 4 is rarely kept, being displaced by Mothering Sunday, a piece of folk religion maintained despite what is often, these days, the almost complete absence of children. If we look at the texts for Lent 4, however, we once again find a great variety of themes, but in the Epistle there is some consistency: "*Once* you behaved like this. *Now* that you are in Christ you behave differently." The Tenakh text for Year B is the plague of serpents in the wilderness, again reflecting on the stories of "revolt in the desert". The importance of this theme, both in Torah and Messianic Writings, is a commentary on the difficulties of discipleship. Well-fed slavery is so much easier, so much less trouble— do we really have to go through with it? In this story, the people are punished for their doubts and their refusal of the call to freedom by a plague of fiery serpents and only saved when Moses makes an image of one and commands people to look at it. The fiery serpents represent the doubts and disagreement of the people (ourselves) with G-d's liberating purpose: "there is no food and water, and we loathe this worthless food" (Numbers 21:5). Discipleship, we say, does not feed us. It is too costly. G-d's purposes are cancelled or annulled. This is addressed by the raising up of the serpent raising up and reaffirming the purposes of G-d. John understands this in terms of the cross (John 3:14—the Gospel for this Sunday). The Epistle is a reminder: "Once you were darkness, but now in the Lord you are light" (Ephesians 5:8). "You were dead through the trespasses and sins in which you once lived, following the course of this world, following the ruler of the power of the air" (Ephesians 2:1–2). Christian discipleship, the Messianic Writings say over and over again, is not a simple struggle to be virtuous, but part of a struggle with the principalities and powers, the forces which structure our world and determine it in dehumanizing ways. When we reconfirm our baptismal vows, we acknowledge where we stand in that struggle and we look to the standard which is raised up for us. It is that which heals us.

Lent 5: Can these dry bones live?

In the East, the Saturday before Palm Sunday used to be kept as "Lazarus Saturday". Today that theme is celebrated on the fifth Sunday of Lent. The Tenakh passages are Ezekiel 37, the valley of the dry bones, Jeremiah 31, the new covenant, and Isaiah 43:19: "Behold I am doing a new thing". As Church, we recognize ourselves only too clearly in the dry bones:

> The hand of the LORD came upon me, and he brought me out by the spirit of the LORD and set me down in the middle of a valley; it was full of bones. He led me all around them; there were very many lying in the valley, and they were very dry. He said to me, "Mortal, can these bones live?" I answered, "O Lord G-D, you know" (Ezekiel 37:1–3).

What would it mean to live? The Gospel is the story of Lazarus. When Jesus calls him out of the tomb he is covered with his grave clothes. Jesus says to those who are there: "Unbind him and let him go" (John 11:44). In order to live we have to be unbound from the grave clothes of our commitments to the things which destroy both us and the planet—the prioritization of money, the belief that only growth or technology will save us, belief in the gospel of superior force and redemptive violence. All these are our grave clothes. They have to be removed before the renewal of our baptismal vows becomes possible.

Ezekiel's vision offers a different metaphor. Here the body has not simply been in the tomb four days so that it stinks (John 11:39) but all that remains is bones scattered about. The process of dissolution, the triumph of death, is very far gone. Israel is scattered and without hope or memory, its identity lost, a valley full of bones. The Spirit of G-d, says the prophet, can even bring those fragments back to life, fill them with hope and give them a new heart. That promise, too, is addressed to the Church.

Palm Sunday

The earliest account we have of the keeping of what later came to be called "The Liturgy of Palms" comes from the pilgrim now known as Egeria, who travelled to Palestine sometime between 381 and 384, when Cyril of Jerusalem was still alive. Egeria gives a detailed account of the liturgy in Jerusalem, and especially of "the Great Week" (Holy Week), which began on the Saturday before Palm Sunday with a visit to Bethany to commemorate the meeting of Jesus with Mary the sister of Lazarus. On the Sunday, there is a service in the morning, she tells us, and then people are told to meet at 1 p.m. at the Mount of Olives. Hymns and antiphons are sung until 5 p.m., when the story of Jesus' entry into Jerusalem is read. She goes on:

> At this the bishop and all the people rise from their places, and start off on foot down from the summit of the Mount of Olives. All the people go before him with psalms and antiphons, all the time repeating, "Blessed is he that comes in the name of the Lord". The babies and the ones too young to walk are carried on their parents' shoulders. Everyone is carrying branches, either palm or olive, and they accompany the bishop in the very way the people did when once they went down with the Lord. They go on foot all down the Mount to the city . . . but they have to go pretty gently on account of the older women and men among them who might get tired (Wilkinson 1971: 133).

They made their way to the church built on the supposed tomb of Christ where they held the *Lucernare*, the lighting of lamps, before being dismissed.

In Rome no such celebration was kept, but the Sunday was kept as Passion Sunday, and traditionally the Passion according to Matthew was read (today the three liturgical years follow the Passion in each Synoptic Gospel). Palm Sunday is mentioned in Spain and Gaul around 600 but not until the end of the eleventh century in Rome. Today the lectionary mentions both the Liturgy of Palms and the Liturgy of the Passion, and by and large the Passion is read, and the story of the entry into Jerusalem is omitted, and only referred to through the distribution of palm crosses. This is a real loss. It is true each of the Passions should be read, and to read the three Synoptic accounts over three years is a good practice, but equally we ought to reflect on the special significance of the entry into Jerusalem, as they did in the fourth century in Jerusalem itself.

The usual heading in our Gospels for this incident, "the triumphal entry", is a wonderful piece of unconscious irony—for this is exactly what it is not. Myers calls it, with some justification, "political street theatre". The context of the story is the healing of Bartimaeus at Jericho, on the way to Jerusalem, who twice hails Jesus as "Son of David". Jesus and his followers approach Jerusalem, and at the Mount of Olives Jesus sends two disciples to bring a "colt" (*pōlon*—Matthew corrects to *onon*, ass, citing Zechariah 9:9). In Zechariah, we find a prophecy of a great battle in Jerusalem in which half the population will be exiled, but:

> Then the LORD will go forth and fight against those nations as
> when he fights on a day of battle. On that day his feet shall stand
> on the Mount of Olives, which lies before Jerusalem on the east;
> and the Mount of Olives shall be split in two from east to west by
> a very wide valley; so that one half of the Mount shall withdraw
> northward, and the other half southward (Zechariah 14:3–4).

So to biblically literate readers the Mount of Olives is a place from which deliverance might be expected. Myers points out that Simon Maccabeus entered Jerusalem "with praise and palm branches . . . and with hymns and songs" (1 Maccabees 13:51) and that in the revolt against Rome in AD 66 the Jewish leader Menahem "returned in the state of a king to Jerusalem", as Josephus reports in his account of the Jewish wars. So the entry of a military conqueror into Jerusalem might be what was expected. But the passage Matthew cites speaks of victory of an unexpected kind:

> Rejoice greatly, O daughter Zion!
> Shout aloud, O daughter Jerusalem!
> Lo, your king comes to you;
> triumphant and victorious is he,
> humble and riding on a donkey,

on a colt, the foal of a donkey.
He will cut off the chariot from Ephraim
and the war-horse from Jerusalem;
and the battle bow shall be cut off,
and he shall command peace to the nations;
his dominion shall be from sea to sea,
and from the River to the ends of the earth (Zechariah 9:9–10).

This sounds as if the triumph of the king would proceed by his elimination of weapons of destruction, and his humility is stressed. A contrast between military intervention and what Jesus is doing might, then, be what is intended.

As Jesus enters he is once again hailed as "the Son of David", and the crowds call out "Hosanna", "Save now" (Psalm 118:25), a cry applied to kings (2 Samuel 14:4; 2 Kings 6:26). We should not forget that the claim to salvation was appropriated by the Third Reich ("Heil Hitler"). The crowds look forward to the coming of David's kingdom.

In Matthew and Luke Jesus' entry is followed by the cleansing of the Temple, but in Mark Jesus simply retires to Bethany. The "triumphal entry" is nothing of the kind. In this story, the Synoptic Gospels make clear in their own way that "my kingdom is not according to the standards of this world" (John 18:36). This turning upside down of the pomp of military triumph prepares the way for Good Friday.

Holy Week

In the Great Week in fourth-century Jerusalem, there were services every day, attended, according to Egeria, by most of the people. Today, in celebrating Holy Week, the readings from the Tenakh take us through the Servant Songs of Isaiah, culminating on Good Friday with Isaiah 53, the song we know as "the suffering Servant". As in Lent, the Gospel takes us through John, and includes the betrayal by Judas. All these days are designated "holy", but for most Christians the observance of Holy Week centres on Maundy Thursday and Good Friday.

Monday of Holy Week

The reading from the Tenakh we have come across before: it is Isaiah 42:1–9, the Servant whose job it is to bring light to the nations:

> I have given you as a covenant to the people,
> a light to the nations,
> to open the eyes that are blind,
> to bring out the prisoners from the dungeon,
> from the prison those who sit in darkness (Isaiah 42:6–7).

Probably in its original context the prisoners may have referred to the exiles, and the servant to Israel, but now it is understood as referring to Christ. The prisoners were often thought of metaphorically, but we need to think of them literally as well. As we shall see in Part 3, this was a crucial concern of the Church during the imposition of the "national security state" in Latin America in the 1970s and 80s, a concern which was sometimes ducked.

The Epistle is Hebrews 9:11–15—Christ the High Priest, offering himself for sins once for all. Usually read as affirming a sacrificial understanding of Christ's death, it can also be read as meaning the end of all sacrifice. In Jesus the Messiah, we no longer have the blood of goats and bulls but the total offering of the person who offers, sacrificing himself totally to giving up his own blood, his own life. By sacrificing himself, this high priest made the perfect offering which needs no renewal but is performed once and for all (Hebrews 7:27). In the same way, as G-d's son, Jesus makes a total break with the established idea of priesthood; it is not inherited since he is descended from Judah not from Levi; and it is not traditional since he is a priest after the order of Melchizedek (Hebrews 7:1–28). What remains instead of sacrifice is *the concrete act of witness and confession of faith, as well as a service of love* (Hebrews 13:15)—an idea we find in Paul as well (Romans 12:1; Philippians 2:17).

The Gospel is the story of the anointing in Bethany, a story which John shares, at points, word for word with the Synoptics, echoing both the Markan and Matthean version and Luke's version (where the point is the forgiveness of sins). Here it is preparing Christ for burial.

Tuesday of Holy Week

The passage from the Tenakh is Isaiah 49:1–7, another Servant passage, the promise that G-d's salvation will reach to the ends of the earth. This is a reiteration of the theme of Epiphany, reminding us that the promise of "salvation"—the realization of G-d's order of peace and justice—is not for Christians, or for the religious, but for all people.

The Epistle is Paul's word to the Corinthian congregation about the wisdom and power of G-d, both known in the cross. It is often said that the only definition we have of G-d is that "G-d is love" (1 John 4:8), but here Paul is talking about what we learn about G-d through the story of Jesus. Blithely ignoring the passage, many of the greatest theologians of the Church reached for Greek accounts of what "must" be true of "that than which a greater cannot be conceived" (Anselm) and spoke of G-d in terms of omnipotence, omniscience and eternity, a projection based on our own human limitations. Paul made no such mistake. If you want to know what G-d's power and wisdom look like, he told the little group in Corinth, then it is the crucifixion you must look to.

The Gospel is John's echo of Gethsemane (John 12:20–36), a passage which both conveys the same insight as Paul's, but in narrative form, and takes up the promise mentioned in Isaiah:

> Now my soul is troubled. And what should I say—"Father, save me from this hour? No, it is for this reason that I have come to this hour. Father, glorify your name". Then a voice came from heaven, "I have glorified it, and I will glorify it again". The crowd standing there heard it and said that it was thunder. Others said, "An angel has spoken to him". Jesus answered, "This voice has come for your sake, not for mine. Now is the judgment of this world; now the ruler of this world will be driven out. And I, when I am lifted up from the earth, will draw all people to myself". He said this to indicate the kind of death he was to die (John 12:27–33).

As we have already seen, the crucifixion is the lifting up of the sign which saves people from the fiery serpents of denial and espousal of the standards of this world; it is the fulfilment of the prophecy of Isaiah; and, adding to Paul's comments on wisdom and power, it is the true account of what we mean by G-d's glory.

Wednesday of Holy Week

The text from the Tenakh is another Servant passage, this time Isaiah 50:

> The Lord G-D has given me
> the tongue of a teacher,
> that I may know how to sustain
> the weary with a word (Isaiah 50:4).

Jesus is Reb Joshua, the teacher of Israel, the Rabbi whom people flocked to hear, who spoke, and continues to speak, in parables. He is, as Hebrews puts it in the Epistle for today, the "pioneer and perfecter of our faith", who, for the joy set before him, endured the cross (Hebrews 12:2). "Joy" is a key word of the Messianic Writings, following from the resurrection, and frequently used by Jesus in the "Farewell Discourses" in John (John 15:11; 16:20–4; 17:13). Here the joy is that of fulfilling the Servant's mission, the offering of salvation to all.

The Gospel is John's account of the betrayal of Judas, leaving the meal, and going out into the "night" which John understands as a symbol of the rejection of G-d and G-d's purposes. The paradox is that the "handing over" of Jesus by Judas (*paradidōmi*, John 13:11) is what enables the handing on of the gospel (*paradidōmi*, 1 Corinthians 11:2; 15:3), the fulfilment, in another way, of the Servant's mission.

Maundy Thursday

On the Thursday of Holy Week, in fourth-century Jerusalem there were services in the morning, and then at 2 p.m. began a round of services which lasted until dawn on Friday. There was a Eucharist, but Egeria does not have anything special to say about it.

As things developed in the West, Thursday began with a Chrism Mass, at which oil for anointing was blessed, and then in the evening, the main service commemorated Jesus' Last Supper with his disciples, usually read as the "institution" of the Eucharist. The reading from the Tenakh is Exodus 12, the rubrics for the Passover, and the Epistle is Paul's account of the Last Supper, and Jesus' charge to "remember" (1 Corinthians 11:23–6).

I have argued elsewhere that to regard the accounts of the Last Supper as *alone* the institution of the Eucharist is mistaken: the Eucharist derives *also* from the fellowship meals of Jesus, the great feedings, and the resurrection meals. Jesus was recognized by the disciples at Emmaus when he broke bread—a characteristic action which he clearly invested with significance. Luke, in that story, makes immersion in the Scriptures and the recognition of the way in which Jesus embodies G-d's promises, on the one hand, and the breaking and sharing of bread on the other, the hallmark of Jesus' risen presence. Of course, as Paul and the Synoptic accounts make clear, the Last Supper left an indelible mark. In his study of the Eucharistic words, Joachim Jeremias argued that the words of interpretation—Jesus' form of the Passover *haggadah*—were a reference to his forthcoming sacrificial self-offering:

> Jesus made the broken bread a simile of the fate of his body, the blood of the grapes a simile of his outpoured blood. "I go to death as the true Passover sacrifice", is the meaning of Jesus' last parable (Jeremias 1966: 224).

In the light of Isaiah 53, Jesus understood his death as atoning for all people, and ushering in the final salvation which effects the new covenant. Jeremias understands the command to remember as a prayer "that G-d may remember me". It is a version of the Lord's Prayer: "May your kingdom come on earth ... " It has the meaning: "Keep joining yourselves together as the redeemed community by the table rite that in this way G-d may be daily implored to bring about the consummation in the *parousia*".

Because the Gospel is John's account of the Last Supper, the celebrant washes the feet of some at least of the congregation, as Jesus washed his disciples' feet according to John. This is important but becomes a mockery if it is a mere liturgical vestige and does not lead to daily "footwashing", i.e. care for, solidarity with, the poor, and the struggle for G-d's righteousness which both the prophets and Jesus insisted on.

At the end of the service, all hangings are stripped off, leaving the church completely bare—the "stripping of the altars"—preparing the way for the humiliation of the crucifixion. The congregation leaves in silence. It is a profound and moving service and the lectionary offers no alternative. That there might be an alternative is, I believe, suggested by the reading from the Tenakh, which is Exodus 12:1–14, the origin of the Passover, with another charge to "remember":

> This day shall be a day of remembrance for you. You shall celebrate it as a festival to the LORD; throughout your generations you shall observe it as a perpetual ordinance (Exodus 12:14).

As we know, John does not believe the Last Supper was a Passover meal: he says that Jesus' accusers did not enter the praetorium as they did not want to be defiled, because they wanted to eat the Passover (John 18:28). Jesus was crucified, therefore, on the day *before* Passover. According to the Synoptics, however, the Last Supper *was* a Passover meal (Mark 14:12,14,16 and par.). The Latin Church has assumed the Synoptics were right, and therefore uses unleavened bread at the Eucharist; the Greek Church assumes John was right and therefore uses leavened bread. Today it is generally agreed that the Last Supper was a Passover meal—it was held in Jerusalem, at night, they reclined at table, Jesus broke bread during the course of the meal, they drank wine, and above all Jesus offered an interpretation of his actions—based on the Passover *haggadah*. Because this is the case, many Christians have for some time kept Maundy Thursday as a Passover meal. Many of the earliest Christians did this, but they kept it as a fast and not as a feast. The advantage of keeping it as a Passover, however—read with the Last Supper in mind—is, first, that it puts Jesus back in his Jewish context, and puts the Eucharistic words back in the context of Passover—namely, G-d's liberating action in saving Israel from slavery, and looking forward, like Second and Third Isaiah, to its final accomplishment. Not least it reminds us that our Jewish neighbours are "the rock from which we are hewn" and that, however uncomfortably, we remain yoked together with them throughout history. There was a tendency, in the third and fourth centuries, for Christianity to become a mystery cult, a tendency which developed in a different way when all the attention focussed on the miraculous "change" of "the elements". Reminding ourselves that Jesus, Paul and all the rest were Jews, that the Tenakh was their Scripture, that, as Paul insists, the promises to Israel (not to be confused with the contemporary nation state) are irrevocable, anchors us back in history, in the story of the long road to freedom (and indeed some of the songs to be sung at a Christian Passover are "Negro spirituals", full of a longing to escape from bondage to freedom informed by the exodus story). Passover reminds us that, as the Jew Paul knew, sin is not simply an individual affair, but is first of all structures of oppression of which we are all a part and which (and as we have seen this is the meaning of all the stories of "revolt in the desert", Numbers 11:4ff. and often) is such a struggle to get free from. These structures of oppression can be Pharaoh—unjust and cruel rulers—there are plenty of them; but it can also be, as the Numbers story plainly says, the lure of the commodity, the longing for bread and circuses rather than the discipline of the long road.

Good Friday

Ave crux, unica spes! ("Hail, O cross, our only hope!"), a verse inserted into the famous Passion hymn, the *Vexilla regis*, in the tenth century. What does it mean? In what sense is the cross "our only hope"?

In her account of "the Great Week", Egeria records how prayer, worship and readings continued without a break from Maundy Thursday morning to Friday evening. An absolute fast was observed by everyone except pregnant women, infants and the sick (they were allowed bread and water!). At cockcrow on Friday, people moved from the supposed place of Ascension to Gethsemane, where they stayed until morning, reading the Gospel accounts, singing and praying. At about 7 a.m., they moved to the place of the cross and after a short break regathered for the veneration of the "true cross", which had (supposedly) been discovered in 320. From midday to 3 p.m., the Psalms, Epistles and Gospels relating to the cross were read. They then went to the church built over Jesus' tomb until the evening, when they were dismissed. These Christians, who in any case fasted two days of every week, had spent virtually two whole days in fasting and prayer, focussed on the Passion.

Egeria does not tell us what the substance of the reflections was, but coming forward more than a thousand years we have a famous sermon of Martin Luther from 1519, when he was still an Augustinian Friar. He distinguishes between true and false views of Christ's sufferings. To his credit (given his anti-Jewish treatises later), he begins by saying that the first false view is to blame Christ's sufferings on the Jews; also false are various ways in which these sufferings can be understood superstitiously. The true view of Christ's sufferings, however, is first of all to realize that our sins caused them, that on account of that we deserve eternal death, that Christ has borne our punishment for us, that we need to lay our sins on Christ, that the love of God shines from these sufferings and that we should keep them before us for our whole lives (Luther 2000: 183–92).

This sermon, reprinted many times in Luther's own lifetime and over and over again reprised in pietist hymns, gives one answer to the question why the cross might be taken to be "our only hope". It has to be admitted that there are many texts from the Messianic Writings which seem to justify this view. But do they do so *necessarily*? That is a different question, and many Christians today have their doubts.

After two thousand years of Christian piety, with the cross, often of silver or even gold, sometimes studded with jewels, at many points in every church, worn as jewellery, even as earrings, the horror of crucifixion has faded. It was death by torture and intended to shame. Victims were usually tied rather than nailed and died from thirst and asphyxiation. They were crucified naked and died covered in their own excrement. The Roman historian Tacitus noted grimly that in virtue of its use conquered peoples "feared our peace". After the Spartacus rebellion in 71 BC, 6,000 slaves were crucified along the 120 miles of the Via Appia and their bodies left to rot—as a warning to others. Josephus tells us that after the capture of Jerusalem in AD 70 the city was ringed with crosses—so many that the whole area was denuded of trees. It was a punishment reserved for slaves and rebels, and it was this death Jesus suffered. If the Gospels are to be believed Jesus' disciples had come to believe that he was "Messiah", G-d's anointed one, during his lifetime. At first convinced by the crucifixion that the whole thing had been a dreadful mistake (Luke 24:21), the resurrection led them to believe that, after all, it was true. All the same it was an immense paradox, a tremendous stumbling block. What we have in the Messianic Writings is the product of an intense combing of the Tenakh by the earliest community to prove to fellow Jews that yes, despite everything, this crucified rabbi was in fact G-d's Messiah. On examination, they found, every strand of their Scriptures pointed in this direction. This involved taking the absolute negative of crucifixion and putting a "plus" sign in its place. They appealed to texts of liberation—G-d's paradigm act of delivering Israel from Egypt; to sacrificial texts; to texts about reconciliation; to all the prophetic texts of G-d maintaining G-d's righteousness. All these texts were used to show that the worst possible death, a death by shame and torture, was in fact yet another example, indeed the paradigm example, of G-d acting to save G-d's people—and not just that, but all people.

Through the lectionary, the Church engages with this struggle to understand. Exploring the same texts, but also the texts which the first community itself produced, it seeks to come to grips with the possibility that this death might be redemptive. This goes on throughout the year, but Good Friday has it at its heart. How, then, should Good Friday be kept? We have seen two examples: by retracing the steps of Jesus and the disciples in the last days of his life, or by reflecting on the word, in Luther's case, by a sermon. Today there are two usual options. The first is to keep the "three hours" from midday to 3 p.m. This practice is not far from the practice of the early Church which kept the day with readings from Scripture and meditations. The present form of it originated with a Jesuit priest in early eighteenth-century Peru, from whence it spread to Rome and then to the rest of Europe. It gives scope for reflection on the variety of responses to the crucifixion in the Messianic Writings. It often draws on the Seven Last Words, culled from the four Gospels, and sometimes makes use of Haydn's setting of those words, or indeed the whole range of the poetry and music by which Christians have reflected on the crucifixion over two millennia.

An alternative is to keep the Good Friday liturgy, whose roots lie in the veneration of the cross Cyril of Jerusalem practised in the fourth century. People gather in a church stripped of all its usual appurtenances—candles, crosses, flowers etc. They hear a series of readings, beginning with the fourth Servant Song (Isaiah 52:13–53:12) where the servant is understood straightforwardly as Jesus.

The song tells us that

> Chastisement that led to our welfare lay upon him
> And by means of his stripes there was healing for us (Isaiah 53:5).

Five verses later the technical word *asham*, guilt offering, occurs. The servant "made his life an offering for sin". In verse 12, we are told that he poured out his soul (*nephesh*) to death.

From the beginning the community has felt that these verses touch the heart of redemption—but how? In the ancient world, suffering was thought to follow wrongdoing (classically in the friends of Job). Could suffering be borne for others, and did this mean that suffering had a positive value? Paul's assertion that "Christ died for our sins" (1 Corinthians 15:3), and the claim, by other writers, that he was the atoning sacrifice for our sins (Hebrews 13:12; 1 Peter 2:21) were read in this way. It appeals to two profound realities. The first is that the life of each is bound up with the life of all—the presupposition of any vicarious reading of human experience. We are not isolated individuals. All of us are bound up with myriads of others—a fact rather gruesomely illustrated by the Covid pandemic, but obvious to a moment's thought: how many thousands of people stand behind every single fact of our everyday lives, from the clothes we wear, the tables we eat at, the beds we sleep on, the food we eat—and on and on. In Walt Whitman's words, but in a very different sense to what he intended, we "contain multitudes". But vicariousness is the category we need for the conscious decision to live for others, rather than to give priority solely to our own agenda. Jesus is, as Bonhoeffer put it, "the man for others".

At the same time Jesus, if understood through Isaiah 53, dies as a victim. What is odd about the vicarious role of the victim is that it implies the creative use of something forced upon us, for the very idea of victimhood is passive. Whether or not Isaiah 53 was used by Jesus himself, or by the New Testament community to understand the significance of his story, there is no doubt that Jesus was an innocent victim, crucified for no crime. As with the Joseph story, victim status is not a purely negative category but has redemptive significance for the whole community. If Isaiah 53 is our lens, then the suffering of the victim is vicarious. The danger with this idea is that it can evoke a mysticism of suffering which understands pain in itself as something positive. This is an elephant trap into which Christianity has constantly fallen. At the same time, hanging on to Isaiah 53, it has tried to make sense of vicarious suffering. Iris Murdoch reflects on this in her novel *The Unicorn*. Two of the characters reflect on the position of Hannah, who has power because she has to exercise forgiveness. Recalling the Greek idea of *atë*—folly, delusion or blindness—she suggests that this is the name of "the almost automatic transfer of suffering from one being to another". This is a use of power, often rationalized in the picture of the all-powerful G-d, but this is, in fact, sacrilegious. She goes on, "But Good is non powerful. And it is in the Good that Ate is finally quenched, when it encounters a pure being who only suffers and does not attempt to pass the suffering on" (Murdoch 1977: 9). Perhaps it was something like this which Bonhoeffer had in mind when he wrote that "only the suffering G-d can help".

It is also true that in dying as a victim G-d in Jesus puts G-dself alongside the victims of history. We have already seen, in the nativity stories, how they reprise G-d's identification with the poor, the nobodies, the underside of history. The Servant Songs, and the community following them, underline this: not just the poor, but the victims of history. But to find G-d there is not to hand the palm to the executioners, but on the contrary to nullify their power.

Reflecting on Isaiah 53, Jürgen Moltmann suggests that G-d's patience and capacity for suffering is the root of G-d's creative activity in history. Through this, G-d creates chances for liberation from isolation and for the evolution of open life systems:

> It is not through supernatural interventions that G-d guides creation to its goal . . . it is through G-d's passion and the opening of possibilities out of G-d's suffering (Moltmann 1985: 211).

These ideas are taken up in the psalm which follows, Psalm 22, which Jesus quoted on the cross: "My G-d, my G-d why have you forsaken me?" Perhaps this was a cry of absolute despair. Perhaps Jesus himself believed that G-d would vindicate him, and in his agony had been failed. On the other hand, the psalm turns from lament to affirmation:

> For he did not despise or abhor
> the affliction of the afflicted;
> he did not hide his face from me,
> but heard when I cried to him (Psalm 22:24).

Whether or not Jesus intended this on the cross it opens the door to the perception that this may not be just another judicial murder, the powerful stamping on those who challenge them as they do every single day.

The Epistle is one of two possible passages from Hebrews, either 10:16–25 or 4:14–16 and 5:7–9. The first passage begins by citing Jeremiah 31, the new covenant, with the promise that G-d will remember our lawless deeds no more. The author then alludes to Leviticus 16: it is the blood of Jesus which allows us to enter the sanctuary, and he has opened a way through the curtain of the Temple, adding "that is to say, through his flesh" (10:20).

The second of the two passages emphasizes that "Jesus, the Son of G-d is able to deal gently with the ignorant and wayward" and then, with a reference to Gethsemane,

> In the days of his flesh . . . he offered up prayers and supplications, with loud cries and tears, to the one who was able to save him from death . . . he learned obedience through what he suffered; and having been made perfect . . . became a source of eternal salvation to all who obey him (Hebrews 5:7–9).

This is the letter which begins by affirming Jesus' absolute identity with G-d. The author, therefore, is talking about the fact that salvation is only available by G-d's absolute solidarity with the creature, sharing their sufferings and weakness, learning obedience, and only in that way, through sharing the sufferings of the creature to the deepest depths, able to save them from death.

The Passion according to John is then read, beginning with the arrest (18:11) through to Jesus' burial. All four Gospels record the fact that one of Jesus' disciples drew a sword and cut off the ear of one of the High Priest's servants, but they deal with the incident differently. John, who names Peter as the hothead, has: "Put your sword back into its sheath. Am I not to drink the cup that my Father has given me?" (18:11). Tertullian comments: "In disarming Peter Christ thus disarmed every soldier."

John's account of the trial differs from the Synoptics, allowing John to reflect on what it means to say Jesus is a "king". As in the Synoptics, Pilate puts this question to Jesus. In John, Jesus replies: "My kingdom is not according to the standards of this world (*ek tou kosmou toutou*) . . . If it were my followers would be fighting to keep me from being handed over to the Jews" (18:36). Jesus thus clearly affirms non-violence as his way, making any kind of crusade impossible.

John's account goes on:

> Pilate asked him, "So you are a king?" Jesus answered, "You say that I am a king. For this I was born, and for this I came into the world, to testify to the truth. Everyone who belongs to the truth listens to my voice". Pilate asked him, "What is truth?" (John 18:37–8).

What is at issue, Lehmann comments, is the ultimate point and purpose of power—the question which is also raised in the Temptation narratives in Matthew and Luke. Truth, in John's Gospel, is used in a political not a theoretical sense, that is, it is not a question of philosophical speculation but a question of how human beings orient their lives. Pilate stands for power which has abandoned truth. John's Jesus has said, "I am the truth"—that is, the revelation of love of G-d which works through forgiveness and not through violence. The trial exposes the weakness of power before the power of weakness. It manifests the light of the darkness of the gospel.

As the trial proceeds, John underlines the rejection of Jesus' claim to kingship: "We have no king but Caesar!" (19:15)—a cry the Church has bellowed from the fourth century onwards, and still does, in its honouring of militarism and even of nuclear weapons! Again John returns to the theme. Pilate insists on the titulus: "The king of the Jews" (v. 22), refusing to qualify it.

John alone of the Gospels has Jesus' mother at the cross. The word to his mother and to the beloved disciple is the fulfilment of the new relationship that his followers will have (15:12–17). Jesus then fulfils Scripture (Psalm 69:21) by drinking vinegar and then dies with the word, "It is fulfilled" (*tetelestai*)—all the discourses in which the Johannine Jesus has set out G-d's purposes through him are now complete.

In John, Nicodemus, the hesitant disciple, joins Joseph of Arimathea in burying Jesus. Traditionally this has been read as a gesture of incipient discipleship, but Myers suggests, however, that the concern is simply to make sure the Sabbath is not profaned and that "the authorities . . . have prevailed after all . . . Jesus is dead, the Powers have taken over the story, and the disciples are nowhere to be seen" (Myers 1988: 395).

Following the reading of the Passion the solemn intercessions follow, including prayers for Christian unity, for the Jews, for Muslims, for those who do not believe, and for those in all kinds of need.

A cross is then brought in and whilst it is held up the reproaches, deriving from Micah 6, are sung:

> O my people, what have I done to you?
> In what have I wearied you? Answer me!
> For I brought you up from the land of Egypt,
> and redeemed you from the house of slavery (Micah 6:3–4).

G-d's redemptive acts in the exile are rehearsed: "I fed you in the desert"; "I planted you my vineyard"; "I raised you as a nation". After each verse the people sing G-d's refrain:

> My people, what have I done to you?
> How have I offended you? Answer me!

Micah, of course, was speaking to Judah, but these reproaches are directed to the Church which, as in the case of its endorsement of militarism and its playing the stock market game, betrays its Lord. The cantor sings the final verse:

> Then listen to my pleading, do not turn away from me.
> My people, do not reject me, for I suffer bitterly!

The cross is then venerated and after that, in the Catholic tradition, hosts consecrated on Maundy Thursday are received.

The practice of venerating the cross began with the supposed finding of the cross on which Jesus was crucified by Helena, the mother of Constantine, at the beginning of the fourth century. Fragments of "the true cross" were sent all over Christendom, and Cyril of Jerusalem had to keep an iron grip on what remained to make sure it was not stolen. Even today, in a distinguished study of liturgical practice, it can be suggested that if at all possible the veneration of the cross should be practised where such a fragment is available. "Without it, the words and gestures of the ritual lose their immediacy and cease to convey their intended meaning"(!). This is an astounding piece of liturgical fetishism, quite apart from the fact that Roman practice would have left no such remains, nor would they have survived the destruction of Jerusalem by Hadrian, when the city was put under the plough. The point, of course, is to remind ourselves, and to venerate, not a relic, but the way in which G-d is revealed and salvation wrought.

The silence which follows is broken by the insistent prayer: *Veni creator spiritus* (often sung to the Taizé chant). That is it. Jesus is in the tomb and the stone of irrevocable death is rolled against the door—which means the end of the narrative. The rest is silence.

Easter

Since the fourth century, Easter has been the axis of the Christian year, and it is a surprise to find that this was not always the case. Jesus was crucified at Passover time, and some Christians continued to remember that. They called the commemoration Pascha, a name which survives in French *Pâques*—and kept it on 14 Nisan, along with their Jewish neighbours. The name actually derives from Pesach, Passover, but they erroneously derived it from the verb *paschō*, to suffer, and their Pascha centred on the death of Jesus. At Nicaea, it was decided that the Pascha should be kept on the Sunday after 14 Nisan, keeping Jewish Passover in view, but celebrating the resurrection "on the third day". There was now a focus on the resurrection, though in some circles the priority of the Passion remained for at least another century.

Bede derives the name Easter from Eostre, the name of a Saxon goddess who used to be commemorated at this time. Others derived the name from "east", as the rising of the sun was a figure for the resurrection. Contemporary scholars think it might derive from a corruption of *hebdomada in albis*—week in white vestments—where *in albis* was understood as the plural of *alba*, "dawn", translated in Old High German as *eostarum*.

Once Easter was celebrated on the Sunday there was a gradual move to separate the events of Holy Week and Easter, and the keeping of the Triduum emerged—Good Friday, Holy Saturday and Easter Day. Good Friday and Easter Day interpret each other. Good Friday without Easter is the record of just another martyr, just another dot on the historical record, one of the thousands of slaves crucified after the defeat of Spartacus, whose names we do not know (and Jesus refers to himself as a *doulos*, a slave). Easter without Good Friday, however, would be meaningless, a piece of mythology which we could consign to Frazer's *Golden Bough*. As it is, Holy Saturday is the first record we have of the

Madres de Plaza de Mayo, the women who demand from the authorities to know where their loved ones are, who sorrow as those without hope. For that reason, it is not true that Christianity has no room for tragedy. Whatever it was which happened at Easter, however, is what changes all this. For that reason, many books on the Christian year choose to begin with Easter. It is true it is this event which means that there is such a thing as Christianity at all. However, for reasons I have explained, I think the decision to make Advent the start of the Christian year is not a mistake. Easter, then, on my understanding, is the axis of the year or, to vary the metaphor, it is the sun around which the planets of this particular galaxy circle. The Messianic Writings as a whole "breathe resurrection"; every line is predicated on that event.

The date of Easter

As we have seen, Bede wrote his *De temporum ratione* to settle the question of the date of Easter. He would be astonished to know that the question is still under discussion. The difficulty first arose from harmonizing the lunar and solar calendars, as indicated in Part 1.

The issue was as follows: Easter should coincide with the Jewish Passover, but at Nicaea it was decided it should always be celebrated on a Sunday, whereas 14 Nisan can be any day of the week. In that case, what is the range of dates when it is permissible to celebrate Easter? Nisan is "the first month" (Exodus 12:2) and falls in spring, but when does spring begin? Does it begin from the Spring Equinox, as Alexandria believed? Or was it the day the sun entered the constellation of Aries, as Rome believed? Further, Rome dated the equinox on 25 March, Alexandria on 21. The difficulty was compounded by the fact that the Egyptian New Year began in September and the leap year day was inserted in August, whilst the Roman one began in January and the leap year day was inserted in February. Alexandria came up with the best proposal, based on a nineteen-year cycle, and a Scythian monk, living in Rome, Dionysius Exiguus, adapted it to the Roman calendar. Britain, and especially the obdurate community of Iona, was the last to adopt it, and Bede wrote his treatise to finally bring over these benighted northerners.

For him, Easter has to be celebrated when there is an equinox and a full moon, which lines up the resurrection with the creation of sun and moon. The date of Easter is not just historical but also symbolic, or as we would say, sacramental.

For some time, there has been discussion about committing to a fixed date for Easter. Many scholars argue that the most probable date for the crucifixion is 7 April, AD 30, and therefore the resurrection happened on 9 April. It has therefore been suggested that Easter should be celebrated either after the second Saturday in April (9–15) or on the second Sunday in April (8–14). The Second Vatican Council endorsed this proposal, and many Protestant denominations have also expressed approval, but so far the Orthodox have not. Critics have alleged it represents a capitulation to the need for regularity of an industrial or post-industrial society. Favouring the proposal, Adam comments: "To seek the best possible division of time is . . . an exercise of that right of domination which the Bible tells us G-d has given to the human race" (Adam 1979: 299). We could argue to the contrary that conforming to the needs of the market society is no proper exercise of our responsibility, and climate change more than ever requires us to pay attention to nature's cycles. More serious, in my view, is that it represents another step away from our Jewish roots. Though Easter and Passover frequently do not coincide the present system of dating means that we keep them in view, like two ships at sea sailing in the same direction.

The Easter Vigil

Liturgy is not life. It helps us to reflect on life. It interpolates our day-to-day story with G-d's story. As such it illuminates what is often the darkness of our everyday reality, as John suggests in his Prologue. Nowhere does it do so more clearly than in the Easter Vigil, the greatest and most important celebration of the Christian year—but a celebration increasingly forgotten. Until sixty years ago, and probably still in theory, "Easter communion" was the minimum mark of church membership. Mass car ownership and the priority of leisure in bourgeois life has now called this into question. Easter is now a time for the family to "get away".

The two most popular services of the Church's year are now Christmas midnight—appealing, as we have seen, to a largely sentimentalized and domesticated account of the nativity—and Remembrance Sunday, not kept, as was originally intended, as a way of recalling the horrors of war and a determination never to go that way again, but as a frankly idolatrous worship of the nation and the "glory" of its military past, with any criticism treated as blasphemy. Justin Martyr's sharp word to the pagans of his day, that Christians "do not worship the gods of the state", has been entirely forgotten. We only have to recall what John meant by "glory" to see that the Church should refuse to go along with these idolatrous practices: services committing to peace and recalling the wickedness and folly of war would be another matter.

This explains, to some extent, why the Easter Vigil has been forgotten. If I say we urgently need to recover it as part of an essential Christian discipline, this is not because I put liturgy in place of life but because, in its signifying role, it puts cross and resurrection back at the heart of our corporate life. Often Maundy Thursday, the commemoration of the Last Supper, is referred to as "the institution of the Eucharist". In my view, this is a mistake: every Eucharist is, rather, an echo of Easter Day, of the Triduum, the darkness of Good Friday but also the joy of Easter morning. Easter is when we remember and celebrate this in all its splendour.

The Vigil starts outside the church building: "outside the city gate" (Hebrews 13:12), where Jesus taught, healed, disputed, was crucified, buried and rose again, where G-d works and calls disciples to work. A fire is kindled there—traditionally struck from flint, fire struck from the bones of the earth, the elements of creation, recalling the fire from which we all come, which is also a symbol of the Spirit. The Paschal Candle, inscribed with the year, with the symbols alpha and omega (Revelation 1:8), and with five grains of incense to symbolize the five wounds of Christ, is lit and carried into the unlit church—still in the darkness of Easter Saturday, the darkness of the grave, of death and of mourning. The celebrant sings: "The light of Christ", which the whole congregation echoes. He or she carries it halfway up the church and repeats it, a semitone higher; one more time at the place where the Paschal Candle will be placed. Then candles are lit from this candle until every worshipper is holding a lighted candle and the building is full of light. Only at this stage, if the building has artificial light, are the lights turned on.

The Cantor then sings the *Exsultet*, the ancient hymn of praise for what G-d has done in the resurrection, asking that the Easter Candle may be a sign of that. It contains the famous words: "O happy fault which merited such, and so great a redemption", and ends with praying for the *Parousia*: "May he still find us here, your Son your only Son, our Lord Jesus Christ, living and reigning for ever."

After a hymn of acclamation, the congregation's candles are extinguished and the liturgy of the Word begins—the original "nine lessons", beginning with creation, the fall and then—essential for Easter night—Exodus 14, Israel's escape through the sea. On Friday, we have listened to Isaiah 53. Now we turn to Isaiah 54–5, "Glad tidings to Sion", and to Ezekiel—the promise of a new heart (Ezekiel 36:16–28). Romans 6:3–11 is then read—baptism as a parable of death and resurrection—and finally one of the Synoptic accounts of the resurrection. Each reading is preceded or succeeded by a song.

After the address, the congregation's candles are lit again, baptismal vows are renewed, and the congregation sprinkled with water into which the Paschal Candle has been immersed three times. The intercessions follow, the offertory, the Eucharistic Prayer, the offering of peace, and communion. In the course of the service, there may be as many as a dozen hymns, quite apart from the Gloria, the Sanctus and the Agnus Dei. Easter is not a time to be niggardly, to look at our watches and yawn. It is a time for Christians to respond to the astonishing story of the resurrection. That astonishment is buried in a bourgeois tomb and needs to be liberated. As a token of that we need to recover the medieval practice of the *risus paschalis*—the Easter laughter—marking the resurrection. In the Middle Ages, congregations were expected to laugh "long and loudly" on Easter Day, and clergy were supposed to help them do this by telling jokes, not always decorous. If we take the resurrection seriously, how could we not laugh? Laughter and seriousness are not opposed, but both express the other. Easter is the laughter of G-d over death, and those who believe need to share it.

As a coda, feasts are made to be shared, and Easter is the great and central feast of the Christian Church. The evening of Easter Day is the time to have a huge bonfire and for Christians to invite the community to come and share with them—to eat, sing and dance—not to knock people on the head with testimony but simply to share their joy. The word "comedy" probably derives from *komos*, the processional dance which ended the plays of Aristophanes and which marked the resolution of the difficulties of the plot. Christianity is not simply a *divina commedia* in Dante's sense, the triumph of life over death, good over evil, but also the affirmation of *joie de vivre*, which I take to be comprehended in John 10:10—fullness of life. Nietzsche said Christ's disciples would need to look more redeemed before he could take them seriously. Here is the chance!

The Easter Gospel

In the early Church, until the fourth century, Easter was termed "the great Fifty Days". It was forbidden to kneel or to fast for the whole of this period, and Easter celebrations only finished on Pentecost Sunday. With the recognition of the consubstantiability of the Holy Spirit, in 381, however, Pentecost became a feast on its own, and not long afterwards the Ascension was recognized as a separate feast on the fortieth day, following Luke's timing. Vatican II sought to restore the "fifty days" but without changing the feasts of Ascension or Pentecost, which it could not very well do. In the lectionary, we currently have, therefore, Easter Morning, and the following two Sundays are devoted to the resurrection stories. The following three Sundays turn back to John's Gospel, looking at John 10 on Easter 3, and the Last Supper Discourses of John 14–15 on Sundays in Weeks 5 and 6.

In what follows, I will look at what Paul has to say, and then briefly at each of the Gospel accounts.

Paul says that he handed on what he had himself received, that Jesus died for our sins, "and that he was buried, and that he was raised on the third day in accordance with the scriptures" (1 Corinthians 15:4). He appeared to Cephas, to the twelve, then to more than five hundred, most of whom were, Paul says, still alive, then to James, then to all the apostles. "Last of all, as to one untimely born, he appeared also to me"

(1 Corinthians 15:8). Taking their cue from Luke's account of Paul's conversion, this suggests to many commentators that the resurrection appearances must have been visions and can thus be categorized as a form of religious experience.

Mark's Gospel has a promise of resurrection appearances but no accounts of them. Mary Magdalen, Mary the mother of James, and Salome come to the tomb to embalm the body but find the stone which closed the tomb rolled away and a "young man" who has already appeared in Gethsemane (Mark 14:51), who tells them not to be alarmed: "He has been raised; he is not here. Look, there is the place they laid him. But go, tell his disciples and Peter that he is going ahead of you to Galilee; there you will see him, just as he told you" (Mark 16:7). "Galilee" is Galilee of the Gentiles, and so the story looks like a legitimation of the Gentile mission. The story picks up the earlier prediction in Mark 14:27–31, and especially 14:28.

Matthew heightens the drama with supernatural or legendary additions. He tells us that Mary Magdalen and "the other Mary" went to the tomb, there was a great earthquake and a terrifying angel rolled back the stone and sat on it. "For fear of him the guards shook and became like dead men." Where in Mark the angel reminds the women of what Jesus had said, here he tells the women the same message as in Mark, and they run off with fear and joy. "Suddenly Jesus met them and said, 'Greetings!' And they came to him, took hold of his feet, and worshipped him" (Matthew 28:9). Jesus then tells them to tell the disciples to go to Galilee. The eleven disciples go to Galilee to "the mountain"—the scene of Jesus' teaching and of the transfiguration. "When they saw him, they worshipped him; but some doubted" (Matthew 28:17).

Matthew also includes the clearly apologetic story that after the guards reported to the chief priests and the elders what had happened the priests bribed them to say that the disciples had stolen the body.

Luke tells us that Joseph of Arimathea laid the body of Jesus in an unused tomb. The "women who had come with Jesus from Galilee"—Mary Magdalen, Joanna, Mary the mother of James, and other women—came early in the morning after the Sabbath to the tomb and found it empty. Two men in dazzling white now appear and ask the women why they look for the living among the dead. "Remember what he told you whilst still in Galilee." The appearances are no longer to be in Galilee, as in Mark and Matthew, but this was the place where Jesus had told them what was to happen. They run and tell the disciples and meet with disbelief. Peter runs and verifies the story of the empty tomb.

Now follows the story of the walk to Emmaus, in which Jesus walks with two otherwise unknown disciples, is recognized by them when he gives thanks and breaks bread, and immediately "vanished from their sight". On the walk, the risen Jesus expounds the necessity of the Messiah's suffering and later exaltation. They run back to Jerusalem and find that Jesus has appeared to Simon Peter. Jesus then stands amongst them and greets them with the conventional "Shalom". They are terrified and think they see a "spirit" (*pneuma*). Jesus asks why they are terrified and why they doubt. "Look at my hands and my feet; see that it is I myself. Touch me and see; for a spirit does not have flesh and bones as you see that I have." He shows them his hands and feet, and he then eats a piece of broiled fish in their presence. They are then told to wait in Jerusalem for Pentecost.

John seems to share a source with Luke. Here Joseph of Arimathea and Nicodemus together embalm Jesus' body. The next day (which we call Sunday) Mary Magdalen goes to the tomb and finds it empty. She runs and tells Peter, and he and "the beloved disciple" run to the tomb and also find it empty. They return home. Mary remains and sees two angels who ask her why she is weeping. She then encounters Jesus, whom she does not recognize. Her suspicion that the tomb may have been robbed echoes Matthew's story but also looks back to the story of Lazarus. Mary knows Jesus when he calls her by name (a dramatization of John 10:3f. that the good shepherd calls his own sheep by name and they hear his voice). In complete contrast to the following story, she is not allowed to touch him because "I have not yet ascended to the Father" (John 20:17). The word ascend (*anabainen*) lays the emphasis on exaltation as the meaning of resurrection. Mary is told to "go to my brethren" with the news of the resurrection.

In the evening of the same day, Jesus appears in the middle of a locked room and gives the greeting of peace. We then have John's version of Pentecost: Jesus breathed on them and said, "receive the Holy Spirit". Thomas is absent and is incredulous. A week later, Jesus reappears through shut doors and invites Thomas to put his finger into his hands and side and says: "Do not doubt but believe" (John 20:27). The need to combat Docetism is evident here. Thomas responds, "My Lord and my G-d"—possibly a response to Domitian's demand to be addressed in the same terms.

In the final chapter, which may or may not be by John, Jesus appears to the disciples whilst they are fishing in the Sea of Galilee. The story of the miraculous catch of fish, which in Luke is a call story (Luke 5:1–11), here becomes a resurrection story, which includes a shared meal. "This was now the third time that Jesus appeared to the disciples after he was raised from the dead" (John 21:14). John, therefore, includes appearances both in Jerusalem and in Galilee.

The Gospel accounts, though differing in detail, share some aspects in common. All four accounts prioritize the witness of the women: they are the first witnesses to the resurrection—a fact all the more significant because in no existing culture did their evidence count for anything. Secondly, in Matthew, Luke and John the theme of doubt is prominent. We read about doubt (Matthew 28:17), scoffing (Luke 24:11), resignation (Luke 24:21), and fear and dismay (Luke 24:37). Luke records the incredulity Paul's talk of resurrection sparked in Athens (Acts 17:32), and the story of Thomas suggests that this was not limited to non-Christians. All four Gospels mention the empty tomb, but Paul does not (though he does not exclude it).

Christians are still divided about how to make sense of the resurrection stories. Schweizer speaks of the story of the guard on the tomb in Matthew as "a wrong-headed narrative". It is an attempt to prove the truth of the resurrection, which is a mistake because only faith can respond to it. The resurrection takes place in the hearts of the faithful (Schweizer 1976: 521,527). Others think primarily in terms of visions or religious experiences. The emphasis on the bodiliness of the resurrection, however, need not be understood as an attempt to prove anything but rather as a countercultural and counter-intuitive emphasis on the place of the body in G-d's redemptive purposes. The presupposition of many commentators is that the understanding of "natural" events, about what is or is not possible as "science" describes it, is absolute. If, however, G-d exists, called all things into being, is to be found at the heart of all reality, overriding our understanding of what is spiritual and what is material, then perhaps the way is open to understand the resurrection appearances as an eschatological sign, which is what the imagery of Matthew suggests. The Messianic Writings, and in particular Paul (in 1 Corinthians 15) and John (in the story of Lazarus), think of the resurrection of Jesus as the earnest of the promise in Isaiah 25, that death will be no more. More particularly the context of the resurrection is not any old death, but death by torture. Jon Sobrino, whose colleagues were murdered in El Salvador in 1989, speaks of the resurrection as generating a hope *against* death and injustice (the biblical model) rather than simply a hope *above and beyond* death and injustice (the Greek model). The hermeneutic is political rather than ontological, or ontological only as it is political. It is not abstract but grasped in discipleship (Sobrino 1978: 380). The Easter appearances are "phenomena of vocation".

Ascension

What we call "the Ascension" is recorded only in Luke. If we only had the Gospel, it would look as if this event was the conclusion of Easter Sunday. Jesus appears to the disciples, leads them out to Bethany and blesses them, withdraws, "and was carried up into heaven" (Luke 24:51). In Acts, however, Luke corrects this possibility: he writes that "After his suffering [Jesus] presented himself alive to them by many convincing proofs, appearing to them during forty days and speaking about the kingdom of God" (Acts 1:3). Then, from an unspecified place, "as they were watching, he was lifted up, and a cloud took him out of their sight" (1:9). Two men in white appear (not "in dazzling clothes", as in the resurrection narrative) and tell them not to stand gazing into heaven, but to expect the Second Coming. Jesus will come "in the same way as you saw him go" (1:11). Although John's Gospel clearly reflects on Pentecost, Luke is the only one who gives us the story, and Pentecost occurs forty days after the resurrection. The Ascension, then, punctuates the narrative between Easter and Pentecost: it gives a clear terminus to the appearances, and, in implying Jesus' glorification, prepares the way for the gift of the Spirit at Pentecost.

As a festival, Ascension was just part of the fifty days after Easter into the fourth century, not becoming universal until the fifth.

By way of comment, the reading from the Tenakh is Daniel 7:9–14. Daniel has just had a vision of beasts from the abyss, the last of which is small, has human eyes and is speaking arrogantly. The heavenly court is convened, the books are opened, and this beast is condemned to death, and dominion removed from the other beasts, "but their lives were prolonged for a season and a time" (7:12).

The immediate context of the passage is Antiochus Epiphanes and his idolatrous taking over of the Temple, but overall it is a judgement on the power of the world empires Israel had experienced: Babylon, the

Medes and the Persians (Egypt is missing!). G-d condemns their brutal and idolatrous exercise of power, though the writer acknowledges that it is still around—but without a legitimate claim to dominion.

Then

> I saw one like a human being [a "son of man"]
> coming with the clouds of heaven.
> And he came to the Ancient One
> and was presented before him.
> To him was given dominion
> and glory and kingship,
> that all peoples, nations, and languages
> should serve him.
> His dominion is an everlasting dominion
> that shall not pass away,
> and his kingship is one
> that shall never be destroyed (Daniel 7:13–14).

Luke uses the term "Son of Man" more than any other writer and it is very likely that he has this passage in mind. The passage set for the Epistle, Ephesians 1:15–23, implies the same. The author prays that his readers may know the greatness of G-d's power:

> G-d put this power to work in Christ when he raised him from the dead and seated him at his right hand in the heavenly places, far above all rule and authority and power and dominion, and above every name that is named, not only in this age but also in the age to come. And he has put all things under his feet and has made him the head over all things for the church, which is his body, the fullness of him who fills all in all (Ephesians 1:20–3).

This is the same power that Daniel speaks about, a power known in Jesus the Son of Man, the human one. To all intents and purposes at the crucifixion the beastly power of empire is reaffirmed. According to the Church's understanding, however, that is not the case. The claim, but not the reality, of dominion is given them "for a time and a season". Divine power, the power known in Jesus who, according to Luke, died praying for forgiveness for his executioners, is quite different and it is "far above all rule and authority and power and dominion". We hear the laughter of the heavenly court at all human pretension (Psalm 2:4).

In the Messianic Writings as a whole, but particularly in Ephesians, Colossians, Hebrews and the Prologue to John's Gospel, we have the astounding claim that the man Jesus of Nazareth, whose brother James was the senior figure in the Jerusalem church for a while, is "seated at G-d's right hand in the heavenly places". This is what is such a stumbling block to both Judaism and Islam, for it seems to be idolatry, identifying the creature with the Creator. As we have seen, thinking around the incarnation sought to address this problem. With the Ascension, the Church speaks, stumblingly and in poetic form, of the G-d who can become creature. At Christmas, the emphasis is on the *creature*; at Ascension it is on *G-d*. More specifically it is about the humanity of G-d. "G-d became human that human beings might become divine", said Athanasius. "G-d has raised humanity to G-d's throne", says Karl Barth. "G-d's most proper space is itself the space which this man occupies in the cradle and on the cross, and which he cannot therefore leave or lose again, for, as his resurrection and ascension reveal, it is now his permanent space" (Barth 1957: 486). Here we have the culmination of what we spoke of in Part 1 as "the meaning of history". Again we are in the realm of poetry and what "heaven" might possibly mean we do not know. Certainly not "to lie before Thy starry throne and gaze on Thee", but a sharing in G-d's time and in G-d's fullness of life. This is the promise of Ascension.

Pentecost

After Nicaea had affirmed that the Father and the Son were "one substance" in 325, it took another fifty-six years before the same was done for the Spirit, at the Council of Constantinople. Thereafter, and to the continued regret of some, Pentecost became a separate feast, and it acquired its own octave after the sixth century.

The witness of the Tenakh to the Spirit is extremely rich, and not entirely reflected in the Pentecost readings. The great story in Numbers 11 is set, in which the Spirit is given to help Moses with the burden of leadership, and which concludes, "Would that all the Lord's people were prophets". Exodus 33 is given, intimating that the gift of the Spirit is to inspire craftsmanship. Ezekiel 37 is given—the Spirit bringing the despairing and hopeless people of Israel back to life. Joel 2 is given, looking forward to the gift of the Spirit on all.

Other texts which need to be explored include the gift of the Spirit to the "Judges" of Israel (e.g. Judges 3:10; 8:23), enabling them—men and women—to lead struggles for freedom; the Spirit of YHWH coming to Micah enabling him to "declare to Jacob his transgression, and to Israel his sin" (Micah 3:8); the promise that the Spirit will bring a future rule of justice and peace (Isaiah 32:14–17, cf. 11:2ff.); the promise that the Spirit will enable servant Israel to bring forth justice to the nations (Isaiah 42:1); the promise that the Spirit sends the prophet "to bring good news to the oppressed, to bind up the broken-hearted, to proclaim liberty to the captives", and the realization of the Jubilee (Isaiah 61:1); the promise that the Spirit will enable a new exodus (Isaiah 63:11,14). Failure to consider some of these texts has led to a restriction of the Spirit's work to Church and sacraments, when in fact "Spirit" is a way of speaking of what G-d does to make and to keep human beings human, especially at the level of what we call political community.

Luke frames his account of Pentecost (Acts 2:1–21) in terms of Joel's prophecy when the dream of Numbers 11 is realized and when those ever denied a voice—even maidservants—"prophesy", which is to say, share in rule. This outpouring begins the realization of the new age, when the new humanity comes into being. The lectionary invites us to understand the story through Genesis 11. Myers brilliantly reads this as a story about the problem of imperial monoculture:

> Life in Babel is fundamentally characterized by centralization of purpose (the construction of a tower) and cultural conformity (they all spoke one language). The metropolis exerts an overwhelming gravitational force (both economic pull and military push) to bring human and natural resources into its orbit, expropriating and concentrating economic and social assets (Myers and Colwell 2012: 23).

On this reading the diffusion of peoples and the multiplicity of languages is part of the original divine purpose (cf. Genesis 1:28; 9:1). In that case, Pentecost reaffirms that purpose for all the different nations present hear the gospel *in their own language*. The point is that the recognition of one humanity is not at the expense of cultural difference. Cultural difference is affirmed. To use the slogan of the contemporary world we can have unity without uniformity. Myers speaks of "insurrectionary heterogeneity", pointing out that ecologists insist that biodiversity is essential to survival. In this respect humans, too, are part of nature. The McDonaldization of culture is a strategy of death.

The outpouring of the Spirit has concrete results in terms which are outlined in Torah. Deuteronomy had envisaged that in the Jubilee year those who were well off would open their hand to the poor brother so that there will be "no poor among you" (Deuteronomy 15:4). Luke echoes this as he tells us that the Jubilee sharing of the community of the Spirit meant that there was not a needy person among them (Acts 4:34–5). The story of Pentecost must not, then, be understood primarily as a story of religious ecstasy and of the empowering of Christian witness, though it may also be both those things. Rather, the fundamental continuity with the gospel is maintained: it is the Messianic Spirit which empowers the community and the new humanity which begins to emerge.

Whether Luke's story of Pentecost has a historical basis or not, it is obvious that Paul's constant talk of "Spirit" represents a new experience of G-d at work, and this is the reality of "Pentecost". It is the Spirit which enables people to see that the wisdom and power of G-d is known in the cross (1 Corinthians 2:4,10–16). Paul draws a direct connection between the nature of G-d revealed by the Spirit and the nature of the community the Spirit creates, which consists largely of the unlettered, the weak, the non-influential, the low and despised, through whom Paul sees G-d working to bring to nothing the things that are (1 Corinthians 1:26–8). Given the class conflict in the Corinthian community we appreciate the revolutionary significance of the remark that "by one Spirit we were all baptized into one body—Jews or Greeks, slaves or free—and all made to drink of the one Spirit" (1 Corinthians 12:13). By the same token, the promise that all G-d's people are prophets is realized, and it is essential to realize that the humblest gifts may be the most important (1 Corinthians 12:22).

In Romans, Paul is led to a description of behaviour in the new society, behaviour led by the Spirit. On the one hand, there are works of the flesh, and on the other fruits of Spirit. Paul speaks of "the Spirit of life" and argues that "If the Spirit of him who raised Jesus from the dead dwells in you, he who raised Christ from the dead will give life to your mortal bodies also through his Spirit that dwells in you" (Romans 8:11). Paul warns that the kingdom of G-d is not food and drink but righteousness and peace and joy in the Holy Spirit, where the connection of righteousness and peace made by the prophet and Psalmist must surely be in the background (Psalm 85:10; Isaiah 32:15–16; Malachi 2:6). The Spirit in this letter is a spirit of hope for G-d's future (Romans 15:13). Paul says Christians have the firstfruits (*haparchē*) of the Spirit (8:23). This means to be under the law of the Spirit of life, rather than under the law of sin in the flesh, where "flesh" means every attempt to live without G-d, especially the attempt in the name of grace to live without grace. The Spirit of G-d in Christ does not make us quiescent and satisfied with the way things are, but makes us groan inwardly, intercedes within us with sighs too deep for tears. The Spirit gives us courage for the toil of overcoming evil with good through revolutionary patience and solidarity with the lonely (12:12,16). In the spirit of hope, Paul can counsel submission to the authorities, confronting the weakness of power with the power of weakness. Beyond both of these is the debt to the neighbour by which the state is itself judged and which is fulfilled in the kingdom of G-d, the situation where G-d's will as expressed in Torah and in Jesus is concretely recognized.

Paul tells us that "where the Spirit of the Lord is there is freedom" (2 Corinthians 3:17). To the Galatians he writes, "For freedom Christ set us free" (Galatians 5:1). Paul's context is discussion about freedom from the law, but Paul is no antinomian. The fruit of the Spirit, he reminds the Galatians, is love, joy, peace, patience, kindness, generosity, faithfulness, gentleness and self-control (Galatians 5:22). At the same time, Paul's understanding of freedom needs to be put in a paschal context: Christ is our "Passover" (1 Corinthians 5:7), the rock from which Israel drank in the wilderness (1 Corinthians 10:4), leading us to the new social reality of a united, free humanity living under the law of love and forgiveness.

John tells us that the Spirit proceeds from the cross where G-d's glory and attractive power are manifested (John 7:39). Only through the cross will Jesus draw all people to himself (John 12:32). This happens through the witness of Jesus' disciples (John 14:12) which is made possible by the Paraclete, the Spirit of truth which is Jesus, the crucified Messiah. It is only when this truth indwells the community that it can do greater works than Christ. It is the work of the Paraclete in the strict sense to enable the community to understand and enter into the work of G-d in Christ (John 14:26). Naturally the peace which follows this gift is not as the world gives, the peace based on terror, the peace of compromise with the status quo, of turning a blind eye to evil, the flight into religious realities away from the raw facts of political torture and execution. Like everything else this peace comes only through the cross, and it is this the Spirit witnesses to (John 15:26).

The Paraclete, says John, will convince, convict or expose the world in respect of sin, righteousness and judgement (John 16:8). In Ephesians, the author uses the same verb (*elenchein*) to speak of the exposure of the works of darkness (Ephesians 5:11,13) and in Colossians it is the public exposure of the powers which is the means of Christ's triumph

(Colossians 2:15). The Spirit of the crucified judges the ruler of this world by exposing the weakness of power; the Spirit convicts people of sin, because they insist on relying only on these power structures and refuse to trust in the power of weakness, which is at the same time the righteousness of G-d, the way in which G-d keeps faith with G-d's creation by bringing salvation. It is deeper into the mystery of the divine powerlessness, of the truth available there, that the Spirit guides the disciples (John 16:13), and it is this Spirit which both abides in Jesus and which Jesus bestows on the disciples (John 20:22).

The work of the Spirit

The work of the Spirit, as understood by Christian doctrine, has only too often been narrowed and domesticated. To be sure the Spirit's role in creation has been recognized, both in the creation at the beginning and in artistic or literary creation. Too often, though, the Spirit's work has been limited to sanctification—a process which began with Origen, at the beginning of the third century—and otherwise it is thought of in terms of church and sacraments. Pentecost, we are told, is "the birth of the Church". These trends are intensified by the opposition of "spiritual" and "material", the use of the word "spiritual" to describe especially pious or holy people, and thus the idea that the Spirit has nothing to do with realities like political freedom, or the rebirth of a nation, which is precisely where the Tenakh sees it.

This way of understanding the Spirit's work was encouraged by the tendency of enthusiast movements to identify their millenarian hopes with the Spirit—Joachim of Fiore spoke of the inauguration of "a third age of the Spirit". The disaster this led to at Münster, with Thomas Müntzer, and the adoption of the third-age terminology by the Third Reich, brought all this into disrepute. The result, however, is that the baby is thrown out with the bathwater. The horizon of Scripture, we have to insist, is not a religious movement edified by an ever so beautiful liturgy but a new humanity, the world made otherwise, action springing from the daily prayer, "Your kingdom come on earth".

According to the Scriptural witness, Spirit language is a way of saying that "G-d" makes history *through men and women*. G-d makes history but not history in general with all its slavery and oppression but a history directed to peace, justice and freedom. To speak of the Spirit is to speak of the openness of history, to deny that it is controlled by iron laws, and to assert that its future may be infinitely better than the present—precisely because the G-d who loves in freedom is the beginning and end of all things. The NAME, we may say, especially in its third iteration, grounds an order of peace, beauty, excitement and freedom and calls all creation and history to follow. Within history, G-d is the creator of hope, the source of all generous visions, of all human openness. G-d inspires dreams of justice, peace, love, fellowship, dreams of a society where the rule of G-d will be realized. Spirit language speaks of G-d revealing G-dself as merciful, gracious, long-suffering and loving and this revelation, grasped little by little and set down in this and that, inspires hope for human behaviour which is likewise compassionate and loving.

Spirit language, therefore, speaks of G-d's presence to and within historical process, but presence only discerned through action like that of the Judges, social critique and warning like that of the prophets, and through a life lived for outcasts like that of Jesus. G-d accomplishes G-d's purpose only through his presence to women and men. Beyond any question the early Christian community, in the wake of cross and resurrection, had an extremely vivid experience of the power of G-d at work amongst themselves which, following their reading of Joel and Isaiah, they spoke of as "Spirit".

Trinity Sunday

The second main block of time of the Church's liturgical calendar ends on the Saturday before Trinity Sunday. With Trinity Sunday, "ordinary time" begins. This seems to me a huge mistake, quite apart from the objections I have already sketched to the idea of ordinary time.

As we have seen, many liturgical developments only clarified in the fourth century, partly as a result of the new political settlement, and partly as a result of great church councils such as Nicaea and Constantinople. These established that when we speak of Messiah Jesus or the Spirit, we speak of G-d. How that was possible had already been the subject of much discussion from the second century onwards. Did it mean Christians were not monotheists? No it didn't, Christians asserted. What then? Tertullian already spoke of "three persons in one substance". In the discussions which led up to the Council of Constantinople in 381, the three Cappadocian Fathers, Basil of Caesarea, Gregory of Nyssa and Gregory of Nazianzus, all explored how it might be possible to speak of G-d as both one and yet known in three manifestations. At the very end of the century, Augustine, in North Africa, began his mammoth rumination on the Trinity. Astonishingly Trinity Sunday is described as an "ideas feast", a "solemnity", alongside the feasts of Corpus Christi and the Sacred Heart. But these feasts should not be mentioned in the same breath. As Karl Rahner, a theological expert (*peritus*) at Vatican II, insisted in his 1967 essay, the doctrine of the Trinity is a mystery of *salvation*. When G-d engages with us, it is as triune that G-d does so. The doctrine of the Trinity says, at a minimum, what we have to say if what is affirmed at Christmas and Easter is true. The texts for Trinity Sunday cite the various triune formulae to be found in the Messianic Writings, but the real foundation for this doctrine is a series of *events*: the revelation to Moses and the command to lead Israel to freedom (Exodus 3:1–15); the cross and resurrection of Jesus; the outpouring of the Spirit on the infant Church. It is grounded, that is to say, in G-d's revelation in history. Every historical event is interpreted. Passover, Easter and Pentecost all represent interpretations of historical phenomena. They can all be read in a purely sociological, or even a mythological, way. Their interpretation can be described in terms of "ideas", but instead we properly describe them as grounded in narrative. Exactly the same is true of the Trinity, only here three sets of stories are involved. What a miserably inadequate theology it is to describe it as an "ideas feast"! "Trinity", for Christians, is the divine NAME, as YHWH was and is for Jews. The feast is the capstone of those two great periods of the liturgical year which commemorate G-d's self-revelation, and not some transition to supposedly ordinary time.

As Rahner observes, for much of Christian history, the Trinity has been a dead letter and Christianity has been effectively Unitarian. There are many reasons for this, but one is that the doctrine was not fitted to provide the ideological support for monarchical societies. That is why many of the medieval representations of the Trinity feature a king, with a child (the king's son) on his lap, and a pigeon floating about. All the more remarkable, then, that Rublev (c.1360–1427) turned to Genesis 18 and depicted the Trinity as three pilgrims around the Eucharistic table, with the tree from which the cross was fashioned in the background. All doctrines of G-d function to underwrite a particular social order, and this doctrine speaks of three persons where "none is before, or after another; none is greater, or less than another, but one perfect equality". The nineteenth-century Christian socialists added, "in whose image we are made". What corresponds to the Triune G-d, therefore, is "the community of men and women without privileges and without subjugation . . . a community in which people are defined through their relations with one another and in their significance for one another, not in opposition to one another, in terms of power and possession" (Moltmann 1981: 198). This is a version of the Messianic community envisaged by Paul.

Every theologian who has written on the Trinity has confessed the difficulty of knowing what language to use, but this is because G-d is an absolute mystery, not because the doctrine is a mystification. Tertullian, at the beginning of the third century, talked of "three persons". A "person" is for us an independent centre of consciousness, so this would imply tritheism, but on the other hand whatever G-d is, G-d lives and loves, and so "person" seems less inadequate than most other words.

The Cappadocians, followed by John of Damascus, spoke of the divine *perichoresis*, mutual interpenetration. Reflecting on the Latin translation of this (*circuminsessio*), Richard of St Victor, in the twelfth century, suggested that it was necessary to think of G-d as triune because otherwise we would not be able to say, as we have to, that G-d was love. This should not be taken to imply that the doctrine is derived from the logical implications of saying "G-d is love", for the doctrine is a reflection on revelation, but it is true that it illuminates revelation. *Caritas* (the Latin term for the *agape* of the Messianic Writings), he says, cannot exist where love is not directed to another. "In order for *caritas* to be the supreme good, it is impossible that there can be lacking either someone who communicates *caritas* or someone to whom *caritas* is communicated" (Richard 2011: 249). The pleasures of *caritas* are the greatest possible and without fellowship G-d would lack these pleasures. This axiom might yield binity, but, Richard argues, in fact the logic of love requires a third, because for love to be perfect, the two must share their love. The Spirit is, as it were, the breaking open of the divine love for otherness, a realization that that love cannot be an egoism *à deux*. What the doctrine says, therefore, is that relations of love are the ultimate foundation of reality. The unity of the Three is of will, love and purpose, which is not "consensus" but constitutive of the divine identity.

The Trinity and the Cross

There is a persistent suspicion that the doctrine of the Trinity represents a departure from Scripture but "Whoever talks about the Trinity talks about the cross of Jesus, and does not speculate in heavenly riddles" (Moltmann 1974: 207). If Moltmann had written nothing but that one sentence he would still be a great theologian. In Hosea (11:8), we have a picture of G-d's heart agonized over Israel. This could suggest that G-d suffers. Origen, at the beginning of the third century, already talks of the suffering of G-d in terms which suggest the Trinity in his homily on Ezekiel: "G-d suffers our ways as the Son of God bears our sufferings.

Even the Father is not incapable of suffering." Such a view could appeal to the fact that Jesus died believing he was G-d-forsaken (Mark 15:34), and also to John's interpretation of the cross in terms of the intensity of G-d's love. Simone Weil reflects on this in ways which take up Richard's account of the Trinity of love. G-d is love, and before all things G-d loves G-dself, and this love is the Trinity. In this divine love there is infinite nearness or identity, but, resulting from creation, incarnation and Passion, there is also infinite distance. Lovers, she says, desire both to love each other so much that they enter into each other and only make one being, but also to love each other so much that, having half the globe between them, their union will not be diminished in the slightest degree. "The unity of G-d, wherein all plurality disappears, and the abandonment, wherein Christ believes he is left whilst never ceasing to love his Father perfectly, these are two forms expressing the divine virtue of the same Love, the Love which is G-d himself" (Weil 1951: 70).

John tells us that the Spirit is only given after the crucifixion (John 7:39). It is possible therefore to say that the Spirit is "the unconditioned and therefore boundless love which proceeds from the grief of the Father and the dying of the Son and reaches forsaken human beings in order to create in them the possibility and the force of new life" (Moltmann 1974: 245). Paul already pointed out that this Spirit embraces the life of oppressed nature as well (Romans 8:18–25). Though "the doctrine of the Trinity" was not even a twinkle in Paul's eye his thought is profoundly Trinitarian, recognizing, like John, the reality of G-d's salvific presence in Son and Spirit. As Moltmann likes to say, in the sending of the Son and the Spirit, and in G-d's eternal *perichoresis*, or mutual love, G-d is open for human beings, the world and time. To use the terms which the fourth-century theologians struggled to articulate, the *unity* of the Three constitutes an eschatological hope for all reality, when "G-d will be all in all" (1 Corinthians 15:28).

In the eighth century, an unknown Celt—probably a monk—wrote a poem or hymn, the lorica or breastplate of St Patrick. It begins:

> I bind unto myself today
> The strong NAME of the Trinity

The song recognizes that the Trinity is the name of G-d, which we cannot go behind. Precisely because it is Trinitarian the poem is also Christocentric—the second verse traces all the main events of Christ's life (as in Paul—without the teaching) whilst the eighth verse puts Christ at the heart of all Christian experience:

> Christ before me, Christ behind me
> Christ in quiet, Christ in danger . . .
> Christ in mouth of friend and stranger.

In this lyrical verse the revelation of G-d in Christ is seen as the *fons et origo* of our understanding of G-d as Trinity.

The Transfiguration

The feast of the Transfiguration falls on 6 August, peak holiday time in Europe, when families are away, and therefore it gets little attention, but, with consummate irony, it is also the date when the atomic bomb was dropped on Hiroshima, "with a blinding flash", as survivors recalled, "with a whiteness no bleacher on earth could equal" (Mark 9:3), killing 70,000 people instantly, and another 70,000 in the days thereafter. In the nineteenth century, war had been cynically described as "diplomacy by other means", but this moment transfigured our understanding of war, though in 2019 Westminster Abbey held a service of thanksgiving for fifty years of nuclear "peace keeping".

In Mark's account the lead up to the transfiguration begins with the second great feeding, after which Pharisees come and ask Jesus for "a sign from heaven". Jesus "sighed deeply in his spirit and said: 'Why does this generation ask for a sign? Truly (Amen) I tell you, no sign will be given to this generation'" (Mark 8:12). There follow stories concentrating on hearing (8:14–21) and seeing (22–6) correctly. Jesus asks the disciples: "Do you not yet understand?" At this point, we have the confession of Jesus as Messiah followed by the warning of what will happen to the Son of Man ("the Human One") and the need for Jesus' disciples to deny themselves and take up their cross. Myers reads the story in the light of Daniel 7 which we have already considered above. Two courts are projected—the one which condemns Jesus (Mark 8:31) and the one where those who are ashamed of Jesus are condemned (8:38). We are asked: Which side are you on? This applies equally to us as to the first disciples. "Myth collapses time (past, present, future) and space ('heaven' and 'earth') into the one 'moment of truth'" (Myers 1988: 249).

Jesus concludes his words with another "amen": "Truly I tell you, there are some here who will not taste death until they see that the kingdom of G-d has come with power" (Mark 9:1). We have already seen that John understands the crucifixion as the manifestation of Christ's glory and so Mark (and the other Synoptics) here.

After six days (Mark and Matthew) or eight days (Luke) Jesus takes Peter, James and John up a mountain to pray. Jesus is transfigured before them, appearing in dazzling white clothes which will later mark the angels at the tomb and with which Revelation clothes the martyrs (Revelation 3:5,18; 4:4; 6:11; 7:9,13). He appears with Elijah and Moses (that way round)—prophets and Torah. Jesus' option for the cross sums up the whole of the Tenakh. Luke tells us the substance of the conversation: "they spoke of his departure (exodus) which he was to fulfil in Jerusalem" (Luke 9:31). Luke wants to make sure there is no doubt about what is intended. But Peter and his fellow disciples still do not understand: Peter does not know what to say: "let us make three huts [the booths of the wine harvest, Sukkoth]—one for you, one for Moses and one for Elijah". Myers (1988: 250) suggests that Peter proposes a cult of adulation—the transformation of the way of the cross into liturgy and cult, so that what matters is "celebrating the holy mysteries". But as at the baptism a voice from heaven affirms Jesus and tells his disciples to "listen to him"—to the teaching about the way of discipleship which he has just been giving.

Just as, at Caesarea Philippi, Jesus had commanded the disciples to tell no one, so now he tells them not to speak of this vision until after the resurrection—in Mark Jesus' going ahead of the disciples to Galilee, Galilee of the Gentiles. They do not understand what is meant by resurrection and ask whether Elijah has to come first. Jesus confirms that Elijah has already come—in the person of John the Baptist—"and they did to him whatever they pleased, as it is written about him" (9:13). The same will happen to the human one.

Lehmann comments of the Transfiguration story that "the politics of G-d has transfigured the politics of man" (Lehmann 1974: 83). Once again, the darkness of the gospel is affirmed over against the darkness of violence, whether of the Establishment or of revolution.

Creation Season

We saw in Part 1 that there were three major agricultural festivals in ancient Israel: Passover, which was joined with ingathering, celebrating the barley harvest; the Feast of Weeks, celebrating the wheat harvest; and the Feast of Tabernacles, celebrating the olive and grape harvest. Rome had a number of agricultural festivals through the year: a sowing festival in January; the offering of a pregnant cow to "Earth", a wine festival, and Robigalia, a propitiatory festival to ward off rust on the grain crops, in April; Ambarvalia, to purify the fields, in May; and a festival to Ceres, the goddess of Harvest, on 4 October. These festivals are typical of the way what we call "ancient societies" marked the production of food. There is a propitiatory element but above all is the sense of thankfulness for the gift of life, and what makes life possible. Christianity, though it spread through the urban centres, inherited this practice, drawing both on the Tenakh and on the practices of local cultures, Roman and otherwise. Pope Calixtus (217–22) ordered fasts, presumably as forms of intercession, on three Saturdays at the seasons of grain, wine and oil. One of the later Rogation days may have taken over from Robigalia. From the eleventh century on, ember days were kept on Wednesday after the First Sunday of Lent, after Pentecost, after the Exaltation of the Cross on 14 September, and after St Lucy's Day. Some of these line up with harvest time, and were indeed occasions for thanksgiving for harvest. In medieval Europe, 2 August was celebrated as Lammas Day, a celebration of the wheat harvest, when new wheat was used for the Eucharistic bread. Harvest home was celebrated, but often castigated by moralists as a time of riot and excess. Harvest, however, was not given its own place in the lectionary on the grounds that "the all-inclusive basis for the Christian celebration is the saving action of Christ" (Adam 1979: 189). This is part of that tendency to focus on redemption in Christ, at the expense of thinking of G-d's role in creation, which is so marked a feature of Western Christian theology. This tendency was taken over and indeed emphasized by the Reformers who, in spite of their increased attention to Scripture, and in spite of Luther's lectures on Genesis, failed to make creation an important locus in theology. The notorious accusation that Christianity stands at the root of the ecological crisis, though based on the supposed importance of the "dominion" verse (Genesis 1:28), could actually appeal more generally to this neglect. Growing awareness of the crisis has finally led to some attempt to remedy the omission.

The book of Revelation speaks of four horsemen who will destroy the earth (Revelation 6), traditionally understood as war, famine, plague and death. In our day, they stand for overpopulation, loss of biodiversity, resource depletion and climate change. These four factors could, and if we do not take action will, make the earth uninhabitable for humans. Together they constitute what I have called "the global emergency" (Gorringe 2018).

Responding to this danger, in 1989 the Orthodox Patriarch Bartholomew adopted 1 September as a World Day of Prayer for Creation. After meetings with Bartholomew, Pope Francis established the Season of Creation in the Catholic Church in 2015, running throughout the whole of September to 4 October, the Feast of St Francis, the patron saint of ecology. The idea of this, I take it, is to redress the balance in the theology of the liturgical year, so that creation is given its own due weight, and in view of the immense dangers of the global emergency the importance of this cannot be overemphasized. The following year this was adopted by the World Council of Churches, including the Anglican churches. However, the liturgical calendars of both the Roman Catholic and Anglican churches have not yet incorporated this into their lectionaries and have not produced relevant readings for the five Sundays involved. So called "ordinary time" is still followed. In Australia, Norman Habel, of the Uniting Church, has proposed a creation lectionary, organized over three years around Spirit (Matthew), Word (Mark) and Wisdom (Luke) and covering only four Sundays. Each Sunday is themed and over the three years it goes: Forest, Land, Wilderness, River; Earth, Humanity, Sky, Mountain; and Ocean, Fauna, Storm and Cosmos. These themes give congregations an opportunity to reflect on threats posed to different parts of creation, but it means readings are tied rather artificially to each of these aspects, and it is very odd to have a "humanity Sunday", given that there is no aspect of the natural world which could be considered outside its relation to humanity, for good or ill. Also, in a world where more than half of the total population lives in cities, it fails to engage with the relation of city and country which can already be found in Scripture.

Alternative lectionaries, of course, need to be produced through consultation. I take Norman Habel's model to be an invitation to such a consultation, and I propose my own five-week model as another such. The fifth Sunday of creation season I mark as "Harvest", which could be kept any week of the season. I have followed the Common Lectionary, slightly amended. My lectionary for Creation Season would need alternative readings found for Sundays in ministry time, but this could be addressed. The importance of responding to the global emergency liturgically (as well as politically) ought to be obvious.

Year A (Matthew)	Year B (Mark)	Year C (Luke)
Week 1	**Week 1**	**Week 1**
Genesis 1:1–31	Genesis 2:4b–22	Daniel 7:1–8,11–14
Psalm 33:1–9	Psalm 40:4–8	Psalm 29
Acts 17:22–8	Philippians 2:1–8	Ephesians 6:10–17
John 1:1–14	Mark 10:41–5	Luke 4:1–13
Week 2	**Week 2**	**Week 2**
Deuteronomy 30:11–19	Isaiah 55:6–11	1 Kings 19:9b–18
Psalm 19:7–11	Psalm 16:5–11	Psalm 82
Romans 12:1–13	Romans 10:5–21	James 2:1–8
Matthew 25:14–30	Mark 4:1–20	Luke 6:17–28
Week 3	**Week 3**	**Week 3**
Hosea 4:1–6	Deuteronomy 15:1–5	Exodus 32:1–14
Psalm 39:4–13	Psalm 68:4–6	Psalm 31:1–8
Hebrews 12:18–29	Acts 4:32–5	James 5:1–8
Matthew 25:31–46	Mark 6:30–44	Luke 16:10–13

Year A (Matthew)	Year B (Mark)	Year C (Luke)
Week 4	**Week 4**	**Week 4**
Genesis 7:11–8:22	Leviticus	Genesis 11:1–9
Psalm 104:24–33	25:1–7,18–24	Psalm 78:1–8
2 Peter 2:4–9	Psalm 72:1–7	Hebrews 11:8–13
Matthew 24:32–42	2 Corinthians 8:8–15	Luke 19:29–44
	Mark 10:17–31	
Harvest	**Harvest**	**Harvest**
Joel 2:21–7	Deuteronomy 26:1–11	Deuteronomy 8:1–18
Psalm 126	Psalm 100	Psalm 65
1 Timothy 2:1–7	Philippians 4:4–9	2 Corinthians 9:6–15
Matthew 6:25–33	John 6:23–35	Luke 12:16–30

In drawing up this lectionary, I have borne in mind Kate Raworth's justly celebrated image of doughnut economics. Raworth mapped the planetary boundaries onto social ones, taking up some of the demands of the 1948 UN Declaration of Human Rights, like food, education and health, and adding concerns about gender equality, social equity, having a voice and resilience. Moving into a safe and just space for humanity, she argues, means both reducing global resource use and eradicating poverty. One cannot be done without the other.

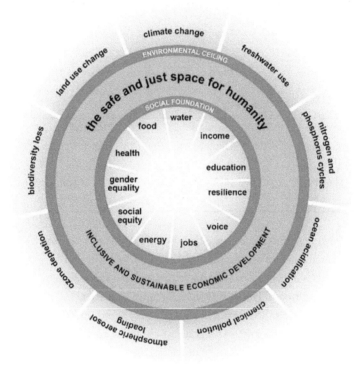

The greatest burden in both directions falls on the world's richest consumers, namely ourselves. This model helps us to approach Creation Season: the inner ring is a justice index, familiar from the prophets; the outer ring is the creation index, marking the dangerous, and possibly terminal, overshoots.

In order to survive and thrive we have to address both the justice issues and the creation issues. "The principal objective of reading the Bible is not to interpret the Bible", said Carlos Mesters, "but to interpret life with the help of the Bible." In this case, we read Scripture to help us address the most urgent social, political and economic issue of our day.

In Year A, the first week gives us the account of creation in the first chapter of Genesis. We have probably had this before, at Christmas or Easter, but here it speaks to us of humanity's place within creation as a whole. We can note two things in particular: the repeated emphasis that creation is good (*tov*) as opposed to the idea that it is a great mistake, or disgusting, or evil, or that, as in the Babylonian Atrahasis epic, human beings simply exist as slaves of the gods. Secondly there is the famous verse which speaks of humans having dominion over the rest of creation. In 1969, Lynn White notoriously suggested that the ecological crisis derives from taking this very seriously. Today, biblical scholars suggest that the verb translated as "have dominion" (*redu b-*) rather has the meaning of the shepherd travelling around with his flock. No one who has actually done this would ever suggest that it involves dominion. In the Acts passage, Luke suggests that Paul draws on Stoic ideas to think of G-d engaged at all points in creation. And John's Prologue we have already seen is a Midrash on the Genesis creation story.

The second week draws attention to the human need to obey Torah if we are to thrive. This is not naive biblical literalism but simple common sense. "Torah" stands for a recognition of fundamental principles based on gratitude and humility; its opposite is precisely the *libido dominandi* which Augustine thought was the essence of sin. The passage from Deuteronomy 30 sums up the great sermon of the book and insists that if humans obey Torah, that is to say, if they care for and nurture creation, then they will thrive. If they do not, on the other hand, they incur a curse. The Matthew passage suggests that our task as humans is to use our gifts in the service of others, but this also includes the service of what these days we call the planet. In Romans, Paul urges us to appreciate the difference of gifts, to let love be genuine, and to rejoice in hope. Obedience, therefore, is a joy—the yoke is light, and not a curse.

The third week picks Deuteronomy's warning of judgement. In Matthew 25, the judgement is incurred in failures in relation to our neighbour, but today we realize that our neighbour includes, first of all, the poor all over the world, many of them impoverished by unjust trade policies and whose livelihoods have been ruined by climate change, but also future generations who may have to live in far more difficult circumstances than we do today, and in the worst case might not survive at all. Hosea talks about the land mourning as a result of wicked human behaviour, and Hebrews insists that if we turn down the divine gift, then we receive it as judgement. Many people (and not just Christians) have learned from the global emergency that there has to be a place for lament in liturgy. It could fruitfully come here. The prophets use the "prophetic perfect" to speak of a catastrophe that will come if people do not repent (Jeremiah 9:10; Amos 5:1–2,16–17; Micah 1:8). These warnings are identical to the warnings of James Hansen, Kevin Anderson and Greta Thunberg about what we can expect if we too do not repent, which is to say, change our ways. We celebrate creation, but we also have to lament the enormous damage we have inflicted on it, the injustice this represents to the poor of the earth, and the ingratitude to G-d it represents. Week 3, then, could be the week for lament within Creation Season.

The last week of Year A gives us the Noah story, which needs to be read from beginning to end, a mythic way of saying that human wickedness (Genesis 6:5–6) incurs near-extinction. In Matthew, Jesus takes up the flood story as a way of thinking about the imminence of the coming kingdom and of the judgement that it implies. 2 Peter does the same. These texts ask us to think about the extreme seriousness of the crisis we face and to act appropriately.

In Year B, we again begin with Genesis, but this time with the second account of creation. Genesis 2 is certainly the right place to start and in understanding it we have to bear in mind the fundamental hermeneutic rule—Redactor is Rabbenu—the redactor is our teacher. We are certainly intended to read the first account of creation through the second. In the first account, human beings are the last work of creation before the Sabbath. Here human beings are fashioned from the primal dust: "Adam" is taken from *adamah*, soil. "Adam", we could say, means "compost". He is placed in a "garden" (*gan*)—a metaphor for the whole earth. His job is to till and keep it. The verb translated "till" is the verb *abad*, which means to work, serve or worship. It is not only human beings who do this, but G-d as well. "I have not made you serve", says G-d in Isaiah, "but you have made me serve with your sins" (Isaiah 43:24). The noun from it is *ebed*, servant, fundamental for the theology of Second Isaiah and taken up by Jesus in Mark: "The Son of Man came not to be served but to serve" (Mark 10:45). Serving, in Scripture, is key to being fully human; and farming, serving the earth, serving the whole human community, is part of this.

The verb "to keep", *shamar*, is invariably used for keeping G-d's commandments. It is the root of the word Cain uses when he asks: "Am

I my brother's keeper?" To keep in this sense likewise goes to the very heart of human identity. To be truly human is to keep my neighbour; it is to keep the commandments and thus to keep the gift, G-d's earth. Keeping the earth, in fact, is the practical application of keeping the commandments. The poet, farmer and theologian-philosopher Wendell Berry notes:

> The agrarian mind begins with the love of the fields and ramifies in good farming, good cooking, good eating and gratitude to G-d ... the industrial-economic mind begins with ingratitude, and ramifies in the destruction of farms and forests (Berry 2002: 241).

The Epistle is the famous passage in Acts where Paul, in Athens, cites the Stoic poet Aratus:

> The G-d who made the world and everything in it, he who is Lord of heaven and earth, does not live in shrines made by human hands, nor is he served by human hands, as though he needed anything, since he himself gives to all mortals life and breath and all things.... "In him we live and move and have our being", as even some of your own poets have said, "For we too are his offspring" (Acts 17:4–28).

Whether or not this is an accurate quote from Paul we know that Paul had done a module in Stoic philosophy at Tarsus University from the first chapters of Romans. Stoicism was part of the common currency of the age. Here we begin not from the fact that humans are "of the earth, earthy" but that G-d is at the heart of all reality—not just of humans, but of the entire natural world, the entire cosmos. It is saying the same thing as the Genesis passage, but from the other end.

The second week draws attention to the importance of hearing the word—the word of life, the word which sets out the conditions of life. In Mark's account of the parables, the disciples have to be helped to hear what it is Jesus is saying; in Romans Paul talks about the fundamental need for the word to be carried and spread. This is not so that a number of individuals can be saved, but so that humans can orient themselves in a life-enhancing direction. The prophet who wrote Isaiah 55 insists that G-d's word never returns empty and always accomplishes what it seeks—a word of hope in desperate times.

Week 3 begins with Deuteronomy's account of Jubilee and the promise that "there will be no poor amongst you". Mark 6 is the account of the feeding of the Gentiles and suggests how this might be possible. As Ched Myers has rightly suggested, this is about the miracle of sharing rather than a miracle of the multiplication of particles. This is a moral issue as an economic issue: it is not primarily telling us not to be selfish and greedy but to recognize that the miracle of sharing points to an economy beyond the global marketplace. In 2 Corinthians, Paul understands the need to share what we have as fundamental to the existence of Christian community. Put together these texts suggest a picture of a world order based on mutuality rather than on competition.

Scripture gives us a picture of the world made otherwise. The fourth week illustrates this promise. Leviticus 25 gives us a fuller account of the Jubilee year which includes rest not only for humans and animals but for the fields. Keeping fields fallow for a year has long been recognized as a way of allowing land to recuperate and today regenerative agriculture again stresses the need to rest land in order to keep it in good health, which means at the same time able to provide food for the human population. In verse 23, the writer tells us: "The land shall not be sold in perpetuity, for the land is mine: with me you are nothing but migrant labourers (*gerim*) and tenants." Ton Veerkamp has called this "the most important verse in Scripture". It makes clear that the earth exists for all creatures and cannot be appropriated for profit or domination.

In Mark's account of the rich man who wants to "inherit" eternal life, Jesus challenges him to sell what he has, give to the poor and enter on the path of discipleship. Jesus cites Leviticus to remind the man that the issue is not charity but redistribution—which is what the Jubilee year was. All those who had lost their inheritance (*nachala*) through debt had it restored to them. As Myers puts it, Jesus invites the man "to receive the kingdom as that 'social state' of redistributive justice where the dominant relations of power are turned upside down". Both the man and the disciples are shocked. The disciples protest that they have left everything to follow Jesus. Jesus responds:

> Truly I tell you, there is no one who has left house or brothers or sisters or mother or father or children or fields, for my sake and for the sake of the good news, who will not receive a hundredfold now in this age—houses, brothers and sisters, mothers and children, and fields, with persecutions—and in the age to come eternal life (Mark 10:29–30).

Myers argues that this is not a utopian proposal. The hundredfold harvest promised in the sower parable is not a pipe dream of indebted peasants but "the concrete result of redistributive practice". "Surplus is created when the entitlements of household (basic productive economic unit), family (patrimonial inheritance) and land (basic unit of wealth) are 'left'—which is to say, restructured as community assets (10:29f.)" (Myers 1994: 167).

We can note that land reform is under discussion all over the world and is a precondition of our survival as a species. Without any reference to Mark 10, Colin Tudge has recently suggested that all land should be bought (not "brought") into common ownership. "Land should be owned by everybody and rented to individuals or companies that are contracted to use it well, which means for the common good" (Tudge 2020: 244). To do this properly would require fostering true respect for the natural world which implies a sense of the sacred, exactly what the Creation Season is seeking to foster.

In the Acts passage, we have Luke's famous account of the sharing amongst the early Christian community whilst the Deuteronomy passage imagines a world in which because Torah is obeyed "there are no poor amongst you".

The first Sunday of the third year in the cycle begins with an account of the powers. Luke's temptation story depicts the temptation to manipulate, to achieve ends through worldly power. Daniel 7 depicts the empires which Israel was up against as mythic beasts who can only be overcome by war in heaven led by the Archangel Michael. In Ephesians, the author speaks of the principalities and powers which, as Walter Wink has argued, is language about the "interiority" of cultures, nations, churches and movements. This does not mean that the powers are not objective entities. They may very well be. In terms of our experience, however, what is important is that there is no way we can escape their influence. As the spiritualities of movements and cultures, they shape our lives to their deepest depths. Thus the spirituality of nationalism was a "power" responsible for many of the bloodiest conflicts of the twentieth century. In prophetic preaching, and in the life and teaching of Jesus, Wink argues, we find an outline of G-d's domination-free order. The New Testament words *kosmos* (world), *aeon* (age) and *sarx* (flesh) are various ways of speaking of the domination system. They represent society organized against G-d, operating according to assumptions which are contrary to G-d. For this reason, they become the focus of G-d's wrath and redemptive activity. In Wink's terms, the powers are good, fallen, and can be redeemed. The powers represent the institutional structures without which we cannot exist. The first step in redemption is unmasking the "delusional assumptions" of the domination system. Amongst the delusional assumptions of our society, Wink lists the following: money is the most important value; the possession of money is a sign of worth; the production of material goods is more important than the production of healthy and normal people; property is sacred and property ownership is an absolute right.

These assumptions are what underlie the global emergency and they have to be overcome and replaced.

Week 2 thinks in terms of the inner circle of Kate Raworth's diagram, of the poor who lack food, education, adequate health care and so on. According to Luke, Jesus blesses the poor; there is, as liberation theology wanted to say, a preferential option for the poor in Scripture. The Magnificat speaks of the poor being raised up and the rich being sent away empty. In the passage from 1 Kings, Elijah is commissioned to set up a whole series of revolutions, which were certainly bloody enough. We should not take this as an invitation to armed struggle, but we should note that Scripture warns us of the need for a change in the social and political order.

The third week contains Luke's account of the warning that human beings cannot serve both G-d and Mammon. This is dramatically illustrated by the story of the golden calf in Exodus, an image of the money which we all too easily worship. James also warns us against that danger. In 2014, Naomi Klein published a book called *This Changes Everything*, which she subtitled *Capitalism Versus the Planet*. Fundamentally it is the pursuit of money which has driven the global emergency. It has given us a situation where three or four billionaires own and earn as much as half of the rest of the world's population, a situation where growth is obligatory. In his Large Catechism, Luther commented on the First Commandment: "the faith of the heart makes both G-d and idol". He went on: "A G-d is that to which we look for all good and in which we find refuge in every time of need ... Many a person thinks he has G-d and everything he needs when he has money and property; in them he trusts and of them he boasts so stubbornly and securely that he cares for no one. Surely such a man also has a god—Mammon by name, that is, money and possessions—on which he fixes his whole heart. It is the most common idol on earth" (Luther 1967: 11).

Nowhere is this more true than in the contemporary affluent world, classically expressed by Victor Lebow's analysis the *Journal of Retailing* in 1955:

> Our enormously productive economy... demands that we make consumption our way of life, that we convert the buying and use of goods into rituals, that we seek out spiritual satisfaction, our ego satisfaction, in consumption ... we need things consumed, burned up, worn out, replaced and discarded at an ever increasing rate (Lebow 1955).

"Pleasure" is our cultural dominant, and even the counterculture seeks for "happiness" (without asking, in any particular case, whether we should be happy or sad). The craving for pleasure, like the craving for money, as the myth of Croesus recognizes, cannot recognize limits. It is this failure to recognize limits which is destroying us. As is well known, it is the minority of extremely affluent people who contribute most to the ecological crisis. The issue is idolatry. When we use the word "G-d", we are speaking of the origin and image of the values we live by. What marks the difference between G-d and idol is not the existence or non-existence of G-d so much as whether the understanding of G-d leads to life or death: in the biblical narratives, at any rate, death dealing practices are always characterized in terms of idolatry. The "God" who is mentioned on the dollar bill was believed to be life-giving for 200 years, and particularly for the last eighty. People pointed to rising standards of living: better food—for some, better medical care—for some, better housing—for some, and the claim was that this would be generalized, that a rising tide would lift all boats. But, in a savage irony, a literal rising tide is now eliminating Pacific communities, and is set to eliminate cities and harbours all around the world. Ultimately, it turns out, this "God" delivers death and not life. We need another account of G-d, and this is precisely what we have in Scripture.

The last week of Year C draws our attention to the role of the city. More than half the world's population now live in cities, and this is both a good thing and a bad thing. On the one hand, cities enable people to live in close community, and where they are well organized this means that their footprint may be lighter than, for example, suburbia. On the other hand, they depend on their hinterlands, which today includes the whole world of cheap labour, especially in agriculture. We have to think about this when we are thinking about our relationship to the planet and those with whom we share the planet, seeking a way of living and of feeding ourselves which maintains both people and planet in justice and in good social, cultural and political health.

Harvest

As noted at the beginning of this section, ancient Israel had three harvest festivals. When the Church came to draw up its calendar the emphasis was, first, on the events of Christ's life, and then on the commemoration of those who bore witness to Christ. Creation receded into the background. The Reformers made no formal arrangement for celebration of harvest. Today, in Common Worship, harvest is referred to as a "local celebration" which may be kept provided it does not supersede any principal feast. This is a serious mistake, and in this respect ancient Israel was much better informed. A harvest festival is first and foremost a way of expressing our joy and gratitude for the gift of creation, and our commitment to caring for it. In the present context, however, it also calls for repentance and amendment of life, more particularly in our farming, eating and consuming practices. The current lectionary offers three sets of readings, which I have altered to put Matthew in Year A and Luke in Year C; John replaces Mark in Year B.

Wherever we live harvest invites us to think about food, the way it is produced, and what and how we should eat. After World War II, and particularly from the 1960s onwards, it began to look as if the problem of hunger, which had bedevilled human cultures since the end of the hunter-gatherer phase, had been solved once and for all. There were "butter mountains" and "wine lakes", and all of a sudden governments were paying farmers to take land out of production and grub up fruit trees which were no longer needed. The superficial success of industrial agriculture has persuaded governments and some parts of the farming community that this kind of farming is the only way to feed earth's burgeoning population. It turns out, however, that things are not so simple. The Dust Bowl in Oklahoma in the 1930s was the canary in the mine. Deep ploughing led to the loss of moisture-retaining grasses and topsoil was lost over a huge area, making farming impossible. Rachel Carson's

Silent Spring, published in 1962, drew attention to the negative side effects of synthetic pesticides which were, she said, "hurled against life". She was successful in getting DDT regulated, but today industrial agriculture is insistent on using neonicotinoids, which destroy pollinators. Industrial agriculture, it turns out, can bring short-term gains, but threatens to destroy the ecosystem. On top of this, overuse of water for irrigation is leading to growing water shortages in many areas of the world, and as world temperatures rise due to climate change more fertile land is lost and more crops become impossible to grow. If the global temperature rise exceeds 2°C, which it looks set to, there will be a reduction of up to 40 per cent in two of the world's staples, maize and rice. It turns out that if we do not obey Torah, widespread and catastrophic famine may be the result, just as Deuteronomy predicted.

The debate about how best to farm which is going on at the moment is at its heart a debate about Torah, about how we understand the world we have been given and what obedience to social, political and biological reality entails. Just as we cannot be Church and ignore questions of economy and political community, so we cannot be Church and ignore this debate. Harvest is what invites us to reflect on it, and to ask about discipleship, or as Deuteronomy puts it, obedience and disobedience. The agenda of a harvest festival is not to pile up marrows and tins of baked beans in front of the altar but to ask about our food and farming culture in relation both to food poverty and the global emergency. It is to raise, first, the question "What then shall we do?" and then to take steps to act on it (for example by adopting a Community Supported Agriculture project as a congregation, by getting to know farmers and growers, by finding out why it is we have food banks).

The harvest readings include Paul's insistence on the gift in 2 Corinthians. Today this asks us to think about the economy. The word "economy" (from Greek *oikonomia*, household) stands for the organization of a community to provide for its needs. Since no community meets all of its needs, trade began very early on as a way of exchanging goods a community has in abundance for goods it lacks. All imperial economies are extractive. A kingdom of G-d economy, by contrast, understands that the earth and all its resources are gifted to all its people. It takes the Deuteronomic vision—every family under its vine and fig tree, which is to say, with enough to survive and thrive—and applies it to all humans, recognizing, in the light of Pentecost, the importance of cultural difference.

In Year C, the parable of the rich fool addresses precisely the manic pursuit of growth which is the overriding concern of the neoliberal economy, which wants to "pull down its barns and build bigger". Cancer cells do exactly the same and have the same result—death. The neoliberal economy adopts precisely the opposite of what ought to be done. In place of a maximalist we need a minimalist economy, asking: "What is the minimum we need to produce, consume and earn in order to create the kind of world that can remain in good heart for aeons to come" (Tudge 2020: 230)?

The Feast of St Michael and all Angels (29 September)

Creation Season includes the feast of St Michael and all Angels. Is this not a piece of medieval theology which we can now quietly drop? Karl Barth, for one, thinks that "biblical realism" makes this impossible. If we take Scripture seriously, he argues, we have to be prepared to talk about angels. This raises lots of questions about the nature of revelation, about whether ideas which were common currency in parts of the Ancient Near East ought to be regarded as revelation, about the role of metaphor, about whether premodern ideas of the so-called "three-tier universe" should be regarded as the basis, or even a basis, for revelation, and so forth. Without attempting to discuss these critical questions, I will follow the tradition of the Church but ask, in particular, what the angels contribute to the theme of "Creation Season". The texts for the feast are Genesis 28:10–17, Revelation 12:7–12 and John 1:47–51. Hebrews 1:5–14 is offered as an alternative to the Genesis reading.

The passage from Genesis tells the story of Jacob blessed and sent away by his father Isaac to seek his fortune with his uncle Laban. On his first night away, he sleeps and dreams of a ladder reaching from earth to heaven, and the angels of G-d ascending and descending upon it. Although the place already has a name (Luz), he renames it Bethel—house of G-d. In the Gospel passage which is set Jesus promises Nathanael that he will see "the heaven opened and the angels of G-d ascending and descending upon the Son of Man" (John 1:51).

In making sense of these passages, we can note, first, Barth's insistence that when we talk about either angels or the heavenly realm we are using "divinatory" speech, akin to poetry, which is essential for reading Scripture (he expounds this first in exegeting the creation narratives). It is not literal speech, but it is not pure metaphor either. Rather, it gestures to a realm which is real, but not susceptible either to sense experience, or to merely prosaic description. We are talking of realities which can only be seen and grasped imaginatively.

Secondly "heaven" appears in Scripture (and in the Nicene creed) as G-d's "place". It, too, is part of creation. It is the sum of all that which in creation is unfathomable and mysterious.

The angels both in Genesis and John, ascending and descending, represent the constant traffic or passage between heaven—G-d's place—and earth. In Genesis, G-d speaks to Jacob in his dream, and promises that G-d will be with him. As a result, Jacob promises that, if this is the case (it is conditional on results!), he will serve the G-d revealed to him and give G-d a tenth of all his produce. It is a *do ut des* relationship. John, on the other hand, is looking forward to the cross, where the glory of G-d is revealed in the crucified Son of Man (John 12:23–32).

We can recall the angelic host appearing to the shepherds in Luke (Luke 2:13). Barth describes the heavenly host as the heavenly entourage of the G-d who acts from heaven to earth. We are told nothing about their nature or mode of existence, but we do know they exist "in and with the kingdom of G-d coming and revealed to us" (Barth 1960: 451). The Hebrews passage which is set is first intended to put a clear distance between Jesus and the angels, but it then gives as near a definition of angels as we find anywhere in Scripture. They are "spirits in the divine service (*leitourgika pneumata*), sent to serve for the sake of those who are to inherit salvation" (Hebrews 1:14).

The passage from Revelation speaks of war in heaven, led by the angel Michael, a name which means "Who is like G-d?" The struggle is with the "dragon"—an allusion to Leviathan (Isaiah 27:1)—a symbol for the source of evil which oppressive empires such as Rome (for the author of Revelation) draw their strength from and create chaos and destruction (Revelation 12:4). In Revelation, the struggle is won by the Lamb, the one who assumes solidarity with the persecuted people, to whom Michael and the angels witness. The question "Who is like G-d?" refers to the cross, which is G-d's way of achieving victory in the struggle against the powers of evil and chaos. According to the perspective of the writer, the powers know they have no future (12:12).

The work of angels

As we read Scripture, we repeatedly come across angels, and they are everywhere in the art of the Middle Ages and Renaissance, often in an almost Disneyfied form. What are we to think of them? The word *angellos*, like the Hebrew *malakh*, which it translates, originally means "messenger". Angels, then, as we see them in the birth stories in particular, are the messengers or ambassadors of G-d. Barth argues that there are fundamentally two things which need to be said about them. The first is that their function is that of witness. The angels witness to the reality and glory of G-d and human witness lives and is enabled by that witness.

Both Isaiah and Luke speak of the angels praising G-d, and the idea has therefore grown up of the heavenly choir, which human choirs echo. But, Barth argues, we can never forget the warning of Amos 5:21f., in which G-d denounces the cult, and asks instead for justice and righteousness. The ministry and service of humans is in the first instance witness to G-d's incoming rule, the kingdom:

> Where the kingdom of G-d is, there the strict and saving mystery of G-d is at work, and therefore the kingdom of heaven, and therefore, in all their imperceptibility and humility, in the unreserved selflessness and objectivity which distinguishes them from all earthly creatures, the angels (Barth 1960: 516).

Secondly, the witness and presence of angels is the concrete form of the divine mystery perceptible on earth. They are the "atmosphere" in which witness can take place. In other words, the presence of angels is what Rudolf Otto called the numinous, as indeed the story in Genesis 28 seems to suggest. If that is the case, I think it allows us to make a connection between this feast and Creation Season; for the angels, then, are to be encountered both in the glory of the created world, and also in the witness and struggle of those who seek to respect, preserve and honour that glory. This leads us to the closing day of Creation Season, the Feast of St Francis.

Feast of St Francis (4 October)

I shall say something about Francis in the next part of the book. Here I shall simply say something about the *Cantico delle creatura*, which expresses that love for creation which is presumably the reason Francis is named the patron saint of ecology. The song begins:

> Most High, all powerful, good Lord,
> Yours are the praises, the glory, the honour, and all blessing.
> To You alone, Most High, do they belong,
> and no man is worthy to mention Your name.
> Be praised, my Lord, through all your creatures,
> especially through my lord Brother Sun,
> who brings the day; and you give light through him.
> And he is beautiful and radiant in all his splendour!
> Of you, Most High, he bears the likeness.
> Praised be You, my Lord, through Sister Moon and the stars,
> in heaven you formed them clear and precious and beautiful.
> Praised be You, my Lord, through Brother Wind,
> and through the air, cloudy and serene,
> and every kind of weather through which
> You give sustenance to Your creatures.
> Praised be You, my Lord, through Sister Water,
> which is very useful and humble and precious and chaste.
> Praised be You, my Lord, through Brother Fire,
> through whom you light the night and he is beautiful
> and playful and robust and strong.
> Praised be You, my Lord, through Sister Mother Earth,
> who sustains us and governs us and who produces
> varied fruits with coloured flowers and herbs.

Thomas of Celano, Francis' first biographer, wrote:

> Who can explain the joy that arose in his spirit from the beauty
> of the flowers, contemplating the gallantry of their shapes and
> the breathing of the fragrance of their aromas? ... And finding
> himself in the presence of many flowers, he preached to them,
> inviting them to praise the Lord, as if they enjoyed the gift of
> reason. And he did the same thing with fields and vineyards, with
> rocks and forests, and with all of the beauty of the countryside,
> the waters of the springs, the fruits of the orchards, land and fire,
> air and wind, inviting them with genuine purity to divine love
> and to joyful fidelity. Finally he called all creatures his brothers
> and sisters, like one who had arrived at the glorious freedom of
> the children of G-d (*First Life* 81).

The Psalm set for St Francis Day is 148, which forms part of the canticle
known as the Benedicite which combines that Psalm with verses from the
Septuagint version of Daniel 3, the Song of the Three Children (vv. 56–88
included in the NRSV). Francis' poem is a version, in Umbrian dialect,
of this canticle, which is a marvellous Baroque song of praise for all the
wonders of creation, beginning with angels, and working its way through
heavens, waters, powers, sun and moon, stars, showers and dew, winds,
fire and heat, winter and summer, dews and frosts, frost and cold, ice
and snow, nights and days, light and darkness, lightnings and clouds, the
earth, mountains and hills, green things, wells, seas and floods, whales,
fowls of the air, beasts and cattle and at last:

> O you Children of Men, bless the Lord:
>   praise him, and magnify him for ever.

Those who accuse Christianity of responsibility for the ecological crisis
have not only never heard of historical materialism, but they have never
sung this canticle either, which it is impossible to read or sing without
both laughter and tears (the latter because of the ways in which we have
abused the gift of creation). Francis recognized what it had to say, namely
that creation itself is grace, gift, at once in itself a glorious hymn of praise

and, because it is gift, evoking gratitude as the fundamental disposition in regard to it.

Though full of joy, Francis also had more than his fair share of that asceticism which seemed a *sine qua non* of discipleship to all Christians before the eighteenth century. To recover some of that asceticism today in those cultures where consumerism is a creed is an important task but, like Francis, we must not let it dim our delight in the created world. Nowhere is that better recognized than in the work of the Episcopalian priest—and cookery writer—Robert Capon. Capon was not a glutton—nobody who takes food seriously can be. His theological and metaphysical account of slicing an onion ought to be obligatory reading for every Christian cook. We think of an onion as formed of spheres, but once sliced "The myth of sphericity is finally dead. The onion, as now displayed, is plainly all vectors, rivers and thrusts. *Tongues of fire.* But the Pentecost they mark is that of nature, not grace: the Spirit's first brooding on the face of the waters." When you have finished your slicing, "Perhaps now you have seen at least dimly that the uniquenesses of creation are the result of continuous creative support, of effective regard by no mean lover" (Capon 2002: 15,17). What we learn from the onion, says Capon, is that the real human work is to look at the things of the world and to love them for what they are. Just so did the authors of the Benedicite and St Francis.

Leonardo Boff, when still a Franciscan, wrote a long love letter to St Francis. He records visiting Assisi and spending time with the gardener of the Porziuncula, Fra Bonaventure. The day they were together was a celebration, and wine was served at dinner. "Brother Bonaventure drinks his wine in silence and with deep respect. He does so as if he were taking part in a ritual of some sort. 'What is it Brother?' And he, in almost a whisper, says, 'I must honour Brother Wine. I myself made it, six years ago. And it, too, is joyful in our joy'" (Boff 1982: 4). Capon understood precisely that. G-d makes wine, he says—makes, not made. He proposes a toast to that:

> To a radically, perpetually unnecessary world; to the restoration
> of astonishment to the heart and mystery to the mind; to
> wine, because it is a gift we never expected; to mushroom and
> artichoke, for they are incredible legacies; to improbable acids

and high alcohols, since we would hardly have thought of them ourselves; and to all being because it is superfluous ... Let the bookkeepers struggle with their balance sheets; it is the tippler who sees the untipped Hand. G-d is eccentric; G-d has *loves*, not reasons. Salute!

Everything about Creation Season is contained in that joy.

All Saints

I suggested at the beginning of this second part that, if we follow the logic of the lectionary, as well as much ancient Christian practice, Advent would begin seven or eight weeks before Christmas. This would mean that All Saints Day would effectively end the liturgical year, and that would mean that the year both began and ended with promise.

The Gospel for Years A and C for this feast is the Beatitudes, and the questions they raise are: who is addressed? And, what does this tell us about G-d?

Schweizer considers Luke's form of the Beatitudes to be original:

> Blessed are you who are poor. For yours is the kingdom of G-d.
> Blessed are you who are hungry now for you will be filled.
> Blessed are you who weep now for you will laugh (Luke 6:20).

Schweizer comments:

> Two things are being said: Jesus promises to those who are economically poor that their fate will change in the kingdom of G-d, and, in anticipation, in the Christian community ... Hearing the promise of Jesus leads to both the espousal of the cause of the poor, the hungry, and those who mourn, and unlimited hope for the world to come that is contrasted explicitly to the "now". Without this hope, the result would be an outbreak of religious fanaticism that would see everything fulfilled in faith, being blind to the suffering that will never be overcome totally by human efforts. But without the attempt to overcome it, as far as humanly possible, there would be no real hearing of the promise (Schweizer 1984: 120–1).

In Matthew's version, there are another five blessings: on the meek, on those who hunger and thirst for righteousness, on the merciful, on the pure in heart, and on the peacemakers. It is important that these blessings not be appropriated by the Church. Matthew adds another blessing, which I shall come to, but these blessings, as I understand them, are addressed to the whole human community. The blessings answer the question, what does it mean to love G-d, honour G-d and serve G-d? Those who hunger and thirst for righteousness, who show mercy, who seek to make peace, the pure in heart, do this. People like this are found in every creed and none. Peggy Seeger wrote a song, "The Naming of Names", which I have used on occasion on All Saints Day. It names those who have suffered or died as a result of hungering and thirsting for righteousness. It includes the White Rose group, who protested against Nazi terror, and died for it; Rosa Luxemburg, imprisoned throughout World War I on the grounds that her peace activism demoralized the troops, and murdered immediately afterwards by the groups who went on to support Hitler; Patrice Lumumba, the first President of the free Congo, overthrown in a coup and murdered; Carmen Quintana, doused in petrol and set light to by Pinochet's forces; and many others, mostly labour activists. Seeger always said that the names were contemporary and could be varied, and so it is entirely appropriate to insert, for example, the names of Ignacio Ellacuría SJ and the others murdered in El Salvador for supporting the preferential option for the poor, but what is crucial is that it should never be a song which commemorates only Christians, as if they alone instantiated the qualities which Jesus blesses as truly serving the G-d he called "Father". In Jesus of Nazareth, G-d addresses the whole of humanity, and does not set out to form a religious group which can then compete with other religious groups in a mutual cock-crowing as to which is the greatest. What does it mean to be truly human? Christians believe this is revealed to us in Jesus of Nazareth, and he in turn, in the Beatitudes, highlights key aspects of true humanness. This, of course, in turn again, throws light on the G-d we worship—not, over and over again it has to be said, the G-d made in the image of the violent, strong and powerful, but the G-d who blesses, and is to be found among, the poor and the hungry.

To these blessings Matthew appends a word to the Church:

> Blessed are you when people revile you and persecute you and
> utter all kinds of evil against you falsely on my account. Rejoice
> and be glad, for your reward is great in heaven, for in the same
> way they persecuted the prophets who were before you (Matthew
> 5:11–12).

This undoubtedly reflects the experience of the earliest community and
from time to time it reflects the experience of the contemporary Church
but, *nota bene*, only when it witnesses to the kingdom as Jesus describes
it and not when it compromises with the powers that be.

The blessings, then, ask us to call to mind these witnesses to the
kingdom, "nameless millions", in the words of Seeger's song. Yes, the
feast also requires us to remember all those nameless Christians who
have passed on the faith from one generation to another, those whom
each believer knows but whose name is written in no book except the
Book of Life (Revelation 20:12), the "great cloud of witnesses" of whom
Hebrews speaks (Hebrews 12:1). The "saints", we remember, are not in
the first instance those people of exceptional holiness commemorated in
the liturgical calendar, but Paul's form of address to divided and in many
ways not very admirable groups like the congregation in Corinth: "To all
G-d's beloved in Rome, who are called to be saints" (Romans 1:7). "To
the church of G-d that is in Corinth, including all the saints throughout
Achaia" (2 Corinthians 1:1). This is how Paul addresses his congregations.
These are the saints we remember and celebrate—with whom are
included "that great host whom no man can number" (Revelation 7:9, a
text for this feast) which includes all those from every nation and culture
on whom Jesus pronounces a blessing in the Beatitudes.

PART 3

Remembering

Memory and truth

Both Israel and Church stand under the command to "remember". At the Passover, Israel must remember the exodus, the journey from bondage to liberation. At every Eucharist, the Church remembers the events of the Last Supper and the significance of the life, death and resurrection of Jesus of Nazareth. Unfortunately, remembering is not a simple matter. The command to "remember" has become a liturgical formula—the *anamnesis*—but what that remembrance consists in has divided Christians since the tenth century and continues to do so.

Memory is central to identity: when we develop Alzheimer's disease, we forget who we are, and this applies to cultures as well as to individuals. Totalitarian regimes can seek to erase cultural memory, as China has sought to do in Tibet for the past seventy years, and as it is now trying to do with the Uighurs, through "re-education". More than 12 million African slaves were taken to the Americas, deprived not only of their freedom but also of their language and cultural memory. In Australia, many of the problems of the Aboriginal population derive from an all-out assault on its cultural memory: when you lose your roots, what are you to do? The Reformation debates about Scripture and tradition were about the identity of the Church, and about the nature of memory. The watchword *sola Scriptura* arose from the perception that tradition could be manipulated in the interests of papal power, as Lorenzo Valla had demonstrated in exposing the "Donation of Constantine" as a forgery in 1440. But then, as Shakespeare pointed out in the following century, "the devil can cite Scripture for his purpose".

Memory can be manipulated or eradicated but there are closer cultural analogies to Alzheimer's disease. Neil Postman, who was Professor of Media Studies at New York University, cited studies which found that 51 per cent of viewers could not recall a single item of news a few minutes after viewing a news programme; 21 per cent of TV viewers could not recall any news item within one hour of broadcast. He delivered what he calls "the Huxleyan warning":

> What Huxley teaches is that in the age of advanced technology, spiritual devastation is more likely to come from an enemy with a smiling face than from one whose countenance exudes suspicion and hate. In the Huxleyan prophecy, Big Brother does not watch us, by his choice. We watch him, by ours. There is no need for wardens or gates or Ministries of Truth. When a population becomes distracted by trivia, when cultural life is redefined as a perpetual round of entertainments, when serious public conversation becomes a form of baby-talk, when, in short, a people become an audience and their public business a vaudeville act, then a nation finds itself at risk; culture death is a real possibility . . . Huxley . . . was trying to tell us that what afflicted the people in Brave New World was not that they were laughing instead of thinking, but that they did not know what they were laughing about and why they had stopped thinking (Postman 1986: 168).

Liturgical memory is not immune from this, brought on by a wide variety of sentimentality, both Protestant and Catholic, which allows us to sing our hearts out and go straight out and kill Jews or practise apartheid.

Memory is crucial to identity but at the same time memory is famously unreliable, as gently satirized in the song "Oh yes, I remember it well". Like Antonio, the usurping duke of Milan, we can falsify memory

> Like one
> Who having into truth, by telling of it,
> Made such a sinner of his memory,
> To credit his own lie (*Tempest* Act 1 Scene 2).

But we do not have to go to the lengths of "false memory syndrome" to acknowledge that, as individuals, we re-narrate our story constantly, sentimentalizing, damning, blocking out what is inconvenient or unbearable, setting events in new lights. Very often people live with denial, but so do cultures. In 2020, in Britain and other places there was widespread indignation about the tearing down of statues to people who were involved in slavery. "We cannot forget our history" was the cry. But the same people who protest at this applaud when statues of Lenin, Stalin or Saddam Hussein are torn down. The protestors sign up to a mythicized history, scrubbed clean—and built on a lie. In Turkey, a state built on ethnic cleansing, even to mention the Armenian genocide is an imprisonable offence. Probably every culture has sins in this regard, and they can claim biblical authority: the ideology of "the promised land" was used to justify the subjection of "the inhabitants of the land" by David (2 Samuel 5:6–10). It looks like a classic instance of denial.

Historians are either the guardians or the manipulators of memory. In Tudor England, Foxe's *Book of Martyrs* stoked the flames of a bitter anti-papalism, and Catholic records of their martyrs did the same in reverse. History is often, if not always, partisan. Foxe understood it as a weapon of war. Walter Benjamin, whom I cited in Part 1, wrote his theses on the philosophy of history to critique the view of Leopold von Ranke that the job of history was to describe events *wie es eigentlich gewesen war*, just as they happened. Later historians pointed out that even if you go back to primary sources, as Ranke sought to, all history rests on selection. I said earlier that history is time interpreted, but interpretation does not mean bending the facts to suit my view. Ranke is right that the historian's vocation is to struggle for the truth—crucial, for instance, in relation to Holocaust denial and, indeed, in relation to the very survival of a culture at all. This is the sense of the inscription at Yad Vashem: "Forgetfulness leads to exile, while remembrance is the secret of redemption."

There is an intellectual asceticism about all rigorous academic work which is different from Max Weber's claims for the possibility of value neutrality. History needs to interrogate memory in the interests of truth. When the Ukrainian/Russian poet Irina Ratushinskaya arrived in the Small Zone, the area for particularly dangerous ideological enemies of the State in Soviet Russia, she asked her mentor, Tatyana Velikanova, what was the worst thing about the camps. She replied, "The ceaseless lies." Goebbels and Stalin built whole regimes on lies, but they are followed today by governments all over the world. This poisons the wells of political discourse and makes the construction of a common good impossible. A healthy political culture, it turns out, is only possible when there is a serious and committed attempt to speak the truth and this involves a vow of rigour with regard to cultural memory. This applies to liturgical memory as well, and the contemporary sanctoral cycle is by no means clear of partisanship and false memory.

As Foxe shows, memory can be weaponized. In relationships, memories of past hurts can be used to put another down, or exercise power. Memories of past injustices can poison cultures for generations as they have done (not without cause) in, for example, Ireland and the Balkans. Yad Vashem rightly and necessarily remembers the victims of the Nazi Holocaust, but that memory is now turned against the Palestinians, who had nothing to do with it, and who have lost their land, their livelihoods, and live with constant harassment and humiliation on its account, and whose history faces erasure.

For the past forty years, many states have sought to deal with past wrongs through "Truth and Reconciliation" procedures. Building on the idea of restorative justice such procedures work on the assumption that knowing the truth can give closure to victims. It turns out that it is not that simple. In some places (Chile, El Salvador), the perpetrators remained in power. Virtually everywhere existing social injustices have not been rectified. "Thirty-six years of war cannot be fixed with truth alone," said a Guatemalan witness. People want social justice, and they also want to see the main perpetrators punished, as a way of saying that horrendous human rights abuses are indefensible and inexcusable. This, rather than retribution, was the function of the Nuremberg trials, and the trial of Eichmann.

Salvation history, says Metz, is secular history "in which a meaning is conceded to obscured and suppressed hopes and sufferings . . . in which the vanquished and forgotten possibilities of human existence that we call 'death' are allowed a meaning which is not recalled or cancelled by the future course of history" (Metz 1980: 114). In Part 1, I noted that he speaks of this as a "dangerous memory", but Miroslav Volf points out that in the first place remembering does not seem very good at stopping atrocities. More importantly, the Gospel raises the question of whether at some point remembering needs to be replaced by forgetting. The apostle of memory in our culture, Elie Wiesel, insists that we must never forget, whilst recognizing that in some conflicts (he has the Balkans in mind, but he could equally have said Northern Ireland) memory can be an abomination. Volf, however, properly asks whether ultimate redemption is consistent with an undying memory of wrong: "The world to come that keeps alive the memory of all wrongdoing suffered . . . would not be a place of uplifted radiant faces but one of eyes downcast in shame, not a place of delight in one another but a place enveloped in the mist of profound sadness" (Volf 2006: 213). Both the Tenakh (in Isaiah 25) and the book of Revelation, which draws on Isaiah, envisage an ultimate future where G-d will heal all hurts. The Messianic Writings, ruminating on Isaiah 53, think of the death of Christ as the divine accomplishment of this promise, a bearing of wrongs which makes final mutual forgiveness possible. Week by week the Eucharist invites us into this understanding, asking us to begin with the unlovely body of fellow disciples, as a school of forgiving love to be extended to all people.

In the liturgical cycle, the memory of Christ comes first, but from the beginning Christians have also remembered the saints and martyrs. Here, too, memory can be problematic: *who* do we remember, and *why* and *how*? The saints and martyrs are rightly remembered when they place before us redeeming memory, or memory which helps forward redemption. Unfortunately liturgical memory is also often partisan. Liturgy, too, it turns out, needs its own ascesis.

The sanctoral cycle

The liturgical cycle set out in Part 2 constitutes the *temporale*, the foundational narrative of salvation for the Christian Church. This is based on the cultural memory first of Israel and then of the Church as recorded in Scripture. From very early on, this was supplemented by, and occasionally replaced by, the *sanctorale*, the memory of the heroes of the faith, and in particular the martyrs. Peter Brown has argued that in the early Church the cult of martyrs was what Christianity meant for most ordinary Christians. Despite attempts at reform, the Roman Catholic Church prior to Vatican II had 262 saints' days. In a further attempt to prioritize the core history of salvation, the Council reduced the number of days and classified them as either solemnities, feasts or memorials. Only five saints, all from the Messianic Writings (Mary, Joseph, John the Baptist, Peter and Paul) were assigned solemnities.

In the calendar of the Anglican Book of Common Worship (which follows Caesar's calendar and does not begin with Advent!), there is a distinction between Principal Feasts, festivals, lesser festivals and commemorations. There are eleven Principal Feasts, twenty-two festivals, 101 lesser festivals and 112 commemorations (with some doubled up on the same day)—246 festivals and commemorations in all.

The sanctoral cycle is important. Karl Barth introduced his lectures on the history of doctrine by reminding students that Augustine, Aquinas, Luther, Schleiermacher and all the rest were not dead but living. "In him they all live" (Luke 20:38). This is the reality of the communion of saints. We remember the reality of that communion at All Saints, but apart from that feast there are lives which for one reason or another we especially wish to remember. Vatican II decided that local or national churches could celebrate feast days relative to them, but "Only those should be extended to the universal church which commemorate saints who are truly of universal importance". It was pointed out that commemoration of saints needed to be based on "historical truth", and there was also an attempt to recognize saints and martyrs from the whole Christian world, rather than principally from Europe.

Despite the attempt at reform the sanctoral cycle is still crowded, and there is good reason for that because we need to remember the great and heroic figures in our past. It is good to include them in a calendar, but it is not possible that each should have a festivity. The sanctoral cycle on the whole needs to be part of the community's educational work, however that is carried out—whether through weekly pew sheets, through Lent courses or other study days. By and large we do not take this pedagogical work sufficiently seriously.

The sanctoral cycle began with the martyrs, and that is right. Still they are the greatest number of feasts and commemorations (36); after them come Religious (31), teachers of the Church (27) and bishops (24). Some figures, like Augustine for example, fall into two categories or even three, but in my tally I have counted them in just one. The categories in which they appear are a version of Paul's "gifts of the Spirit" in 1 Corinthians 12. Paul makes it clear that no one has to do everything and that there are different charisms. The number of bishops in the list, however, suggests that the Church has not heeded what he has to say about the priority of the weakest and humblest members of the community (1 Corinthians 12:22–3). It must never be forgotten, either, that Paul goes on from the discussion of the charisms to talk about the priority of faith, hope and love—the love which learns from Christ and is imbued with Christ. Some of the teachers commemorated were particularly poor in that respect. In what follows, I want to comment on a number of the categories and suggest some others.

Martyrs

The martyrs commemorated in Common Worship are not uncontentious. In January, as a lesser festival, we have "Charles, King and Martyr". This suggests a take on Charles I, derived more or less from Filmer (the apologist for absolute monarchy in the late seventeenth century), which no contemporary historian would subscribe to. Charles was pious and sincere but also devious and, consistently with his views on kingship, arbitrary. He was executed by men who were equally pious and equally sure they were doing G-d's will. To call him a martyr is to subscribe to one version of that period's history which happens to be the version of the ruling class, sanctified in the Book of Common Prayer. Remembering the martyrs is crucially important but often, as with Foxe, it can be a way of claiming victory for one particular party or position.

In April, St George is celebrated as a festival, but we have no firm evidence that George ever existed. We know that there was a cult of St George, especially in the East, but we have no acta, as we have with the great second- and third-century martyrs. The appropriation of George for military purposes ("G-d for Harry, England and St George!") is deplorable, and even more deplorable is the adoption of the flag by the extreme right wing in England. Far better to keep 23 April, as many of us do, as Shakespeare's birthday!

In November, Catherine of Alexandria has a commemoration. But there is no evidence whatever that Catherine existed. Worse still, her legend may well be a cover-up for the murder, by a Christian mob, of the Neoplatonist philosopher Hypatia in 415. This would be a classic instance of dealing with guilt by blaming it on the victim. There is no excuse for retaining her commemoration in the calendar.

Also commemorated is Dietrich Bonhoeffer. It is right to remember him, but he did not die specifically for his Christian witness. Like a great many others, he was pulled in by the Gestapo because he was tangentially involved in the bomb plot to assassinate Hitler. Until his arrest, he had kept Bishop Bell informed of what was going on. He himself recognized what an absolutely peripheral role he played.

Maximilian Kolbe, who took the place of a family man in going in to the gas chambers, is also rightly remembered. What is shocking is that Paul Schneider is not remembered. In the whole of Christian history so far, he is one of the paradigm martyrs, a record of Christian witness in the face of murderous idolatry. No Christian congregation should be unfamiliar with his story.

Schneider was a Prussian Lutheran pastor who was thirty-six when Hitler came to power in 1933. He was married and had six children. The following year, he joined the Confessing Church when it was formed.

He immediately got into trouble when he had to conduct the funeral of a member of the Hitler Youth and refused to allow Nazi sentiments to be used in the service. This led to his first arrest. In 1937, he excommunicated Nazi members of his congregation for behaviour inconsistent with the gospel. Banned from his parish, he returned to take the harvest service. He was arrested and sent to Buchenwald. There he refused to remove his cap when the Swastika was raised: for him it was a symbol of oppression and to honour it was idolatry and a denial of Christian faith. He refused to give the Nazi salute, "Heil Hitler". "Heil" (salvation), he said, comes only from Jesus Christ. He was stripped and savagely beaten before the whole camp. On Fridays, he fasted and gave the tiny portion of food prisoners received to those he considered more needy than himself. He was put in solitary confinement, but when the camp was assembled, he preached from his window:

> Brothers, our Lord Jesus Christ came into this world to free us from our sins. Whoever believes in him is justified before G-d. We need have no anxiety over what men can do to us because through Christ we belong to the kingdom of G-d. G-d is our Father and Christ is our Brother. Our Lord, who died for us, has promised that we will rise with him if we believe in him. He has said, I am the resurrection and the life—Whoever believes in him will not die. Brothers, have faith. Have faith in Jesus our Saviour and G-d will receive you as his children (28 August 1938) (Foster 1995: 644).

At this point, he was forcibly silenced. He was beaten every time he preached from his window. He knew that Jews were being murdered in the camp and called out from the window: "Murder! People are being murdered in this camp!" When the Swastika was raised, he called out: "You shall not worship idols!" He was beaten and bludgeoned until his face was unrecognizable, and no part of his body was free from bruises. He was murdered with a lethal injection on 29 July 1939. His letters to his wife and children from prison are some of the most moving testaments to Christian discipleship and a response to the frequent observation that celibacy allows you greater freedom in Christian discipleship. He died as a true martyr—a witness to the truth of Jesus Christ. The editors of a collection of records of German martyrs during the Nazi tyranny write of him:

> When confronted by the antithesis of Christianity—the use of the lie as a political force—he called it by its name and thereby forfeited his life. He could not preach the Word without living it. And this he did in all simplicity, without hesitation, even when he found himself alone and at the mercy of his enemies (Gollwitzer 1958: 15).

I wonder whether Paul Schneider is overlooked because he speaks so directly to us. "The use of the lie as a political force." Where, these days, do we not encounter this as a political reality and where do we, as Christians, oppose it?

Archbishop Romero is given a commemoration, and this is proper. But we need to remember, alongside him, the 80,000 civilians killed in El Salvador, which included the massacre of an entire village—500 people—by Roberto D'Aubuisson's troops. The children were hung from trees. Alongside them, we need to remember Rutilio Grande, the first priest to be murdered in El Salvador; Cosme Spesotti, Manuel Reyes, Ernesto Abrego, Mariano Serrano, murdered in 1980, followed by three nuns and a lay woman worker who were raped, murdered and buried by the army—Ita Ford, Maura Clark, Dorothy Kazel and Jean Donovan. All of these were murdered because of their work alongside the poor. And then, in 1989, six Jesuits—Ignacio Ellacuría, Ignacio Martín-Baró, Segundo Montes, Juan Ramón Moreno, Joaquín López y López, Amando López, and Elba Ramos, their housekeeper, and Celina Ramos, her sixteen-year-old daughter, also murdered by the army. The crime of the Jesuits was to be working for a negotiated settlement with the rebel group, the FMLN, and advocating the preferential option for the poor. The army killings were facilitated by the CIA and funded by grants of up to $80 million per year from the US Congress, in the name of defeating communism.

No Argentine martyr appears in the Common Worship calendar, but during the "Dirty War" from 1976 to 1983 between 10,000 and 30,000 people were murdered. Here the hierarchy by and large kept silent, and some positively approved of what was happening. One of the cardinals and the Anglican bishop responsible for the "Southern Cone" both denied categorically that any disappearances were taking place. Among the murdered were priests Alfredo Leaden, Alfredo Kelly and Pedro Duffau, and seminarians Salvador Barbeito and Emilio Barletti, accused of being members of the "Priests for the Third World" movement. Priests Carlos de Dios Murias and Gabriel Longueville, along with lay catechist Wenceslao Pedernera were murdered, and Bishop Angelelli was murdered returning from an investigation of their murder. The daughter of the German New Testament scholar Ernst Käsemann, who was working in the Buenos Aires slums, was also murdered. All this killing was carried out in the name of "Western Christian civilization"—which meant wealth, privilege and power.

In Chile, the British priest Michael Woodward was murdered shortly after Pinochet's coup, for his involvement with work with the poor. His body was never found.

All these died as a consequence of their understanding that the gospel requires solidarity with the poor. None of them were guerrillas or supported guerrilla movements. I have recorded their names because that is what we have to do—the naming of names, as Peggy Seeger said.

Peter Brown notes that the reading of the acta of the martyrs in the early Church "abolished time". They made the deeds of G-d in the Tenakh or Messianic Writings contemporary. They breached "the paper-thin wall between the past and the present" (Brown 1981: 81). But the martyrs also instantiate with their life and death, with their witness, Jesus' words that anyone who wishes to be a disciple must take up their cross and follow. They show us what is meant by the cost of discipleship. It is good that we honour holy women and men, whether Religious or lay, that we honour teachers of the Church, and so forth, but the martyrs come first.

Confessors

Vatican II abolished the category of "confessor", but that seems to me a mistake. A confessor is someone who suffers for their faith, but who does not actually die for it. For examples I turn to Irina Ratushinskaya's account of her four years in the Soviet Gulag, *Grey is the Colour of Hope*. She was arrested and sentenced to seven years in prison and four years of internal exile in 1984. Ratushinskaya was a Christian, but she was imprisoned for her poetry—something we will come to. She tells us of the *babushki* (grandmas). These were "True Orthodox Christians" who refused to recognize the Patriarch the Bolsheviks imposed. They refused to work in any Soviet institution, handle Soviet documents or money. They worked for people who paid them in kind. They were not registered believers, so they were imprisoned, and in the camps they refused to work, so they spent their time in punishment blocks. They were called *babushki* because by the time Ratushinskaya got there, they were very old. Instead of cursing they forgave. Because they could not do hard physical work, they repaired things and made warm clothes from the scraps available. When released they refused their documents, which meant certain re-arrest and sentence:

> From their point of view, this was perfectly normal: were they not suffering for G-d? In their eyes, it is we who act unnaturally: we submit to Satan and his minions—the Soviet government—in order to escape persecution. And Satan, they know, will never give up of his own accord—he shall merely exploit any sign of weakness to his greater gain, penetrate ever deeper into your soul. That was and is the reasoning of the "True Orthodox". Some of them are still alive, living in internal exile . . . Others of them are still to be found in some of the camps, with calm, serene faces, ever ready to lay down their lives for the Lord: to what greater honour can one aspire (Ratushinskaya 1988: 66)?

Ratushinskaya was consigned to a "small zone" for women political prisoners. A number of her fellow political prisoners were there because they were Christians—Pentecostal, Baptist and Catholic. The Catholic

Jadvyga Bielauskiene was a Lithuanian who was sent to Siberia when the Russians annexed her country, and then again sentenced for helping Roman Catholic priests give instruction to children:

> Her faith is the cornerstone of her existence, but she sets no store by denominational differences: there are many confessions, but G-d is one, after all, and it is to G-d we shall all come in the end. He who does not believe now, shall find faith later, in G-d's good time. Jadvyga is a woman of iron character, yet at the same time she takes such care of us that at times we feel almost ashamed: when all is said and done, she is old enough to be a mother to most of us (Ratushinskaya 1988: 98).

When sent to hospital, she spent her time helping people, removing soiled bedding, plucking off lice, "a true Christian".

These women were confessors. They were imprisoned on account of their faith; they suffered for it. Some of the *babushki* died, but those who did not also witnessed to the love of Christ and met evil with good.

Activists

Amongst those who are celebrated or commemorated in the Common Worship calendar are those who are called "social reformers"—many of them women, and including the Quaker Elizabeth Fry. Over one or two of these figures (William Wilberforce for example) there hangs a faint odour of respectability, something which no book of the Bible knows anything about, unless it be in the Sadducees. Freedom (a word often on Paul's lips) and daring are clear marks of the gospel. Rather than the term "reformer", I prefer the word "activist", and my three examples are all from North America and all Roman Catholic. The first is Dorothy Day.

By no manner of means can Day be regarded as respectable, though she came from a solid middle-class background. A passion for social justice led her to anarchism, and a sympathy for communism, but at the same time from childhood on she was called to faith. After a series of love affairs, and a failed marriage, she joined Peter Maurin in founding the Catholic Worker movement, dedicated not only to social justice but to pacifism and non-violence. She engaged for most of her life in non-violent direct action, and was arrested and sent to prison eleven times, the last time when she was seventy-five.

Day was, in her mature years, a conventional but at the same time independent thinking Catholic. She respected episcopal authority but still felt free to challenge Cardinal Spellman over his stand on nuclear weapons. Like so many North Americans, she detested State Social Security and thought charity should come from individuals. She thoroughly disavowed her bohemian youth and felt her abortion was the greatest tragedy of her life. Her anarchism led her to espouse the idea of the small state, characteristic of many on the right in North America. Her advocacy of pacifism in World War II earned her many enemies as, later, did her stand on nuclear weapons. Equally, when McCarthyism was in full swing, she spoke of how much she had learned from communists, and of how they helped her to find G-d in the poor. She visited Cuba after the revolution and defended the Cuban Revolution, endorsing farm cooperatives. "G-d bless Castro and all those who are seeing Christ in the poor", she could write. "G-d bless all those who are seeking the brotherhood of man because in loving their brothers they love G-d even though they deny Him." The apparent inconsistencies in her political views all sprang from her attempt to be true to the gospel, above all to care for the poor and oppressed.

Daniel and Philip Berrigan were the two youngest sons of a North American Catholic family. Daniel, the older of the two, became a Jesuit, Philip a Josephite. Both brothers took a lead in opposing the Vietnam War. Philip eventually spent eleven years in prison for his peace activities and for draft burning. After destroying drafts in Catonsville, Maryland, the Berrigans, and seven others, issued a statement in which they said:

> We confront the Roman Catholic Church, other Christian bodies, and the synagogues of America with their silence and cowardice in the face of our country's crimes. We are convinced that the religious bureaucracy in this country is racist, is an accomplice in this war, and is hostile to the poor (Nepstad 2008: 48).

By contrast we saw, in Part 2, how the Dean and Chapter of Westminster Abbey in Britain in 2019 formally gave thanks for the role of nuclear weapons in "keeping peace".

In 1980, the two brothers were part of the group which started the Plowshares movement, which symbolically damages aircraft or submarines designed to deliver nuclear warheads. In addition to protesting against war, Daniel took up the cause of sufferers from AIDS. Philip, meanwhile, married a former nun, Elizabeth McAllister, also a peace activist (for which they were initially excommunicated), and the two had three children. They set up a commune, Jonah House, dedicated to peace activism. Both continued their peace activism.

Activists like these could be classed as "confessors", but I think it is helpful to have a separate category for them. Like the martyrs and confessors, they witness to the cost of discipleship and show that the gospel is not equivalent to conventional petit bourgeois piety. This ought to be obvious from any reading of the Gospels, but it is painfully easy to forget it, and to confuse Christian discipleship with allegiance to national or other cultural flags.

Religious

There are well over thirty Religious of various kinds commemorated in the Common Worship calendar. As Dogberry remarks, "comparisons are odorous", but I wonder whether, amongst this group, two should be given festivals (whereas George certainly should not). These are Benedict and Francis, who express paradigmatic forms of discipleship in Western Christianity in ways which are especially important for addressing the global emergency.

Benedict is known principally through his rule and the community he founded. The account of him in the Dialogues of Gregory the Great follows the conventional account of the holy man. This is the first difference from Francis, who attracted biographers from the very beginning. We know that he was born about 480, that he was called to an ascetic life, and after experiments with various monastic communities formed a community on Monte Cassino. Gregory says Benedict wrote a monastic rule "notable for its discernment and his clarity of language". This rule was based on an earlier and much longer rule known as "the rule of the Master" and also drew on a tradition of Christian monasticism by then already 200 years old. In this tradition, the monastery takes the place of the desert, and the abbot is the spiritual father whose task is to train others and lead them to salvation. The capital virtues of the monk are obedience, silence and humility. As understood by its contemporary practitioners the rule manifests "a certain liberalism and humanism". Human weakness, even in the abbot, is recognized and accommodated. The monastery is a "fraternal communion in love". It shows "respect for persons and for the mystery of freedom" (Fry 1981: 93). The monk's time is divided between common prayer, the *opus Dei*, seven prayer times during the day, and the night office; four hours of study and meditation so that the Word of G-d would shape the whole of the monk's inner psychology and outward activity; and finally manual labour, in which the monks would provide their own food, and have surplus for the poor, for travellers and for guests. This latter had an incalculable effect on Europe for through it much marginal land was brought into cultivation, and the work of the monks also spread into hospital care and the development of herbal remedies and medicine. The need to work with your hands profoundly challenged the Platonic and aristocratic disdain for manual labour and the privileging of the intellectual over the bodily. The late medieval honouring of agricultural work (in Piers Plowman, for example) probably derives from here. This threefold pattern has provided a model for much Christian thinking on how the life of discipleship should be structured, even if the vast majority of people have no wish for a monastic life. Puritanism had its own form of *lectio* and meditation and a profound respect for craft work and "honest toil". The work ethic probably owed something to it and did not derive just from the need to prove that you were saved, as Weber thought. Today "new monasticism" still looks to the threefold pattern, and the discipline of the monastery is properly recognized as a challenge to the consumerism which underlies so much of global warming.

The Benedictine unity of work and prayer, the discipline of study, the rule of hospitality—vital today in a world of refugees, where borders are increasingly policed and guarded—all speak to a world in the grip of the global emergency. In 1981, Alasdair MacIntyre spoke of "the construction of local forms of community within which civility and the intellectual and moral life can be sustained through the new dark ages which are already upon us". He looked back to the collapse of the Roman empire in the fifth century when

> men and women of good will turned aside from the task of shoring up the Roman imperium and ceased to identify the continuation of civility and moral community with the maintenance of that imperium. What they set themselves to achieve instead—often not recognizing fully what they were doing—was the construction of new forms of community within which the moral life could be sustained so that both morality and civility might survive the coming age of barbarism and darkness . . . What matters at this stage is the construction of local forms of community within which civility and the intellectual and moral life can be sustained through the new dark ages which are already upon us. And if the tradition of the virtues was able to survive the horrors of the last dark ages, we are not entirely without grounds for hope (MacIntyre 1985: 263).

We need, he said, a new and doubtless very different St Benedict. Three years later, and certainly completely independently, the German Green thinker Rudolf Bahro suggested that to respond to the ecological crisis we need a new Benedictine order which will come into being by people relating to G-d. Benedict, then, is one of the patron saints of the movement to respond to the global emergency with hope. The other, as we have already seen, is Francis, named as the patron saint of ecology by John Paul II.

Francis founded his Order in 1210, at the age of about twenty-eight (the year of his birth is either 1181 or 1182), and died in 1226. The first life of Francis was written by Thomas of Celano, at the wish of the Pope, within two years of his death, in 1228. A *Life* by Bonaventure, and the collection of stories we know as the *Fioretti*, not written up until the end of the following century, but probably containing early material, followed. The nineteenth and twentieth centuries saw innumerable further "Lives". With the exception of the Virgin Mary, Francis is the most popular saint in Western Christendom and has attracted a vast mass of sentimental commentary. Beneath this sentiment is an awareness that Francis caught and embodied something of both the challenge but also the freedom and joy of the gospel.

Francis' first rule was simply the verses from the commissioning of the disciples in Matthew 10, which he heard read as the Gospel at Mass. The passage spoke of cleansing lepers and preaching the nearness of the kingdom. Francis had already embraced a leper, the lowest and most disgusting person in medieval society. It went on "Take no gold, or silver, or copper in your belts, no bag for your journey, or two tunics, or sandals, or a staff; for labourers deserve their food." It then spoke of the greeting of peace (Matthew 10:7–13). Francis received this as a command and immediately began preaching repentance and, according to his first biographer, "Whensoever he preached, before setting forth G-d's word to the congregation he besought peace, saying, 'The Lord give you peace.' Peace did he ever most devoutly proclaim to men and women, to those he met and those he overtook."

Francis shared with all the monastic orders both an ascetic vision of Christian discipleship and a vocation to pray and meditate on Scripture, and he also wanted his brethren to work for their living if they were able. They formed a community, but, in contrast to the monastic vocation, Francis wanted to preach on the highways and byways, and eventually took himself off to Palestine to preach to the Muslim ruler Melek-al-kamil and to try and put an end to the crusades. At the heart of Francis' account of discipleship were four things: first, a passionate Christ mysticism which finally issued in the stigmata. Whatever ego Francis may have had was completely replaced by his love of the figure of Christ. Thomas of Celano says: "The brothers who lived together with him know with what gentleness and tenderness, each and every day, he spoke of Jesus. His mouth spoke from the fullness of his heart, the fountain of illuminated love that filled his whole being bubbling forth" (Celano 2000: 114). This included, second, an understanding of the humility of G-d, which the disciple had to follow. This lay behind his focus on the nativity stories and his use of the crib as a teaching aid: the miracle of the G-d who became a helpless child enraptured him—and caught the imagination of

Western Christendom. What made him drunk with love and compassion for Christ is the fact that G-d made G-dself the brother of all people in poverty and humility. Humility, therefore, was an essential characteristic of the Franciscan vocation. The brothers were the Fratres Minores, the little brothers, who showed their humility by their love of lepers and their identification with the poor—the Franciscan tunic was what an Umbrian shepherd might have worn. The First Rule of 1221 said the little brothers should "feel satisfied to be among the common and rejected people, the poor and the weak, the sick, the lepers and the beggars of the street".

Third, Francis wanted absolute poverty—he wanted nothing to do with money which he described as "a demon and a poisonous serpent". Leonardo Boff defines poverty as a refusal of the will to power:

> Possession is what engenders the obstacles to communication between human beings themselves and between persons and things... The more radical the poverty, the closer the individual comes to reality, and the easier it is to commune with all things, respecting and reverencing their differences and distinctions (Boff 1982: 39).

The sentimental vision of Francis cannot withstand even a momentary inspection of the original Lives, for Francis was a rigorous ascetic, and wanted the same from his brethren. He had compassion, but he knew that discipleship meant discipline. Francis wanted to meet the real world with the realism of the gospel, which does not take sin and evil lightly. At the same time all the early biographies, and particularly the *Cantico della creatura*, show an overflowing and infectious love for creation—hence the stories about Francis preaching to the birds and about Francis and the wolf (which may recycle a much earlier story about the proto-monk, Antony). Hence, alongside poverty and humility, joy is an essential characteristic of the Franciscan vocation.

One of Francis' contemporary brethren, Leonardo Boff (shamefully silenced by Cardinal Ratzinger—Boff is now no longer a member of the Order), understands Francis as constituting a response to a world in crisis, a crisis driven primarily by the drive to acquire wealth. Francis, he thinks, was driven by eros, which he defines as that force which with enthusiasm, joy and passion makes us search for union with others, the world, our vocation and with G-d. His asceticism was a result of his channelling of eros, not his denying it. His avowal of poverty was not a glorification of poverty in itself. It is the disavowal of all forms of domination, including the technological domination which currently threatens the planet. As the lack of means to produce and reproduce life with a minimum of human dignity, poverty is "the most painful and bloody wound in the history of humanity" (Boff 1982: 49). In identifying with the outcasts of society Francis seeks to create a church of the poor in order to raise all to fullness of life. His adoption of poverty was the precursor of the preferential option for the poor. His rejection of money follows Jesus' warning against trying to combine the service of G-d and of Mammon. It is a challenge to the Church to understand that salvation cannot be achieved through money, and that if humanity is to survive, a completely new monetary order, a different way of calculating our debts to each other, has to be worked out (see Gorringe 2018: Chapter 7). The joy in creation which he manifests is the driving force for all those who wish to put a spoke in the wheel of predatory capital before it destroys the home which has been gifted to us.

As with Benedict, very few people, and indeed not even his own Order, are able to live with his absolute renunciation of possessions and refusal to have anything to do with money, but Francis' total vision of the gospel caught people from the very beginning. His remodelling as the patron saint of eco-warriors is just the latest manifestation of this attraction. "His image is in harmony with popular culture almost everywhere" (Boff 1982: 115). As with Benedict, the repudiation of money speaks to a society destroying itself through its pursuit of growth and its idolatry of the commodity. People may not be able to dispossess themselves as far as Francis did, but they see the direction nevertheless. They also know that though there is a way of the cross in the Gospels, it is somehow also a manifestation of joy, and that in understanding and living this Francis offers a supremely powerful hermeneutic of the gospel.

Teachers

There are at least twenty-seven teachers commemorated in Common Worship, more if we count those listed as Reformers. Teachers make a modest and not unimportant contribution to the life of the Church. Their job is to elucidate the gospel for their generation, in conversation with those who have gone before them. They share with historians the vocation to struggle for the truth, but, as with historians, this becomes problematic when the struggle becomes violently partisan, a mark of theological work on both sides in the Reformation dispute. The list is very uneven, and giants like Augustine and Aquinas stand alongside relative minnows like F. D. Maurice.

I have three suggestions concerning those who might be added to the list. Doubtless a good lapse of time needs to pass before anyone is added to it; perhaps it needs to be more than a century. But at more than half a century it seems to me we should acknowledge Karl Barth as one of the great teachers of the universal church. Appropriately his magnum opus is a torso, for no one, no matter how great, can address adequately the divine mystery witnessed to by Scripture. Everyone has blind spots, and can sometimes be downright wrong-headed, and this includes Barth. Why should he be included? First because he is, as *Der Spiegel* called him, a "joyful partisan of the good G-d". Joy and humour are, in my experience, more characteristic of the *Church Dogmatics* than they are of any other major work of theology. This is primarily a resurrection joy, but it is a joy which catches the humour of the Scriptures themselves, which Christian piety has often, doubtless prompted by the devil, entombed in black. Barth is pugnacious, especially in his earlier work, but in the small print of the *Dogmatics* he goes to great lengths to be fair to, and to understand, his opponents (the discussion with Pseudo Dionysus and Aquinas in the chapter on angels is a good example). At his best, Barth has an extraordinary capacity to rethink dogmatics from the ground up, above all in the doctrine of election—rescued from the misery of Calvinist double predestination and made a doctrine of grace—and in the doctrine of G-d, where all the old accounts of the "attributes" of G-d are melted down and rethought, leading us, later, to his account of the humanity of G-d. The canon in any discipline—literature, poetry, works of history and so forth—establishes itself over time and time will tell. I believe, though, that Barth should be honoured as one of the great teachers.

Secondly, I want to propose that some Jewish teachers be included in the list. Well, of course, all of our Scriptures are about Jews and by far the majority are written by Jews, but since "the parting of the ways" Jewish teachers have not been honoured. In the twentieth century, however, Martin Buber, first of all, then Abraham Heschel, and, on a more recherché level, Franz Rosenzweig and Emmanuel Levinas, have all been teachers of the Church. Jews and Christians are separated brethren. The history of Christian anti-Semitism makes the separation dark beyond belief but, just as with Jacob and Esau, the fact of brotherhood cannot be undone. Buber spoke of Jesus as "a brother, but very strange". Jacob Taubes said something very similar about Paul and made sure that courses on Paul were taught at the Hebrew University. Buber's *I and Thou* has been a seminal document not just for philosophers, not just for Jews, but for Christian theology as a whole. Whether we like it or not, he is a teacher of the Church. The same goes for Heschel, a friend and ally of Philip Berrigan in his peace campaigning. Heschel's work on the pathos of G-d has contributed to the theology of the Crucified G-d elaborated by Moltmann. To recognize them as teachers will not heal the breach between communities, but it will at least signal that the Jewish voice continues to be heard, not as the voice of an enemy or outsider, but as the voice of those who, alongside Jesus of Nazareth, worship the G-d of Abraham, Isaac and Jacob.

Spiritual guides

Common Worship identifies seven or eight people as spiritual guides. The list includes Seraphim of Sarov, Richard Rolle, William Law, Julian of Norwich, Philip Neri, Evelyn Underhill, the Curé D'Ars and John Bunyan. Of course many people have found Augustine, or Luther or Benedict or Francis, spiritual guides. Here I wish to ask whether, for all sorts of reasons, Simone Weil should not imperatively be added to this list. Weil has been important to an extraordinarily diverse group of people, from Albert Camus to Pope Paul VI, and this says something about the breadth of her experience, thought and interests. She died when she was thirty-four, with a verdict of suicide by self-starvation, but what she achieved is extraordinary. Like Benedict, she insisted on, and practised, manual labour; like Francis, she identified with the poorest and most despised in society; intellectually, although her works are fragmentary, she can hold her own with Augustine or Aquinas; she was a dedicated anti-colonialist and political activist, and understood Marxist thought from the inside; she was a mystic in the great tradition, forced to her knees in the Porziuncula, taken possession of by Christ whilst reading George Herbert in a Benedictine abbey. All this makes her a unique spiritual guide. In this capacity, the most familiar form of her writings is the collection of letters and essays published as *Attente de Dieu* in 1950 (*Waiting on God*, 1951), and it is only this to which I will refer.

After finishing her university studies, Weil taught in a *lycée*; working in factories or on farms she tried also to offer teaching for her fellow workers. In *Waiting on God*, we find an essay called "Reflections on the Right Use of School Studies with a View to the Love of G-d". It begins, "The Key to a Christian conception of studies is the realization that prayer consists in attention." She noticed that when she told her students to "pay attention", they screwed up their brows "in a kind of muscular effort". That, she said, is not attention. Attention (*l'attention*), properly understood, "consists of suspending our thought, leaving it detached, empty and ready to be penetrated by the object . . . our thought should be empty, waiting (*attente*), not seeking anything, but ready to receive in its naked truth the object which is to penetrate it" (Weil 1951: 56). Attention is a self-emptying which allows G-d to take possession of us. Both the love of G-d and the love of neighbour have this attention as their substance. Intercessory prayer is the turning of this attention to a person or a situation who or which needs G-d's healing. Moreover (in a doctrine later taken up by Iris Murdoch), "every time we really concentrate our attention, we destroy the evil in ourselves. If we concentrate with this attention, she said, a quarter of an hour of attention is better than a great many good works."

In a later essay sent to her friend, the Catholic priest Henri Perrin (*Forms of the Implicit Love of G-d*), she reflects on this attention as

constituting the love of G-d in relation to our neighbour, the order of
the world, and religious practices. With regard to the latter, she believed
that "attention animated by desire is the whole foundation of religious
practices", an attention opposed by "the mediocre parts of the soul" which
disguise G-d in all sorts of false comforts.

In "The Love of G-d and affliction [*malheur*]", Weil turns her attention
to extreme human suffering. *Malheur* is what Weil experienced in her
factory work, being ground down, the mindnumbingness of the work, the
sense of being an object or tool (which Marx spoke of as "alienation"),
systematic humiliation. It is not in the first instance what the English
word would suggest, namely an incapacitating illness (though Weil had
this as well—tuberculosis—and it was probably this which really killed
her). Affliction is all this *plus* physical pain. She wrote:

> The great enigma of human life is not suffering but affliction. It is
> not surprising that the innocent are killed, tortured, driven from
> their country, made destitute or reduced to slavery, imprisoned
> in camps or cells . . . It is not surprising either that disease is the
> cause of long sufferings, which paralyse life and make it into an
> image of death . . . But it is surprising that G-d should have given
> affliction the power to seize the very souls of the innocent and
> to take possession of them as their sovereign lord. At the very
> best, he who is branded by affliction will only keep half his soul
> (Weil 1951: 65).

Weil understands affliction as what Christ experienced on the cross. As
we have seen, she understands Trinitarian love through affliction. In
affliction, the infinite distance which separates G-d from the creature is
concentrated into one point to pierce the soul in its centre. She writes:

> He whose soul remains ever turned in the direction of G-d while
> the nail [of affliction] pierces it finds himself nailed on to the very
> centre of the universe . . . In this marvellous dimension, the soul,
> without leaving the place and the instant where the body to which
> it is united is situated, can cross the totality of space and time and
> come into the very presence of G-d. It is at the intersection of

creation and its Creator. This point of intersection is the point of intersection of the branches of the Cross (Weil 1951: 78).

One can see why some critics have understood this (like a great deal of Christian teaching) as a form of intense masochism. Iris Murdoch, again, has taken up this theme. But Weil is wrestling with the central paradox of Christianity, that G-d is encountered in the cross. More than most of the spiritual guides currently commemorated in the calendar, she helps us to make some sense of this in the context of the world in which we live, and in the context of the lives which most people on the planet have, i.e. lives of poverty and toil.

Poets

In Common Worship, at least six poets are remembered—more if we include John of the Cross. George Herbert gets a lesser festival, John Donne and Christina Rossetti a commemoration, Thomas Traherne, Geoffrey Studdert Kennedy and John Keble are also mentioned. Only two of these poets, both priests, are absolutely of the first rank, and why Herbert should get a lesser festival and Donne not is (in a strictly non-Pauline sense) a mystery. However, the prior question is, why might poets have a place in a church calendar?

In the preface to the first volume of Irina Ratushinkaya's poetry published in the West is a protest written by a friend, and circulated in samizdat at the time. The friend recalls the other poets murdered, imprisoned or exiled in Russia. The piece goes on:

> Why is our poetry time and again the subject of such frenzied attacks? A true poet cannot lie. To be silent, or to be reluctant to see the world in which one lives in its true colours—that is also a lie! The calling of a poet is to speak the truth, even though it may be a subjective truth . . . I believe that for a poet in our country to be arrested is a compliment. A peculiar form of recognition for his services to the motherland (Ratushinskaya 1986: 27–8).

Writing from an African American experience Audre Lorde contrasted poetry as a vehicle of ideas with poetry as an expression of feeling. It was not, she said, sterile word play. She went on:

> poetry is not a luxury. It is a vital necessity of our existence. It forms the quality of the light within which we predicate our hopes and dreams toward survival and change, first made into language, then into idea, then into more tangible action. Poetry is the way we help give name to the nameless so it can be thought. The farthest external horizons of our hopes and fears are cobbled by our poems, carved from the rock experiences of our daily lives (Lorde 1984: 37).

Lorde was speaking specifically about the experience of African American women and contrasting it with the experience and views of white men. It seems to me, however, that Ratushinskaya would agree with her, and moreover that what she says is true of all great poetry, as opposed to second-rate poetry.

Why do we read poetry? Why can it move us to tears? What is it which distinguishes great from second-rate poetry? Simone Weil thought that true works of art caught the beauty of the world: "G-d has inspired every first-rate work of art, though its subject may be utterly and entirely secular; he has not inspired any of the others." In relation to poetry, there has to be a necessity as to why this word is used, and not another. "In the case of a really beautiful poem the only answer is that the word is there because it is suitable that it should be . . . The poem is beautiful, that is to say the reader does not wish it other than it is" (Weil 1951:1 12; this is probably the response to critics of the *Four Quartets*).

Great poetry expresses what we know in our hearts as well as our minds to be true. What distinguishes it as poetry, as opposed to prose, is that it expresses the truth with an inner music and with a perception sharper and keener than is available to those of us who are not poets. Poets help us to see the world. Scripture is full of poetry. Not just the Psalms and the Song of Songs, but many of the oracles in the prophets, the Song of Miriam in Exodus, the Prologue to John's Gospel, and Paul's ecstatic celebration of agape in 1 Corinthians 13. The poet helps us to see and to say what we cannot quite see for ourselves and have never been able to express. As such it has an affinity with revelation. Sometimes it is revelation.

For this reason, I think it is right that poets find a small corner, a poets' corner, in the Christian calendar. The choices of Common Worship, however, are odd. Donne and Herbert, of course. No Milton? No Blake? Goodness! Traherne, another priest, and a witness alongside Francis to the glory of G-d as experienced in creation, should of course be there, but so should Henry Vaughan. And coming to the twentieth century, and the recent past, in T. S. Eliot, Edwin Muir and R. S. Thomas we have some of the greatest poets in the language (though I can imagine that Lorde might regard Eliot as "sterile wordplay"). One of them happens to have been a priest. All of them help us to explore and understand our faith. And they are poets, not "religious" poets. They are poets who happen to be Christians, and believers.

Here I depart from my script in order to say a word about Shakespeare. I do not for a moment propose that he should be included in the calendar, but I note that Alan Ecclestone, who was an important spiritual guide to many in the second half of the twentieth century, thought that if our first language was English, we should read Shakespeare through once a year! In the *Church Dogmatics* Barth has a famous encomium on Mozart who, though not a particularly active Christian, who led what appeared to be on all accounts a rather frivolous existence, "knew something about creation in its total goodness that neither the real fathers of the Church nor our Reformers, neither the orthodox nor the Liberals, neither the exponents of natural theology nor those heavily armed with the 'Word of G-d' . . . either know or can express and maintain as he did" (Barth 1960: 298). This does not apply directly to Shakespeare, but there is an analogy. Despite the labours of many armies of scholars, we still know very little about him. He disappears behind his characters and his verse. No outrageous ego forces itself upon us (as it does with Goethe). He has little Latin and less Greek but appears to have a universal knowledge of the human heart and an extraordinarily wide acquaintance with the humanist interests of his day. He alludes to, or cites, Scripture in every play, from several different translations, and knows the Homilies of the Book of Common Prayer, but he never preaches. His themes include sin, grace, reconciliation, the happy fault, forgiveness, providence, kenosis, hell and paradise, but he cannot be placed on any doctrinal spectrum. His account of the human condition in its tragedy and comedy, its nobility, its self-delusion, and its capacity for wickedness, takes us strangely close to the gospel. "The glory of G-d is a living human being," said Irenaeus. This living human being is not sketched only in Scripture or indeed even above all in Scripture. I have taken the meaning of history to be hominization, but it is possible, reading Scripture, to come away with an account in which much of the glory and splendour of humanity is drained away. Thus Aquinas, following Chrysostom, could believe that the fact that Jesus "never laughed" was a proof of his divinity. But comedy, laughter, is certainly part of our humanness and it is hard to conceive of redemption without it, though generations of theologians have had a pretty good try. Where do Bottom, Dogberry, Benedict and Beatrice fit in with humanization? More problematically, where does Falstaff fit in? He is, after all, dissolute, a coward, a compulsive liar—he does not instantiate one of the virtues Paul enumerates. Hazlitt said that he had no malice, but the rag-bag group of soldiers he collected for Hal are almost all killed ("there's not three of my hundred and fifty left alive, and they are for the town's end to beg during life"), which suggests the callousness of a World War I general. "But Falstaff," said Dr Johnson, a moralist, "unimitated, unimitable Falstaff, how shall I describe thee? . . . the man thus corrupt, thus despicable, makes himself necessary to the prince that despises him, by the most pleasing of all qualities, perpetual gaiety, by an unfailing power of exciting laughter, which is the more freely indulged as his wit is not of the splendid or ambitious kind but consists in easy escapes and sallies of levity, which makes sport but raise no envy". The world he represents is firmly put in its place ("I know you not, old man"), but the cheek, the wit and the debunking of the honour code win our affection. Comedy is something we cannot live without and cannot imagine heaven without. Alongside this is romantic, or erotic, love. Shakespeare affectionately sends up its foibles but all the same he crowns most of his comedies with marriage. He knows, as we know, how fragile and self-deceiving erotic love is, but he also recognizes, and celebrates, the way in which it gives us glimpses of transcendence. Dante was right, after all, to include it in the *Divina Commedia*.

To say this is not to make Shakespeare, or any other artist, a mediator of revelation. It is to insist, however, that to trace the highest artistic inspiration in some respect to the Holy Spirit is not mistaken, and to acknowledge that we learn about the meaning of humanness not just in Scripture but in creation which is, in its own way, touched by G-d.

Redeeming the time

The author of Ephesians (if not Paul) writes: "Be careful how you live, not as unwise but as wise, redeeming the time (*exagorazomenoi ton kairon*), because the days are evil" (Ephesians 5:16; cf. Colossians 4:5) (The NRSV has "making the most of the time", but the verb is *exagorazo*, to redeem, or ransom, especially of slaves).

Let me begin with the last phrase, "because the days are evil". In Part 2, I mentioned the four contemporary horsemen of the apocalypse. One of the horsemen is overpopulation, and I noted that there are voices which think a peaceful reduction of world population may be beginning. That is hopeful but other indicators are much more problematic. The Stockholm Resilience Centre identifies nine "planetary boundaries"—climate change; freshwater use; land use change; nitrogen and phosphorus cycles; ocean acidification; biodiversity loss; ozone depletion; atmospheric aerosol loading; and chemical pollution. Nearly all these boundaries have been transgressed, and the Stockholm group are deeply concerned about the capacity of the earth to sustain life if current human impacts continue. They argue that the Holocene era, which began about 11,700 years ago, and has been the background to human history as we know it, has been succeeded by the Anthropocene, a historical phase in which human beings and their demands are at the centre. This phase is associated with major mechanization of production, huge rises in population, and massive increases in energy consumption both overall and per capita. For the past seventy years, the lifestyle of the wealthy members of US society has been projected as what is humanly desirable but, with 5 per cent of world population, the United States (which has plenty of very poor people, not all economic migrants) accounts for 22 per cent of world energy consumption and one quarter of emissions. As economists like Herman Daly have been insisting for years, this lifestyle cannot possibly be generalized.

At the United Kingdom's Tyndall Centre near Manchester, Professor Kevin Anderson has been arguing for more than a decade that governments around the world have vastly underestimated the seriousness of the response needed. Responding to Prime Minister Boris Johnson's Green Energy plan in November 2020, he noted that for a fair chance of staying below 2°C, developed countries, including the UK, must bring about immediate and deep cuts in emissions from all sectors. That is to say, cuts of 10 to 15 per cent year on year and with immediate effect. Elsewhere he has argued that those who argue that a 2° future is possible have "a magician's view of time and a linear view of problems". 4° of warming, which is possible if action is not taken, is incompatible with the continuance of an equitable and civilized global community.

That transgression of boundaries is not being addressed is due primarily, first to the power of corporations, which control more than half of the global market in key areas, and second to the power they in turn exercise on governments of all stripes. We are stuck, Naomi Klein comments, because the actions that would give us the best chance of averting catastrophe—and would benefit the vast majority—are extremely threatening to an elite minority that has a stranglehold over our economy, our political process and most of our major media outlets (Klein 2014: 18). Many governments around the world are led by out-and-out climate change deniers—Brazil, Australia and until early 2021 the United States; we have xenophobic populations determined to keep refugees out; countries run by criminal gangs, to use Augustine's phrase, and a determination just about everywhere to put No. 1 first. The deniers, says Klein, won the battle over which values would govern our societies. The central lie is that we are nothing but selfish, greedy, self-gratification machines (Klein 2014: 62).

This should not surprise us. As Karl Barth wrote after World War II, the Church "knows human beings as sinners, that is, as beings who are always on the point of opening the sluices through which, if they were not checked on time, chaos and nothingness would break in and bring human time to an end" (Barth 1964: 20).

I think, then, that we can agree with the author of Ephesians that "the times are evil". Just because that is the case, he says, you must live "redeeming the time"—that is, bringing it out of bondage. The nature of this bondage is clear. Ultimately it turns on Jesus' perception that it is impossible to serve both G-d and Mammon (Matthew 6:24). Discipleship is concerned with the exodus from this bondage and liturgical formation is designed to help us to do that.

We have seen in Part 2, and in the section on Francis above, that the starting point of Christian discipleship is joy and gratitude. Our fundamental action as a worshipping community is saying thank you (Eucharist). So redeeming the time begins with praise.

At the same time, when Jesus begins his ministry, he issues a call to repent. 1 Peter reminds us that judgement begins with the house of G-d (1 Peter 4:17), so our first task is to learn what repentance in the face of the global emergency means for us, first of all as Church and then, in that context, as individual Christians. It means learning as a community to accept our responsibility for what is happening and doing something about it, so it affects our lifestyle, individually and corporately. It affects our understanding and use of money as well as of energy, both individually and corporately. It puts awkward questions both to the Vatican bank and to the Church Commissioners. It goes beyond charitable aid to the needy and supporting fair trade (though both are necessary). In truth, the "turn about" (*metanoia*) which is repentance bears on every aspect of our life, from farming to politics to gender relations.

Jesus calls us (and all people) to repentance, but he then calls those of us who seek to be disciples to witness to the incoming rule of G-d. The first task here is *discernment*: right the way through Scripture there is the question of distinguishing true from false witness. The prophetic criterion for distinguishing the two was to see which involved righteousness and specifically caring for the poor. We saw several examples of this in Part 2. In the parable we know as "the sheep and the goats", Jesus endorsed this criterion. The task of discernment falls not just on each disciple but on the Church as a whole, and it can issue in confession, as it did at Barmen in 1934 and in the Ash Wednesday declaration in 2012. The first warns us that such discernment often brings division and conflict *within the Church*; the second warns us that denial may not necessarily take the form of outright opposition but simply of an unwillingness to take on anything which will challenge our comfort zone, which at bottom is a rejection of the G-d of life for an idea of G-d as a giant baby's dummy, lulling us to sleep and crying "peace, peace" when there is no peace (Jeremiah 6:14; 8:11).

Discernment means identifying and challenging the kingdom of lies, which does not so much surround us as constitute the atmosphere we breathe: all the assurances with which we are bombarded day by day by the press, social media, governments and corporations that only big money, Mammon, and its offshoot, technology, will save us. The prophets of our own day are often, as we would expect, outsiders, and not very often Christians, but they all witness to the need for justice for people and planet and call out collusion between government and big money. They include climate scientists like Kevin Anderson and James Hansen, journalists and writers like Naomi Klein and George Monbiot, economists like Herman Daly and Kate Raworth, farmers like Wendell Berry and Wes Hall, even some theologians like Franz Hinkelammert, Ulrich Duchrow and Ched Myers.

Following discernment comes witness to G-d's rule, which affects our understanding of what Augustine called the relation of the *civitas Dei* and the *civitas terrena*. We are members of both but in virtue of our membership of the first our loyalty to the second cannot be absolute and will often be critical. The tiny minority which controls the global economy demonizes every attempt both to witness to and work for the world made otherwise our Scriptures call for. We learn the consequences of this from the martyrs, confessors and activists we celebrate and learn from. There is a nice story about Martin Niemöller, another Lutheran pastor who spent the war in concentration camps and barely escaped with his life. Before being shipped off to Sachsenhausen, he was kept in prison in Berlin and was visited by the prison chaplain. "My brother," said the chaplain, "why are you in prison?" To which Niemöller replied: "My brother, why are you *not* in prison!" This story applies to all of us who are not actively taking up the struggle for a world made otherwise.

Our witness, in word and deed, concerns our sense of the inestimable gift we have in creation and therefore of our need to love and cherish it. Loving and cherishing is worked out in farming, in politics and in economy as well as in social life. These are not side issues but central to faith. As Kate Raworth reminds us, cherishing creation involves at the very same time caring for our neighbour. Again that is not simply a matter of getting on with those around us, but involves our care and concern for refugees and for all the "undocumented" amongst whom Jesus was reckoned. It means taking seriously the understanding of *ekklesia* as the First International. Part of that is understanding the role of churches as "cities of refuge" (Joshua 20:1–8)—places to welcome and shelter the refugee.

All this should be obvious, but it seems we have often shrunk our understanding of discipleship to churchgoing, and that of a very undemanding, culturally assimilated, kind. Some critics of liberation theology were quick to hurl the accusation of "Pelagianism", but this is a very disingenuous move. It forgets that faith is, as Luther put it, "a living, busy, active, mighty thing" and that its concern is the kingdom of G-d for which we pray daily. If we allow ourselves to be formed by the Scriptures we encounter in celebrating the liturgical year, I suggest, that will naturally follow. Exactly like the generation the Deuteronomists addressed, we stand before two ways, a way of life and a way of death, only the threat which faces us is vastly greater, and the odds against us are greater. In the greatest sobriety, and fully aware of the immense difficulty, all we can do is live by the same words the writer of Ephesians addressed to his recipients (and if it truly went to Ephesus, they were part of a glittering, highly civilized, but money-driven centre). He noted that we were not up against common or garden foes but "the rulers . . . the authorities . . . the cosmic powers of this present darkness, against the spiritual forces of evil in the heavenly places" (Ephesians 6:12). This is the whole set of assumptions about what constitutes reality and common sense, the mindset which tells us that only money, violence and high-tech really count. Over against that set of assumptions he first of all set truth and a passion for justice (*dikaiosune*, v. 14). Second, exactly like Francis, he put non-violence, "the gospel of peace" (v. 15). The disciple is then armed with trust in the G-d of life and the word of G-d, which he speaks of as "the sword of the Spirit" (v. 17). It is the martyrs and confessors, sometimes also the poets, who show us not only how this counterwitness can prevail, but also at what cost.

Time, liturgy and discipleship

To be human is to be bounded by time but also, according to both Tenakh and Messianic Writings, to live in the hope of an existence with the source of all things ("G-d"), where all our contradictions, failures and cruelties are finally healed. If the Christian claims about incarnation are true, then time is significant and not, as some philosophies have suggested, *maya*, illusion, signifying nothing. We are invited by the Gospels to make sense of time through discipleship, living according to the vision of peace, justice, love and forgiveness that, following Torah and prophets, Jesus of Nazareth sketched out. The job of liturgy is to school us in that vision, but not as a never-ending course in ethics. Rather, it works by including us in a narrative and by inviting us to celebrate, both to feast and to fast, and sometimes to mourn. The so-called "liturgical year" gives us a structure for remembering and celebrating the story which gives us our identity as Christians. The dazzling perception of Paul was that all humans have Abraham as their father, that the work of redemption cannot be defined in terms of ethnicity. His sense of being called to be an apostle, one who is sent (Romans 1:1), was not about founding a new religion, but about sharing a vision of the way to human solidarity, so that all could be fully human because all were fully human. Jakob Taubes said that Paul's key word was "all"—all human beings were included—but key words were also love, gift, forgiveness, peace, freedom. How shocking that this vision, which he wanted to share with anyone who was ready to hear, should become the possession of small and rabid groups ready to burn each other in disagreement and to persecute those who followed their own way. When this happened, "Christianity" (what an idea!) got shunted onto a siding which led nowhere. The same has happened (for different reasons) with modern-day Zionism. At the same time, the founding narratives remained for both Israel and Church, always pointing the way back from the siding to the main track, to the gracious vision of redemption. The *lectio divina*, the reading, hearing and celebrating of the narrative day by day and week by week, invites us back to this vision, constantly challenging the ways in which we seek to colonize and appropriate it. This process is the pedagogy of the Spirit, fashioning redemption, making sense of time.

Sources

Times and seasons

The dawn of time

Butterfield, H. Christianity and History (London: G. Bell and Sons Ltd., 1940).

Dawkins, R., *The Ancestor's Tale: A Pilgrimage to the Dawn of Evolution* (Houghton, MI: Mifflin Harcourt, 2005).

Hawking, S., *A Brief History of Time* (New York, NY: Bantam Doubleday, 1989).

Levin, H. L., *The Earth Through Time* (New Jersey, NJ: John Wiley, 2010).

Morley, I., "Conceptualising quantification before settlement", in Morley, I. and Renfrew, C. (eds), *The Archaeology of Measurement: Comprehending Heaven, Earth and Time in Ancient Societies* (Cambridge: Cambridge University Press, 2010): 7–18.

Penrose, R., *Cycles of Time: An Extraordinary New View of the Universe* (London: Bodley Head, 2010).

The sense of time

The day

Adam, A., *The Liturgical Year: Its History & Its Meaning After the Reform of the Liturgy* (New York, NY: Pueblo, 1979).

Barth, K., *Church Dogmatics* III/1, tr. J. W. Edwards, O. Bussey and H. Knight (Edinburgh: T. &T . Clark, 1958): 117–33.

Bede, *The Reckoning of Time*, tr. with Introduction, Commentary and Notes by Faith Wallis (Liverpool: Liverpool University Press, 1999): 21–4.

De Vaux, R., *Ancient Israel: Its Life and Institutions* (London: Darton, Longman and Todd, 1961): 180–3.

De Vries, S., *Yesterday, Today and Tomorrow: Time and History in the Old Testament* (London: SPCK, 1975): passim but esp. 344ff.

Koch, K., *The Prophets*, two vols, tr. Margaret Kohl (London: SCM Press, 1982).

von Rad, G., *Old Testament Theology*, vol. 2 (Edinburgh: Oliver and Boyd, 1965): 119–25.

Months and seasons

Bede, *The Reckoning of Time*: 41–54.

Chambers, E. K., *The Medieval Stage*, two vols (Oxford: Oxford University Press, 1903).

De Vaux, *Ancient Israel*: 183–6.

Ordering time

The week

Adam, *The Liturgical Year*.

Bede, *The Reckoning of Time*: 32–41.

Jakobsen, T., *The Treasures of Darkness: A History of Mesopotamian Religion* (New Haven, CT: Yale University Press, 1976).

De Vaux, *Ancient Israel*: 186–8.

Wielenga, B., *Biblical Perspectives on Labour* (Madurai: Tamilnadu Theological Seminary Press, 1982).

The Sabbath and Sunday

Carson, D. A. (ed.), *From Sabbath to Lord's Day: A Biblical, Historical and Theological Investigation* (Grand Rapids, MI: Zondervan, 1982).

Heschel, A., *The Sabbath* (New York, NY: Farrar, Strauss and Giroux, 2005).

Moltmann, J., *God in Creation: A New Theology of Creation and the Spirit of God*, tr. Margaret Kohl (London: SCM Press, 1985): Chapter 11.

Schaff, P., *History of the Christian Church: Vol. II: From Constantine the Great to Gregory the Great A.D. 311–600* (New York, NY: Charles Scribner, 1867).

De Vaux, *Ancient Israel*: 475–84.

Wirzba, N., *Living the Sabbath: Discovering the Rhythms of Rest and Delight* (Grand Rapids, MI: Brazos, 2006).

Hours

Brown, D., "The measurement of time and distance in the heavens above Mesopotamia", in Morley and Renfrew, *Archaeology of Measurement*:183–94.

Mumford, L., *Technics and Civilization* (London: Routledge, 1946): 12–18.

Nonnos, *Dionysiaca*, tr. W. H. D. Rouse, three vols (Cambridge, MA: Loeb, 1940).

How our calendar became

Bede, *Reckoning of Time*: Introduction.

Adam, *Liturgical Year*: Chapter 10.

Markus, R., *The End of Ancient Christianity* (Cambridge: Cambridge University Press, 1990).

Parker, R. A., *The Calendars of Ancient Egypt* (Chicago, IL: University of Chicago Press, 1950).

Scullard, H. H., *Festivals and Ceremonies of the Roman Republic* (New York, NY: Cornell University Press, 1981).

De Vaux, *Ancient Israel*: 170–83; 468–75; 484–515.

Reflecting on time

Augustine, *Confessions*, tr. H. Chadwick (Oxford: Oxford University Press, 1991).

Augustine, *The City of God*, tr. H. Bettenson (London: Penguin, 1972).

Baldovin, J., "The Liturgical Year: Calendar for a Just Community", in M. E. Johnson (ed.), *Between Memory and Hope: Readings on the Liturgical Year* (Collegeville, MN: Liturgical Press, 2000): 429–44.

Barr, J., *Biblical Words for Time* (London: SCM Press, 1969).

Barth, K., *Church Dogmatics* II/1, tr. G. W. Bromiley (Edinburgh: T. & T. Clark, 1957): 608–40.

Barth, K., *Church Dogmatics* III/2, tr. G. W. Bromiley, R. H. Fuller, Harold Knight and J. K. S. Reid (Edinburgh: T. & T. Clark, 1960): 511–53.

Barth, K., *Church Dogmatics* III/4, tr. A. T. Mackay, T. H. I. Parker, Harold Knight, Henry A. Kennedy and John Marks (Edinburgh: T. & T. Clark, 1961): 565–94.

Benjamin, W., *Illuminations* (London: Fontana, 1973).

Duchrow, U. and Hinkelammert, F., *Transcending Greedy Money: Interreligious Solidarity for Just Relations* (London: Palgrave, 2012).

Löwith, K., *Meaning in History: The Theological Implications of the Philosophy of History* (Chicago, IL: University of Chicago Press, 1949).

Markus, R. A., *Saeculum: History and Society in the Theology of Saint Augustine* (Cambridge: Cambridge University Press, 1970).

Metz, J. B., *Faith in History and Society: Towards a Practical Fundamental Theology*, tr. David Smith (London: Burns & Oates, 1980).

Pascal, *Pensees*, tr. A. J. Krailsheimer (Harmondsworth: Penguin, 1966).

Plato, *Timaeus*, tr. Desmond Lee (Harmondsworth: Penguin, 1965).

Pohier, J., *God in Fragments*, tr. John Bowden (London: SCM Press, 1985).

von Rad, G., *Wisdom in Israel* (London: SCM Press, 1972): Chapter 8.

Ricoeur, P., *Time and Narrative*, tr. Kathleen McLaughlin and David Pellauer (Chicago, IL: University of Chicago Press, 1984).

Scott, J. F. and Baltzly, A., *Readings in European History Since 1814* (New York, NY: F. S. Crofts & Co., 1934).

The Christian Year

The liturgical year and the lectionary

Baldovin, J., "The Liturgical Year: Calendar for a Just Community", in Johnson (ed.), *Between Memory and Hope*: 429–44.

Bakhtin, M., *Rabelais and his World*, tr. H. Iswolsky (Bloomington, IN: Indiana University Press, 1984).

Jungmann, J., *The Early Liturgy to the Time of Gregory the Great* (London: Darton, Longman and Todd, 1959), Chapter 21.

Rahner, K., *Theological Investigations*, vol. 14, tr. David Bourke (London: Darton, Longman and Todd, 1976).

Advent

Barth, *Church Dogmatics* III/2: 493–511.

Bradshaw, P. and Johnson, M., *The Origins of Feasts, Fasts and Seasons in Early Christianity* (London: SPCK, 2011): Chapter 18.

Connell, M., "The Origins and Evolution of Advent in the West", in Johnson (ed.), *Between Memory and Hope*: 349–71.

Gorringe, T. J., *Word and Silence is the Climate Emergency: God, Ekklesia and Christian Doctrine* (Lanham, MN: Fortress Academic, 2020): Chapter 3.

Jungmann, J., *The Early Liturgy to the Time of Gregory the Great* (London: Darton, Longman and Todd, 1959): Chapter 21.

Löwith, *Meaning in History*.

Moltmann, J., *Theology of Hope: On the Ground and the Implications of Christian Eschatology*, tr. James W. Leitch (London: SCM Press, 1965).

Myers, C., *Binding the Strong Man: A Political Reading of Mark's Story of Jesus* (Maryknoll, NY: Orbis, 1988): 338–42.

Myers, C. and Colwell, M., *Our God is Undocumented: Biblical Faith and Immigrant Justice* (Maryknoll, NY: Orbis, 2012).

Myers, C. and Enns, E., "Revolutionary Christmas Carols: Luke's Advent Story", <https://chedmyers.org/2015/12/16/121515recordedwebinaradventwomen2015/>, accessed 29 November 2021.

Christmas

Barth, K., *Church Dogmatics* IV/1, tr. G. W. Bromiley (Edinburgh: T. & T. Clark, 1956): 186.

Barth, K., *Church Dogmatics* IV/2, tr. G. W. Bromiley (Edinburgh: T. & T. Clark, 1958): 88, 89, 72.

Bradshaw and Johnson, *The Origins of Feasts, Fasts and Seasons in Early Christianity*: Chapter 15.

Dearmer, P., Williams, R. V. and Shaw, M., *The Oxford Book of Carols* (Oxford: Oxford University Press, 1928).

Gorringe, *Word and Silence*: Chapter 11.

Hengel, M., "Christological Titles in Early Christianity", in J. Charlesworth (ed.), *The Messiah* (Minneapolis, MN: Fortress, 1992): 425–48.

Jungmann, *Early Liturgy to the Time of Gregory the Great*: Chapter 21.

Moltmann, J., *The Way of Jesus Christ: Christology in Messianic Dimensions* (London: SCM Press, 1990).

Myers, M., *Baby Jesus, Refugee: Advent Meditations from Matthew's Story of the Birth of Jesus* (Oak View, CA: Bartimaeus Cooperative Ministries, 2004).

Myers and Colwell, *Our God is Undocumented*.

Myers and Enns, "Revolutionary Christmas Carols".

Schweizer, E., *The Good News according to Matthew* (London: SPCK, 1976).

Roll, S., "The Origins of Christmas: The State of the Question", in Johnson, *Between Memory and Hope*: 273–90.

Epiphany

Bradshaw and Johnson, *The Origins of Feasts, Fasts and Seasons in Early Christianity*: Chapters 16, 17.

Schweizer, *Matthew*.

Schweizer, E., *The Good News According to Mark* (London: SPCK, 1971).

Stendahl, K., *Paul amongst Jews and Gentiles* (London: SCM Press, 1977).

Ordinary time

Gorringe, *Word and Silence*: Chapter 11.

Moltmann, *Way of Jesus Christ*.

Sobrino, J., *Christology at the Crossroads* (London: SCM Press, 1978).

Lent

Bradshaw and Johnson, *Origins of Feasts, Fasts and Seasons in Early Christianity*: Chapters 10–13.

Johnson, M. E., "Preparation for Pascha? Lent in Christian Antiquity", in Johnson (ed.), *Between Memory and Hope*: 207–22.

Jungmann, *The Early Liturgy to the Time of Gregory the Great*.

Lehmann, P., *The Transfiguration of Politics* (London: SCM Press, 1974).

Myers, *Binding the Strong Man*.

Wilkinson, J., *Egeria's Travels* (London: SPCK, 1971).

Holy Week

Gorringe, *Word and Silence*: Chapter 10.

Jeremias, J., *The Eucharistic Words of Jesus* (London: SCM Press, 1966).

Lehmann, P., *The Transfiguration of Politics* (London: SCM Press, 1974).

Luther, M., *Complete Sermons*, vols 1 and 2 (Grand Rapids, MI: Baker, 2000): 183–92.

Myers, *Binding the Strong Man*.

Moltmann, *God in Creation*.

Murdoch, I., *The Unicorn* (St Albans: Granada, 1977).

Regan, P., "Veneration of the Cross", in Johnson (ed.), *Between Memory and Hope*: 143–54.

Wilkinson, *Egeria's Travels*.

Easter

Adam, *Liturgical Year*: Chapter 5.

Bradshaw, P., "The Origins of Easter", in Johnson (ed.), *Between Memory and Hope*: 111–24.

Bradshaw and Johnson, *Origins of Feasts, Fasts and Seasons in Early Christianity*: Chapters 5–7.

Gorringe, *Word and Silence*: Chapter 9.

Schweizer, *The Good News according to Matthew*.

Sobrino, *Christology*: Chapters 8 and 9.

Ascension
Barth, *Church Dogmatics* II/1.

Pentecost
Bradshaw and Johnson, *Origins of Feasts, Fasts and Seasons in Early Christianity*: Chapter 8.
Gorringe, *Word and Silence*: Chapter 13.
Myers and Colwell, *Our God is Undocumented*.
Regan, P., "The Fifty Days and the Fiftieth Day", in Johnson (ed.), *Between Memory and Hope*: 223–46.

Trinity
Richard of St Victor, "On the Trinity", in B. Coolman and D. Coulter (eds), *Trinity and Creation: A Selection of Works of Hugh, Richard and Adam of St Victor* (New York, NY: New City Press, 2011).
LaCugna, C., "Making the Most of Trinity Sunday", in Johnson (ed.), *Between Memory and Hope*: 247–61.
Moltmann, J., *The Crucified God: The Cross of Christ as the Foundation and Criticism of Christian Theology*, tr. R. A. Wilson and John Bowden (London: SCM Press, 1974).
Moltmann, J., *The Trinity and the Kingdom of God: The Doctrine of God*, tr. Margaret Kohl (London: SCM Press, 1981).
Moltmann, J., *The Spirit of Life: A Universal Affirmation* (London: SCM Press, 1992).
Weil, S., *Waiting on God*, tr. Emma Craufurd (London: Routledge and Kegan Paul, 1951).

The Transfiguration
Lehmann, *Transfiguration*: Chapter 7.
Myers, *Binding*.

Creation Season
Adam, *The Liturgical Year*.
Barth, K., *Church Dogmatics* III/2.
Barth, K., *Church Dogmatics* III/3, tr. G. W. Bromiley and T. F. Torrance (Edinburgh: T. & T. Clark, 1960): 369–518.

Berry, W., *The Art of the Commonplace: The Agrarian Essays of Wendell Berry*, ed. and introd. by Norman Wirzba (Washington, DC: Shoemaker and Hoard, 2002).

Boff, L., *Saint Francis: A Model for Human Liberation* (London: SCM, 1982).

Capon, R., *The Supper of the Lamb: A Culinary Reflection* (New York, NY: Modern Library, 2002).

Gorringe, T. J., *The World Made Otherwise: Sustaining Humanity in a Threatened World* (Eugene, OR: Cascade, 2018): Chapter 1.

<https://www.snopes.com/fact-check/letter-to-dr-laura/>, accessed 29 November 2021.

Lebow, V., *Journal of Retailing*, Spring 1955, at <http://www.ablemesh.co.uk/PDFs/journal-of-retailing1955.pdf>, accessed 29 November 2021.

Luther, M., *The Large Catechism*, tr. John Nicholas Lenker, D.D. (Minneapolis, MN: Augsburg, 1967).

Myers, C., *Who will roll away the stone? Discipleship queries for first world Christians* (Maryknoll, NY: Orbis, 1994).

Myers, C., <https://radicaldiscipleship.net/2020/04/10/good-fridays-warning/>, accessed 29 November 2021.

Schweizer, E., *The Good News according to Luke* (London: SPCK, 1984).

Tudge, C., *The Great Re-Think: A 21st Century Renaissance* (Pari: Pari Publishing, 2020).

Remembering

Anderson, K., *Real Clothes for the Emperor: Facing the challenges of climate change* (Norwich: Tyndall Centre, 2012).

<http://kevinanderson.info/blog/category/quick-comment>, accessed 29 November 2021.

Bahro, R., "Dare to form Communes", in *Building the Green Movement* (London: GMP Publishers, 1986).

Baldovin, J., "On Feasting the Saints", in Johnson (ed.), *Between Memory and Hope*: 375–83.

Barth, K., *Church Dogmatics* IV/3, tr. G. W. Bromiley (Edinburgh: T. & T. Clark, 1961).

Barth, K., *Against the Stream: Shorter Post-War Writings* (London: SCM Press, 1964).

Boff, *Saint Francis.*

Brown, P., *The Cult of the Saints* (London: SCM Press, 1981).

<http://dorothyday.catholicworker.org/articles/246.html>, accessed 29 November 2021.

Foster, C. R., *Paul Schneider: The Buchenwald Apostle* (West Chester, PA: SSI Bookstore, 1995).

The Little Flowers of St Francis (Harmondsworth: Penguin, 1959).

Fry, T. (ed.), *The Rule of St Benedict* (Collegeville, MA: Liturgical Press, 1981).

Gollwitzer, H., Kuhn, K. and Schneider, R., *Dying We Live: Letters Written by Prisoners in Germany on the Eve of Execution* (London: Collins, 1958).

Kleiber, Jeffrey S.J., *The Church, Dictatorships, and Democracy in Latin America* (Maryknoll, NY: Orbis, 1998).

Klein, N., *This Changes Everything: Capitalism vs the Climate* (London: Penguin, 2014).

Lorde, A., "Poetry is Not a Luxury", in *Sister Outsider Essays and Speeches by Audre Lorde* (Berkeley: Crossing, 1984).

Loughery, J. and Randolph, B., *Dorothy Day: Dissenting Voice of the American Century* (New York, NY: Simon & Schuster, 2020).

MacIntyre, A., *After Virtue: A Study in Moral Theory*, 2nd edn (London: Duckworth, 1985).

Metz, *Faith in History and Society.*

Nepstad, S. E., *Religion and War: Resistance in the Plowshares Movement* (Cambridge: Cambridge University Press, 2008).

Pêtrement, S., *Simone Weil* (New York, NY: Schocken, 1976).

Postman, N., *Amusing Ourselves to Death: Public Discourse in the Age of Show Business* (London: Methuen, 1986).

Ratushinskaya, I., *No, I'm Not Afraid* (Newcastle: Bloodaxe, 1986).

Ratushinskaya, I., *Grey is the Colour of Hope*, tr. Alyona Kojevnikov (London: Hodder & Stoughton, 1988).

Raworth, K., *Doughnut Economics: Seven ways to think like a twenty-first century economist* (London: Chelsea Green, 2018).

Scholder, K., *A Requiem for Hitler, and other New Perspectives on the German Church Struggle*, tr. John Bowden (London: SCM Press, 1989).

Thomas of Celano, *First Life of St Francis*, tr. Christopher Stace (London: SPCK, 2000).

Volf, M., *The End of Memory: Remembering Rightly in a Violent World* (Grand Rapids, MI: Eerdmans, 2006).

Weil, *Waiting on God.*

Lightning Source UK Ltd.
Milton Keynes UK
UKHW020816230622
404852UK00012B/646